✑ W9-BWX-267

Music Library Association Technical Reports Series

Edited by H. Stephen Wright

Uniform Titles for Music

Michelle Koth

Music Library Association
Technical Reports, No. 31

The Scarecrow Press, Inc.
Lanham, Maryland • Toronto • Plymouth, UK
and
Music Library Association, Inc.
2008

SCARECROW PRESS, INC.

Published in the United States of America
by Scarecrow Press, Inc.
A wholly owned subsidiary of
The Rowman & Littlefield Publishing Group, Inc.
4501 Forbes Boulevard, Suite 200, Lanham, Maryland 20706
www.scarecrowpress.com

Estover Road
Plymouth PL6 7PY
United Kingdom

British Library Cataloguing in Publication Information Available

Library of Congress Cataloging-in-Publication Data

Koth, Michelle S.
  Uniform titles for music / Michelle Koth.
    p. cm. — (Music Library Association technical reports ; No. 31)
  Includes bibliographical references (p.   ) and index.
  ISBN-13: 978-0-8108-5281-5 (pbk. : alk. paper)
  ISBN-10: 0-8108-5281-0 (pbk. : alk. paper)
  1. Uniform titles (Cataloging) 2. Cataloging of music. I. Title.

ML111.K67 2008
025.3'22—dc22   2007047995

Contents

Abbreviations and Acronyms

A	alto voice
AACR2	*Anglo-American Cataloguing Rules*, 2nd ed., 2003 revision
acc.	accompaniment
ALA	The American Library Association
arr.	arranged, arranger
Aufl.	Auflage
Ausg.	Ausgabe
B	bass voice
Bd.	Band
bk.	book
bőv.	bővített
ca.	circa
cb	contrabass
čís.	číslo
CPSO	Cataloging and Support Office
ed.	edition, editor
eds.	editors
enl.	enlarged
fol.	foliation
Gb.	Generalbass
kiad.	kiadás
LC	The Library of Congress
LCRIs	Library of Congress Rule Interpretations
LCSH	Library of Congress Subject Headings
MARC	machine-readable cataloging
min.	minor
MOUG	Music OCLC Users Group
ms.	manuscript
n.	numero
NACO	The Name Authority Cooperative Project
Neuausg.	Neuausgabe
no.	number

nos.	numbers
Nr.	number
núm.	número
OCLC	The Online Computer Library Center
OLAC	OnLine Audiovisual Catalogers
op.	opus
OPAC	online public access catalog
PCC	Program for Cooperative Cataloging
posth.	posthumous
pt.	part, parte
ptie.	partie
r	recto
RDA	*Resource Description and Access*
rev.	revised
RISM	*Répertoire International des Sources Musicales*
S	soprano voice
sér.	série
sz.	szám
T	tenor voice
T.	Teil, Theil
Tr	treble
t.p.	title page
unacc.	unaccompanied
v	verso
vcl	violoncello
vl	violin
vla	viola
vyd.	vydání
WoO	Werke ohne Opuszahl

List of Tables

Preface

The genesis of this book occurred during my first professional position, which was a grant-funded project to convert card catalog records of scores into electronic format at the Indiana University Music Library. The prospect of teaching the concepts of uniform titles for music to others on the project, along with everything else one must know to do the job, was overwhelming. It was then that I began a series of guides about music cataloging for the uninitiated. The guide on uniform titles and subject headings grew into a two-hour sound recording cataloging presentation for the 1994 joint meeting of the Online Audio-Visual Catalogers (OLAC) and the Music OCLC Users Group (MOUG). Two years later, it was expanded into a twelve-hour workshop for catalogers in public libraries in Connecticut, none of whom had music expertise. Of all the sections of the workshop, the four-hour part on uniform titles was the most difficult, and the participants struggled. After that, the next section on music subject headings was a breeze, and the participants visibly brightened, understandably, given the complexities of uniform titles for music.

In 2003, I was invited to give a workshop on uniform titles to the Utah Library Association. As with the public librarians in the Connecticut workshop, some of the Utah catalogers had no music background. For this workshop, I expanded the section on uniform titles into two four-hour parts for the thirty or so catalogers attending. Out of these teaching experiences grew the realization of the need for this longer book version.

My own knowledge of uniform titles for music comes from working with Ralph Papakhian at Indiana. Before working with him, I found uniform titles to be the most fearsome aspect of the music cataloging.

In the process of converting thousands of bibliographic records, it was impossible not to become familiar with useful reference sources for verifying information about composers' works. Working on the list of *Types of Compositions for Use in Music Uniform Titles* while at Indiana and later at Yale University helped me develop the analytical skills needed to deal with the many titles of musical works.

In writing this book, I enlisted the aid and sometimes unknowing participation of many people who deserve acknowledgment. Primary among these are the music catalogers at the Library of Congress (LC), Joe Bartl, Michi Hoban, Lenore Holm, Richard Hunter, Lucas Graves, Sharon McKinley, David Sommerfield, Mary Wedgewood, Valerie Weinberg, Jung Yoon, and others, of whom I have asked questions throughout my career. Jay Weitz of the Online Computer Library Center (OCLC) answered, with humor and authority, many questions in his column in the *MOUG Newsletter*. Those who read preliminary drafts of this book—Charles Herrold, Neil Hughes, Phyllis Jones, Jessica Lang, Diane Napert, Ralph Papakhian, Mark Scharff, and Terry Simpkins—deserve recognition for finding flaws and suggesting improvements. Any errors that remain are, of course, my own.

I also thank my boss at the Yale University Music Library, Kendall Crilly, for generously allowing me the time to work on this project throughout my tenure at Yale, and Yale University, for granting me a research leave to devote to writing the book.

Introduction

In his article "Computer-Assisted Instruction for Music Uniform Titles," Michael Fling wrote,

> "Uniform titles are a vexation to music catalogers, who must spend considerable time on authority work to establish them. They are a menace to unwary patrons not thoroughly schooled in their arcane structure and application. However, they are absolutely necessary to bring together in logical order in the catalog all of the different editions of the same composition."[1]

Vexation and menace indeed! Music uniform titles may be *the* most complex and difficult aspect of music cataloging, even for the cataloger with a strong background in music. This book is directed toward catalogers who deal with music materials and who have some musical background. To effectively catalog music, one must be able to read music, determine key, and recognize musical forms and instrumentation. Because many scores and recordings are in languages other than English, the cataloger must also have a basic understanding of many languages, primarily French, German, Italian, and Spanish, and be able to recognize musical names and terms in those languages. Those working in larger libraries may also need to know the Eastern European languages and languages in non-roman alphabets. Knowledge of the *Anglo-American Cataloguing Rules,* 2nd ed. (AACR2) and the *Library of Congress Rule Interpretations* (LCRIs) is essential. Familiarity with the machine-readable cataloging (MARC) format is important, because of the complexity of subfield tagging within uniform titles. This book was written with these skills in mind, but also with all levels of music cataloging skills, from the fresh-out-of-library-school beginner to the experienced cataloger who wants a refresher.

The order of the book does not follow the order of the rules in AACR2 Chapter 25 and other applicable rules. Rather, the order allows

the reader to progress from generic uniform titles, with the elements needed to make them unique, to distinctive titles, to which, when needed to resolve conflicts, are applied the same elements used in generic titles:
The initial title element (25.27-25.28)
Generic titles
    Formulation of the initial title element (25.29)
    Additions to the initial title element (25.30)
Distinctive titles (25.3, 25.31A-B)
Additions to both generic and distinctive titles (25.32, 25.35)
Collective titles (25.8, 25.34)
Works of unknown or collective authorship (21.5, 21.6)
Manuscripts (25.13)
References (26.1, 26.4)
This book does not cover uniform titles for popular music or for liturgical music entered under a corporate body heading for a church. Nor are series title headings discussed, since the Program for Cooperative Cataloging (PCC) has a series training program in place.

This book is also not intended to replace AACR2, the LCRIs, or any MARC documentation. Instead, this book should be considered an explanation, with examples, of the rules and concepts cited in the sources named above.

In December 2007, the Joint Steering Committee for Revision of Anglo-American Cataloging Rules issued a draft version of sections in *Resource Description and Access* (RDA), including the rules covering "recording attributes of work and expression." In RDA, the phrase "preferred title" corresponds closely to AACR2's "initial title element." The rules for determining the preferred title and making additions to it follow closely the corresponding rules in AACR2, although they are reordered and differ in some areas.

Note

1 Fling, R. Michael. "Computer-Assisted Instruction for Music Uniform Titles." *Public-Access Computer Systems Review*, no. 1 (1990): p. 24.

Chapter 1
Principles of Uniform Titles
for Music

A uniform title is defined in the glossary of *Anglo-American Cataloguing Rules*, 2nd ed. (AACR2), as

> "1. The particular title by which a work is to be identified for cataloguing purposes. 2. The particular title used to distinguish the heading for a work from the heading for a different work. 3. A conventional collective title used to collocate publications of an author, composer, or corporate body containing several works or extracts, etc., from several works (e.g., complete works, several works in a particular literary or musical form)."[1]

Richard Smiraglia described a uniform title as

> "an ordering device . . . consisting of a bibliographically significant title for the work, based on its original [title] as given by the composer . . . to [which] are added musical identifiers (such as opus number and key) to assist with both differentiation and order in a file consisting of all of the composer's works. . . . [T]he name-uniform title citation provides for a alphabetico-classified ordering of a composer's work in an information venue."[2]

A uniform title may be thought of as "the form of a title that has been placed under authority control,"[3] according to Robert Maxwell. He points out the confusion the phrase "uniform title" can cause, since a uniform title may be a title or a name heading followed by a title. Additionally, since "[m]ost uniform titles identify a particular work," Maxwell suggests that "uniform work identifier" might work better.[4] The concept of identifying "a particular work" is important, because the uniform title is the *unique* title *consistently* assigned to all manifestations of a particular work.

Music uniform titles are assigned to musical works. A musical work is "a musical composition that is a single unit intended for performance as a whole, or a set of musical compositions with a group title (not necessarily intended for performance as a whole), or a group of musical compositions with a single opus number."[5]

What Does a Music Uniform Title Do? (25.1A)

A music uniform title:

• Brings together under the heading for a composer all variant manifestations (printed music, sound recordings, arrangements, translations, etc.) of a work under a title unique to that work
• Distinguishes between different works with similar or identical titles
• Identifies a work when the title by which the work is commonly known differs from the title given on the item containing the work.

The use of uniform titles is optional in AACR2. The decision to use a uniform title is based on numerous factors, including the nature of the work (e.g., how well known the work is, whether a translation is involved, and how many manifestations of the work are involved), as well as the purpose of the collection in whose catalog it will appear (e.g., a small browsing collection versus a large research collection).

Given the nature of music publishing, however, using uniform titles for musical works is generally considered to be necessary. Among the vagaries of practices found on published or recorded music are incorrect, incomplete, or misleading information. The fact that a work has been excerpted from a larger work or arranged for a medium of performance other than that originally intended by the composer may not be indicated anywhere on the item. It is not uncommon for a title on an item to consist solely of the name of a type of composition with no other identifying words. The cataloging process begins with the identification of the work.

Rule 25.2A and the corresponding LCRI concern the appearance of a uniform title on a card in the card catalog and in an online public access catalog (OPAC) display. When a uniform title follows the name heading of a composer as main entry, the uniform title is enclosed in brackets, indicating that it has not been transcribed from the item being cataloged.

When the application of the rules in AACR2 Chapter 25 results in a uniform title that is identical to the title proper (disregarding an initial article), the title proper functions also as the uniform title and is not bracketed. It is important to note that the process of determining the uniform title, even when it is not included in the bibliographic record, is routinely done for music materials. When a uniform title alone is the main entry, it is not bracketed, since on a printed card, it would appear above the transcribed information. When used in added entries, neither a uniform title heading nor the title portion of a name/title heading is bracketed. The uniform titles used as examples in this chapter follow this rule for bracketing. In future chapters, most uniform titles appear with MARC tagging, as they would in an online bibliographic record, rather than on a printed card.

A Brief Overview of Uniform Titles for Music[6]

The information included on different publications and recordings of the same work may differ widely as to wording, amount (and possibly accuracy) of information provided, and language. A uniform title is necessary to uniquely identify the work with a heading under which all editions of the work are filed and searchable in the catalog.

Beethoven, Ludwig van, 1770-1827.
[Symphonies, no. 5, op. 67, C minor]
Fünfte Symphonie, op. 67

Beethoven, Ludwig van, 1770-1827.
[Symphonies, no. 5, op. 67, C minor]
Symphony no. 5, C minor, op. 67

Beethoven, Ludwig van, 1770-1827.
[Symphonies, no. 5, op. 67, C minor]
5e symphonie en ut mineur

Uniform titles are generally required for all types of composition (e.g., forms [concerto, symphony, trio sonata], genres [capriccio, intermezzo, nocturne], commonly used terms [movement, piece], and chamber music combinations [trio, quartet, quintet]). Titles of this nature are considered to be "generic" and are given in the plural, unless the composer has written only one work of that type. Instrumentation, identifying numbers, quantitative numbers, and key are given in subordinate positions in the uniform title, or, in some cases, are omitted.

Rachmaninoff, Sergei, 1873-1943.
   [Concertos, piano, orchestra, no. 2, op. 18, C minor]
   Piano concerto no. 2 in C minor, op. 18

Chopin, Frédéric, 1810-1849.
   [Waltzes, piano, op. 69. No. 2]
   Valse in B minor, op. 69, no. 2

Bartók, Béla, 1881-1945.
   [Quartets, strings, no. 4]
   Streichquartett IV

A uniform title may represent a single work or a collection of consecutively numbered works with the same title.

Zaimont, Judith Lang, 1945-
   [Sonata, piano]
   Sonata for piano solo

Sciarrino, Salvatore.
   [Sonatas, piano, no. 2-5]
   Piano sonatas II-V

Titles that include more than the name of a musical form, genre, commonly used term, or chamber music combination and other identifying elements (instrumentation, numbers, key, date of composition) are considered to be "distinctive." The title in the original language is preferred, but not necessarily the original alphabet.

Berlioz, Hector, 1803-1869.
   [Symphonie fantastique]
   Fantastic symphony

Rimsky-Korsakov, Nikolay, 1844-1908.
[Zolotoĭ petushok]
Zolotoĭ petushok
Title on item in Cyrillic: Золотой петушок

An adjective or epithet that was part of a composer's original title are
retained.

Weber, Carl Maria von, 1786-1826.
[Grand duo concertant]
Gran duo concertante = Grosses Duo concertante

Initial numbers that relate serially or quantitatively to the title are
removed from the uniform title.

Maconchy, Elizabeth, 1907-1994.
[Easy pieces]
Three easy pieces : for violin and viola

Numbers in the title that are integral to the title, e.g., not related
serially or quantitatively to the work, are retained in their original
position. Here, the title proper serves as uniform title.

Zechlin, Ruth, 1926-
Die sieben letzten Worte Jesu am Kreuz

The generic uniform title is preferred for a classical work with a
"popular" title, i.e., not the composer's title.

Schubert, Franz, 1797-1828.
**[Quintets, piano, violin, viola, violoncello, double bass, D.
667, A major]**
Trout quintet : for piano and strings, op. 114

Haydn, Joseph, 1732-1809.
[Symphonies, H. I, 103, E♭ major]
The "drum roll" symphony

When a composer's original title is "popular," that title is used as the
uniform title.

Mozart, Wolfgang Amadeus, 1756-1791.
Eine **kleine Nachtmusik**

A separate part of a larger work is hierarchically identified through the uniform title for the larger work. This varies from the practice for uniform titles for parts of literary works, which are entered under the title of the part.

Brahms, Johannes, 1833-1897.
[Symphonies, no. 3, op. 90, F major. Andante]
Andante from Symphony no. 3

Handel, George Frideric, 1685-1759.
[Messiah. Hallelujah]
Hallelujah chorus from The Messiah

An arrangement for a different medium of performance is related to the original version through the uniform title.

Copland, Aaron, 1900-1990.
[Sonatas, violin, piano; arr.]
Sonata for clarinet and piano

Rossini, Gioacchino, 1792-1868.
[Guillaume Tell. Ouverture; arr.]
William Tell overture transcribed for military band

A vocal score, chorus score, libretto, or translation is hierarchically identified through the uniform title.

Mozart, Wolfgang Amadeus, 1756-1791.
Die Zauberflöte : opera, K. 620

Mozart, Wolfgang Amadeus, 1756-1791.
[Zauberflöte. Libretto. English]
The magic flute : libretto

Mozart, Wolfgang Amadeus, 1756-1791.
[Zauberflöte. Vocal score]
Die Zauberflöte / . . . Klavierauszug

Mozart, Wolfgang Amadeus, 1756-1791.
   [Zauberflöte. Vocal score. Italian & German]
   Die Zauberflöte / . . . Klavierauszug mit Übersetzung ins
   Italienische

Collections that are, or purport to be, the complete or partial works of
a composer are identified through collective uniform titles that describe
the extent of the collection. A collection containing a composer's entire
output, or complete works, is given the collective title "Works," qualified
by date of publication.

Brahms, Johannes, 1833-1897.
   [Works. 1996]
   Neue Ausgabe sämtlicher Werke

Collective titles are assigned to partial collections organizing them
according to their contents (e.g., form, genre, or medium of performance),
or identifying them as miscellaneous groups of diverse form, genre, or
medium of performance.

Brahms, Johannes, 1833-1897.
   [Symphonies]
   The four symphonies

Brahms, Johannes, 1833-1897.
   [Piano music]
   Klavierwerke

Brahms, Johannes, 1833-1897.
   [Piano music. Selections]
   Complete sonatas and variations for solo piano

Brahms, Johannes, 1833-1897.
   [Selections]
   Brahms for relaxation

An individual work of unknown authorship is entered under a uniform
title.

Sonata, violins (4), continuo, D major.
Four-violin sonata in D / anonymous

Streets of Laredo.
Laredo

A work of diffuse or collective authorship is entered under the heading of the principal or first-named composer.

Doppler, Franz, 1821-1883.
   [Souvenir de Prague]
   Souvenir de Prague . . . / Franz & Karl Doppler

A manuscript compilation of works of different or unknown authorship that is known by a title given to it after its creation or compilation is entered under that title.

Rusconi codex.
Bologna, Civico museo bibliografico musicale, MS. Q19

Straloch lute book.
The Straloch manuscript

A manuscript that cannot be entered under either a generic or distinctive title is identified through the authorized heading for its repository, followed by the term "Manuscript" and the repository's alphanumeric designation.

Bibliothèque nationale de France. Manuscript. Réserve 1122.
Pièces pour virginal 1646-1654 : fac-similé du manuscrit

British Library. Manuscript. Additional 29369.
Add. ms. 29369

Where Is a Uniform Title Used
in a Bibliographic Record?

Uniform titles may be found in several places in a bibliographic record:
• as the main entry (130) or added entry (730)
• in the 240 field following a 100 field with the heading for the composer (also, rarely, following a 110 field)
• in the 245 ‡a, following a 100 field for the composer. (When the title proper is identical to the uniform title, the 240 field is not used.)
• in a 110 field with the heading for the repository followed by the form subheading "‡k Manuscript" and alpha-numeric designation
• in a name/title added entry (700/‡t) or corporate/form subheading added entry (710/‡k) (also, rarely, 710/‡t)
• in subject headings (600/‡t, 610/‡k, 630)
• in a name/title series added entry (800/‡t).
    The 130/730 field contains a uniform title for:
• single works of no known origin
• named or titled manuscripts
• collections with multiple composers, known by a collective title.
    The indicators for both the 130 and 730 fields are:
1st indicator: 0 = the number of filing characters to be ignored. This number will always be 0, because any initial article is removed from a uniform title.
2nd indicator: ƀ = always blank

Examples

730 0ƀ Shenandoah (Song)
130 0ƀ Glogauer Liederbuch.
130 0ƀ Fitzwilliam virginal book.

    The 100/240 field combination contains the heading for an individual composer in the 100 field followed by the uniform title for a specific work or collection of works in the 240 field. Both indicators are required.
1st indicator: 1 = the uniform title will print on a card or display in an online catalog
                0 = the uniform title will not print on a card or display in an online catalog

2nd indicator: 0 = the number of filing characters to be ignored. This number will always be 0, because any initial article is removed from a uniform title.

According to LCRI 25.1A, a uniform title in the 240 field is not used when it is exactly the same as the title proper found in 245/‡a (and ‡n and ‡p, when used). An initial article in the title proper is disregarded when determining if the uniform title and the title proper are the same.

The 110 field includes the authorized name of the repository, followed by the form subheading "Manuscript" in ‡k and any alpha-numeric designation in ‡n.

1st indicator: 0 = inverted name
                1 = jurisdiction name
                2 = name in direct order
2nd indicator: ♭ = always blank

Example

110 2♭ British Library. ‡k Manuscript. ‡n Additional 10444.

The 700/‡t contains the personal name heading and uniform title for a work contained in an item or for a work related to the item.

1st indicator: 1 = single or compound surname
                0 = entry under forename
2nd indicator: 2 = analytical entry (the work is contained in the item being cataloged)
                ♭ = related entry (the work is not contained in the item being cataloged)

The 710 field includes the authorized name of the repository, followed by the form subheading "Manuscript" in ‡k and any alpha-numeric designation in ‡n.

1st indicator: 0 = inverted name
                1 = jurisdiction name
                2 = name in direct order
2nd indicator: 2 = analytical entry (the work is contained in the item being cataloged)
                ♭ = related entry (the work is not contained in the item being cataloged)

A uniform title heading is used as a subject heading in a bibliographic record for a work about the musical work represented by the uniform title. When a uniform title or name/title heading is used as a Library of

Congress subject heading (LCSH), it is formulated according to AACR2, and not the guidelines for subject headings. A book about Beethoven's fifth symphony would be assigned the same name/title heading under which a publication of the work would be entered. Subject subdivisions necessary to describe the content of the book are added according to LCSH guidelines.

The MARC tags for uniform titles used as subject headings are 600 (name/title heading), 610 (corporate body/uniform title heading or form subheading), and 630 (uniform title heading). The first indicators are the same as when the headings function as main or added entries. The second indicator contains coding for the type of subject heading (e.g., second indicator "0" to indicate Library of Congress subject heading).

The 800 field contains the name heading and uniform title in ǂt for a series traced in a form other than found on the item. (Series headings are not discussed further in this book.)

1st indicator: 1 = single or compound surname
              0 = enter under forename
2nd indicator: ƀ = always blank

Uniform Titles and Authority Records

An authority record contains the established form of the uniform title, references from unused forms of the heading, bibliographic data, and other information. The established form of the uniform title is found in the 1XX field, references from unused forms (formulated according to the same rules for the uniform title) in the 4XX fields, references to other headings in the 5XX field, a bibliographic citation for the item being cataloged and sources for information justifying the heading or further identifying the work in the 670 field, and other information in the 667 and 675 fields, as needed.

Headings and References

An established heading may not appear in the authority record exactly as it appears in the bibliographic record. *Generally* additions to a uniform title in the bibliographic record, such as indication of vocal score, libretto, or language, are not included in the heading in the authority record.

In an authority record, the name/title heading is tagged in the 100/‡t. In a bibliographic record, ‡t is not valid for the 100 field. The uniform title portion of the heading is tagged in the 240 field. As an added entry, the name/title heading is tagged in the 700/‡t. In authority records, the 2nd indicator is always blank.

Authority record:

100 1b̵ Bach, Johann Sebastian, ‡d 1685-1750. ‡t Brandenburgische Konzerte

The same heading as the main entry in a bibliographic record:

100 1b̵ Bach, Johann Sebastian, ‡d 1685-1750.
240 10 Brandenburgische Konzerte

The same heading as an analytical entry in a bibliographic record:

700 12 Bach, Johann Sebastian, ‡d 1685-1750. ‡t Brandenburgische Konzerte.

A uniform title for an individual work of unknown or collective authorship or for a compilation of works of diverse or unknown authorship is tagged as 130 in an authority record, as it is in a bibliographic record. The first indicator is always blank; the second indicator is for the number of filing characters to be ignored. Because initial articles are removed from uniform titles, the second indicator will always be "0."

References from a name/title heading in the authority record are tagged as 400/‡t or 500/‡t. References are discussed in detail in Chapter 15, "References."

Other Fields

Other fields in the authority record rationalize the choice of heading in the 1XX field for the work in hand and may be useful when establishing a uniform title for a similar work by the same composer. The 670 field contains the title proper of the work on which the heading is based, the date of publication of the work, any additional information necessary to justify the heading, and the source of that information. Optionally, main entry from the bibliographic record may also be indicated.

Additional 670 fields may also be used to record further information used to establish the heading or to provide justification for a uniform title that varies from the title found on the item.

When a heading is based on the title proper of the item being cataloged, no further information from the title or other sources is needed to establish or justify the heading.

100 1ḃ Pärt, Arvo. ‡t Passacaglia, ‡m violin, piano
670   Pärt, A. Passacaglia für Violine und Klavier (2003), 2003.

If the title proper of the item is insufficient to establish the heading, information from the rest of the title used to establish or justify the heading is given.

100 1ḃ Berger, Arthur, ‡d 1912-2003. ‡t Duets, ‡m oboe, clarinet; ‡o arr.
670   His Duo, clarinet and piano, c1979: ‡b t.p. (Duo, clarinet and piano; freely transcribed by the composer from his Duo for oboe and clarinet)

When information on the chief source of information is insufficient to establish the heading, information from another source in the item that justifies the heading is included in the 670 field.

100 1ḃ Wittell, Chester. ‡t Concertos, ‡m horn, orchestra, ‡n op. 90, ‡r F major
670   Wittell, C. Concerto in F major for horn and orchestra, 2000: ‡b t.p. (Concerto in F major for horn and orchestra) caption of horn part (op. 90)

When information in the entire item is insufficient to establish the heading and information taken from another source is required to establish or justify the heading, an additional 670 field for that source is included.

100 1b Telemann, Georg Philipp, ‡d 1681-1767. ‡t Trio sonatas, ‡m
flute, violin, continuo, ‡n TWV 42:e7, ‡r E minor
670   His 39. Triosonate in e-Moll für Flöte (Oboe, Violine), Violine
und Basso continuo, 1992.
670   Telemann-Werkverzeichnis, Instrumentalwerke: ‡b Bd. 2
(42:e7; Sonate e-Moll für Querflöte, Violine und Gb.)

The 670 field can be a gold mine of information useful for
establishing uniform titles for works other than that represented in the
1XX field. For example, the second 670 field above indicates the source
in which the cataloger found information to establish the heading for the
work. That same source of information may be useful in formulating the
uniform title for a similar work by the same composer.

In the second 670 in the authority record below, the citation of a
second string quartet by Rauchenecker justifies the plural form of the
initial title element as well as the serial number in the uniform title.

100 1b Rauchenecker, Georg, ‡d 1844-1906. ‡t Quartets, ‡m strings,
‡n no. 1, ‡r C minor
670   Rauchenecker, G. Quartett in c-Moll für 2 Violinen, Viola, und
Violoncello, 1997.
670   Pazdírek ‡b (also a 2nd string quartet in D)

In this authority record, the second 670 field justifies adding a
numeric identifying element (opus number) to a distinctive title and gives
the key signatures of individual sonatas within the work. This information
may be useful when cataloging individually published sonatas.

100 1b Hoffmeister, Franz Anton, ‡d 1754-1812. ‡t Sonates
concertantes, ‡n op. 2
670   Hoffmeister, F.A. 3 konzertante Sonaten, c1998: ‡b t.p. (3
konzertante Sonaten : aus op. II für zwei Querflöten) p. 2 (from
Six sonates concertantes pour deux flûtes traversières oeuvre II)
670   RISM A,I ‡b (Six sonates [D,B,G,C,F,D] concertantes pour
deux flûtes traversières oeuvre II; also Six sonates concertantes
pour deux flûtes traversières oeuvre I)

The 667 field includes explanatory information for other catalogers
using the authority record. The information may relate to similarly titled
but different works by the same composer, concern problems with

numeric identifying elements, or provide information about the nature of the uniform title.

100 1ხ Hummel, Johann Nepomuk, ‡d 1778-1837. ‡t Sonatas, ‡m piano, ‡n op. 20, ‡r F minor
667 Serial numbering deferred.
670 Hummel, J.N. Sonate no. 2 pour le piano forte, oeuvre 20, 1824.

100 1ხ Handel, George Frideric, ‡d 1685-1759. ‡t Quel fior che all'alba ride, ‡n HWV 154
667 Owing to complexity of mediums in cantata settings of this text, use only HWV nos. in uniform titles.

100 1ხ Gabrieli, Giovanni, ‡d 1557-1612. ‡t Sacrae symphoniae
667 Use this uniform title for 1597 publication; use Symphoniae sacrae for 1616 publication.

100 1ხ Lanman, Anthony Joseph, ‡d 1973- ‡t Sonata 46
667 Title apparently reflects the name of the group for which the work was written, rather than location within a sequence of works.

The recognized thematic index for a composer will be cited in a 667 field along with an example of how any numbering is to be formatted.

100 1ხ Danzi, Franz, ‡d 1763-1826
667 Thematic-index numbers used in uniform titles for works without opus numbers are from Pechstaedt, V. *Thematisches Verzeichnis der Kompositionen von Franz Danzi (1763-1826)*, 1996, e.g., [Concertos, bassoon, orchestra, P. 234, C major]

The 675 field cites sources that were consulted, but which did not include information useful for establishing the heading, and alerts other catalogers that they need not consult the sources listed there. Not every source that was consulted is included in the 675 field; only those sources that would be expected to include information, but did not, are cited in the 675 field.

Abbreviations, Capitalization, and Punctuation

Abbreviations

The use of abbreviations in bibliographic records is explained in Appendix B of AACR2. The rules for titles proper are not the same as for uniform titles. For the former, an abbreviation is transcribed in the 245 field only when it appears on the item as such, with the exception of "i.e." and "et al." Abbreviations may be used in uniform titles when the word is spelled out in full in the title proper of the work and the rules for music uniform titles require the abbreviation.

LCRI 25.30C requires the word "opus" to be abbreviated "op." in the uniform title, even when it appears spelled out or in another language in the title proper.

Title:	Sonata for piano, **opus** 19
Uniform title:	Sonata, ‡m piano, ‡n **op.** 19

Title:	Sonate flûte et piano, **œuvre** 10
Uniform title:	Sonata, ‡m flute, piano, ‡n **op.** 10

When "opus" is a Latin word not referring to a work number, it is not abbreviated.

Musicum **opus**
Novum et insigne **opus** musicum

The prescribed abbreviation for the word "number" is "no.," "Nr.," etc., according to the rules for numeric identifying elements for works and parts of larger works with serial numbers associated with them (discussed further in Chapters 7 and 11). The word "arranged" is abbreviated "arr."

25.30B10 prescribes two other abbreviations, "acc." and "unacc." for "accompaniment" and "unaccompanied," in uniform titles with the initial title element such as "Songs," "Lieder," etc.

Songs, ‡m violin **acc.**
Gesang, ‡m **unacc.**

Not all prescribed abbreviations listed in AACR2 Appendix B are used in uniform titles. In some cases, a term that is found in the source on which a uniform title is based is used in spelled-out form even if there is an abbreviation for that term in AACR2 Appendix B. The AACR2 abbreviation "bk.," for "book," may be found in older uniform titles, but is not used in newly established headings.

Older headings	Current practice
Madrigals, ‡n **bk. 1**	Madrigals, ‡n **book** 1
Madrigals, ‡n **bk. 2**	Madrigals, ‡n **book** 2

The AACR2 abbreviation "pt.," for "part," may be found in older uniform titles, but is not used in newly established headings.

Older headings	Current practice
Solos, ‡m flute, continuo, ‡n **pt. 1**	Solos, ‡m flute, continuo, ‡n **part 1**
Solos, ‡m flute, continuo, ‡n **pt. 2**	Solos, ‡m flute, continuo, ‡n **part 2**

LC practice is to use abbreviations such as "bk." in new headings when they have been used in older headings for a composer's works. This is discussed further in Chapter 7, "Numeric Identifying Elements."

Other abbreviations that are integral to the title are retained in the uniform title.

Mass in honor of **St.** Cecilia   **Mrs.** Madison's minuet

Capitalization

Capitalization within bibliographic records is covered in AACR2 Appendix A, rules A.3-4 and A3.C1. The words in a uniform title are capitalized according to the conventions for the title proper.

Capitalize the first word of the title.

Suites, ‡m oboe, piano

LCRI A.4A1 applies to titles beginning with an introductory word or phrase. The introductory word or the first word of the phrase is capitalized. The first word of the title following the introductory word or phrase is also capitalized. Subsequent words in the title are not capitalized unless required by the rules for the language of the title.

Missa Surrexit pastor bonus	Missa L'homme armé
Sonata La pastorella	Sonata "L'abondance"

    The first word of a title within a title is capitalized.

Missa super Christ lag in Todesbanden
Variaciones sobre El carnaval de Venecia
Variationen über Kommt ein Vogel geflogen
Pot-pourri sur des motifs favoris de l'opèra Zampa d'Hérold
Prelude on Psalm 143

    Note that "psalm" is not capitalized when it is not the first word of a title.

Meditations on the 23rd psalm

    Ellipses appearing in a title are replaced with a dash. According to A.4B1, when the first word of a title follows a dash, it is not capitalized.

—huésped de las nieblas—

    Capitalize other words according to the rules for the language of title, e.g., in German, all nouns are capitalized.

Introduktion, vier Variationen über ein Originalthema und Finale

    English words and abbreviations that are added to music uniform titles, such as medium of performance, words accompanying numeric identifying elements, and statement of key, are not capitalized unless the word or abbreviation is, or stands for, a proper name.

Duets, ǂm English horns
Concertos, ǂm ondes Martenot, orchestra

    Adjectives derived from country names are capitalized in English, but not in other languages.

Variations on a French folksong
Variationen über ein französische Volkslied
Variations sur une chanson folklorique française

Titles given to post-nineteenth-century works often include unusual capitalization. General practice is to follow the capitalization used by the composer.

Wissahickon poeTrees   LON/dons
NONAAH   BAROKsoundscapes
SCHerZOid

Single Letters

Single letters, such as "I," when used as the English pronoun, and "O," when used in any language to mean the interjection "oh," are capitalized.

Fain would I change that note   O, O, O, O, that Shakespeherian rag
Take, O take those lips away   Turn thou us, O good Lord
Schmücke dich, O liebe Seele

Other single letters representing words or roman numerals are also capitalized:

E plus A   Psalm CL

Single letters indicating key are capitalized.

Sonatas, ‡m piano, ‡r D minor   Sonatas, ‡m piano, ‡r A♭ major
Sonatas, ‡m piano, ‡r C# minor   Sonatas, ‡m piano, ‡r G

Capitalization in Titles for Sacred Music

AACR2 Appendix A.19 covers capitalization of religious names and terms in English. These instructions apply to all other languages covered in AACR2 Appendix A, as there are no contradictory rules concerning religious names and terms in any other language that would apply to music uniform titles. The initial letter is capitalized in the following types of terms in sacred or liturgical titles. Examples of titles follow each type of term.

The name of a deity	Terms referring to God
Hallelu Yahweh	O Rex gloriae
Invocation to Aphrodite	Coeli enarrant gloriam Dei
The three names of Shiva	Diligam te, Domine
	Christ, unser Herr
	O Vater aller Frommen
	J'ai mis mon espoir en toi, Seigneur
	Notre Dieu est une forteresse

Note that a pronoun referring to the name of a deity is generally not capitalized. A pronoun may be capitalized to clear up ambiguity about to whom the pronoun is referring.

O praise God in his holiness   Let thy merciful ears, O Lord

Terms referring to Mary	Terms referring to Jesus Christ
Alma Redemptoris Mater	Natus est Iesus
Stabat Mater	O Domine, Jesu Christe
Beata Vergine	Vingt regards sur l'Enfant Jésus
Hodie Beata Virgo Maria	Prayer to the Infant Jesus
Ave Maris Stella	

Terms referring to the Christian Trinity and others	Terms referring to groups of people
O lux beata Trinitas	Adoration of the Magi
Mass of the Holy Trinity	Actes of the Apostles
Mass of the Holy Spirit	Vesperae de Apostolis

The name of a major Biblical or religious event or concept	
Stations of the Cross	In die festo Epiphaniae
Stations de la Croix	Triptyque pour la Noël
Oratorio per la Settimana Santa	Oratorio for Holy Week
Carols for the Nativity	Variations on carols for Advent
Ikon of the Crucifixion	Messe de la Pentecôte
Villancicos de Navidad	The Last Judgment
Cantilena de Nativitate Domini nostri Jesu Christi	

Punctuation

The three punctuation marks that may be added to a uniform title to indicate hierarchy within the structure of the uniform title are the comma, period, and semicolon.

Comma

A comma separates the elements of a title used to identify a work. These elements might be the name of a type of composition (such as symphony, concerto, etc.), medium of performance, identifying number(s), key, etc. For example.

Quartets, ‡m strings, ‡n no. 1, op. 1, ‡r D major

The first element names the type of work, a quartet. In order to identify which of Tchaikovsky's quartets it is, the medium of performance, identifying numbers, and key are included. There are two numbers, because the quartet is both Tchaikovsky's first string quartet as well as his opus 1. All the elements of this uniform title act together to uniquely identify the work.

In these two examples, the comma separates the elements of the title of a part of a larger work.

Sonate d'intavolatura. ‡n Pt. 1. ‡p Canzona, ‡r E minor
Album für die Jugend. ‡n Nr. 32, †p Sheherazade

Period

A period can occur in three places, other than at the end of an abbreviation. The period serves to hierarchically set off the uniform title from other information pertaining to the work. A period signals the end of the title that identifies the whole work in its original form. The first letter of the word immediately following the period is capitalized.

1. A period sets off the title of the work as a whole from the title of a part of the work. The uniform title for the work as a whole is first established:

Quartets, ǂm strings, ǂn no. 1, op. 1, ǂr D major

A period is added to the uniform title with the title of the part of the work following:

Quartets, ǂm strings, ǂn no. 1, op. 1, ǂr D major. ǂp Andante cantabile

"Mio Tesoro" is an aria from the opera *Don Giovanni*. The period following *Don Giovanni*, the name of the opera, signifies that "Mio Tesoro" is a part of the opera.

Don Giovanni. ǂp Mio tesoro

The title of the part of the work may be a designation of numbering of a part:

Concerto from bagatelles. ǂn 1st movement

or both number and title. A period separates the number and title of the part from the title for the work as a whole.

Sonatas, ǂm piano, ǂn op. 1. ǂn No. 1, ǂp Rondo

The title of a part of a part of a larger work is also preceded by a period.

Trio sonatas, ǂm violins, continuo, ǂn op. 1. ǂn No. 1. ǂp Preludio
Licht. ǂp Dienstag. ǂp Invasion-Explosion mit Abschied

2. A period sets off the title of the work as a whole from the indication of vocal score, chorus score, libretto, translation, or selections. These elements may also be separated from each other with periods:

Don Giovanni. ǂl English
Don Giovanni. ǂl English. ǂk Selections
Don Giovanni. ǂs Libretto
Don Giovanni. ǂs Libretto. ǂl English. ǂk Selections
Don Giovanni. ǂk Selections

Semicolon

A semicolon is used when the work or a part of the work has been arranged. This is indicated by adding a semicolon followed by the abbreviation "arr." to the uniform title for the original work. It can be added to any uniform title.

Quartets, ǂm strings, ǂn no. 1, op. 1, ǂr D major; ǂo arr.
Quartets, ǂm strings, ǂn no. 1, op. 1, ǂr D major. ǂp Andante
    cantabile; ǂo arr.

Other Punctuation

Other punctuation is used in music uniform titles, but is usually not structurally significant.

A slash is used to separate titles of polytextual works:

Aucune gent/Qui plus aimme/Fiat voluntas tua

A colon may be found in thematic index numbers:

Concertos, ǂm oboe, string orchestra, ǂn TWV 51:D5, ǂr D major

An ampersand is the prescribed punctuation when indicating two languages.

Zauberflöte. ǂl English & German

An ampersand or plus sign may also be used to represent the word "and" when that is the composer's original title:

Prelude & fugue, ǂm clavichord

Parentheses are used to enclose qualifiers, such as a date or phrase, or a quantitative number indicating instrumentation:

Prometheus (Symphonic poem)
Sonatas, ǂm flutes (2), ǂn op. 4 (Walsh)

Sonatas, ‡m harpsichord ‡n (1732)
Estro armonico. ‡n N. 8. ‡p Allegro (1st movement)

A dash is used to replace ellipses when transcribing the title proper. It also replaces ellipses in the uniform title. When a dash precedes the first word of the title, there is no space after the dash (LCRI 1.1B1).

On item: ... huésped de las nieblas ...
Uniform title: —huésped de las nieblas—

In all other cases, add a space following the dash.

On item: Erdenklänge ... Sphärenklänge
Uniform title: Erdenklänge— Sphärenklänge

On item: A la manière de ... Chabrier
Uniform title: A la manière de— . ‡p Chabrier

On item: ... Sine nomine super nomina ... III
Uniform title: —Sine nomine super nomina— , ‡n no. 3

When a dash appears in the title on the item, and the words on either side of the dash will form part of the title proper, include the dash in the title proper, with no space before or after the dash. Omit spaces that appear on the item (LCRI 1.0C).

On item: Erdenklavier — Himmelklavier
Uniform title: Erdenklavier—Himmelklavier

On item: D'oú venons-nous — que sommes-nous — oú allons-nous
Uniform title: D'oú venons-nous—que sommes-nous—oú allons-nous

When to Include a Composer's Original Punctuation in the Uniform Title

Other internal and final punctuation marks (or lack thereof) are retained when they are in the source on which the uniform title is based.

"Vincent" sonata
Variationen über ein Thema aus der Opera "Marie" von Hérold
Why patterns?
!?dialogues suffisants!?
Variations on the villanella Alma che fai? by Luca Marenzio
Tönet, ihr Pauken! Erschallet, Trompeten
Carry on, Caramoor!
Corinthians: XIII
Variationen (über ein Wiener Lied)
Music; that it might be—
Piano, piano— !
Flageolett+Passacaglia=Blues???

Punctuation Between the Name and Title Portions of a Heading

Guidelines for the punctuation between the name and title portions of the
heading are the following. These conventions are for display; input may
vary, depending upon standards of each local system and bibliographic
utility.

When the heading ends with	Precede the uniform title with
period	one space
closing parenthesis	a period and one space
open date	one space (but no period)
question mark	one space (but no period)

Ending Punctuation

Within Elements of a Uniform Title

When an internal unit of a heading or reference ends with a quotation
mark, any other mark of punctuation is placed inside the quotation mark,
according to LCRI 1.0Cd:

Pictures from Radiguet's "The devil in the flesh," ǂm piano
Gedichte aus "Liebesfrühling." ǂp So wahr die Sonne scheinet

This rule is not applied when the quotation mark precedes "ǂo arr."
The quotation mark precedes the semicolon.

Introduktion und Variationen über ein Thema aus "Freischütz"; ǂo arr.
Variations sur "Au clair de la lune"; ǂo arr.
Rapsodi͡ia "Vardar"; ǂo arr.

This is also the practice for other punctuation preceding "ǂo arr."

Schöne Müllerin. ǂp Wohin?; ǂo arr.
Oklahoma! ǂp Oklahoma!; ǂo arr.
Blue skies (Song); ǂo arr.
Wiegenlied ǂn (1881); ǂo arr.
Nocturne, ǂm soprano, guitars (4); ǂo arr.

When a closing parenthesis ends an element within a uniform title, a comma or period follows the parenthesis.

O Ewigkeit, du Donnerwort (Cantata), ǂn BWV 20
Schwanengesang (Song cycle). ǂp Ständchen
Shéhérazade (Song cycle). ǂs Vocal score

An element within a uniform title that ends with an exclamation point or question mark is not followed by the punctuation that usually precedes the next element in the title, except when the next element is "ǂo arr."

Oklahoma! ǂp Oklahoma!
Medjé! ǂl German & French
Mamma mia! ǂs Vocal score
Nozze di Figaro. ǂp Dove sono? ǂs Vocal score
Who can from joy refrain? ǂk Selections

However, there are examples in the authority file that contradict this.

Menus propos!, ǂn op. 48
Lord, what is man?, ǂm soprano, continuo

At the End of a Uniform Title

The 130 and 730 fields end with a mark of punctuation or a closing parenthesis. If there is no final punctuation in the title, add a period. If the title ends with quotation marks, place the ending punctuation inside the closing quotation mark. If the title ends with a punctuation mark other than a quotation mark, do not add punctuation.

The 240 field does not end with a mark of punctuation unless the last word is an abbreviation or initialism or when an ending punctuation mark is part of the title.

A name/title added entry (700/‡t) should end with a mark of punctuation or a closing parenthesis. When it does not end with one of these, add a period to the heading. If the title ends with quotation marks, place the ending punctuation inside the closing quotation mark. If the title ends with a punctuation mark other than a quotation mark, do not add punctuation.

Accents, Diacritical Marks, and Special Characters

Rules 1.0G1 (and the accompanying LCRI) and 1.1B1 cover accents and other diacritical marks. When accents or diacritics specific to a language have been omitted from a title in that language, they should be added by the cataloger:

Title: Theme et variations no. 1 pour timpani
Uniform title: Thème et variations, ‡m timpani, †n no. 1

LCRI 1.0G previously prohibited transcribing or adding a diacritic to an initial capital letter in French, Spanish, or Portuguese. In January 2006, this practice was discontinued.

In German, the ess-zet (ß) is transcribed as "ss."

On item: Es, ist, euch gut, daß ich hingehe
Uniform title: Es, ist, euch gut, dass ich hingehe

When a title includes typographical characters that are part of the composer's original title, they are included in the uniform title.

A*B*C   Mirakus^2
1 + 5   2 X 3
0'0"   3 x 60° EACh
Sum=parts

Notes

1. AACR2, Appendix D, *Glossary.*

2. Richard P. Smiraglia, "Musical Works and Information Retrieval." *Notes* 58 (2002): p. 758.

3. Robert L. Maxwell, *Maxwell's Guide to Authority Work* (Chicago: American Library Association, 2002), p. 2.

4. Maxwell, p. 3.

5. AACR2 25.25, footnote 9.

6. Adapted with permission from Wise, Matthew W. *Principles of Music Uniform Titles: A Brief Introduction,* 1995. http://www.music.indiana.edu/tech_s/mla/ut.gui (accessed January 22, 2008)

Chapter 2
The Initial Title Element
(25.27-25.28)

The first step in establishing a music uniform title is to determine the composer's original title in the language in which it was presented (25.27A). The second step is to isolate the initial title element. The initial title element is defined in the glossary of AACR2 as "the word(s) selected from the title of a musical work and placed first in the uniform title for that work. If no additions to the initial title element are required by the rules, it becomes the uniform title for the work."

The third step is to determine whether the initial title element is "distinctive" or "generic." An initial title element is generic when it is the name of a type, or two or more types, of composition. A type of composition can include:
- the name of a form or genre
- a generic term commonly used by composers
- a tempo designation
- a medium of performance.

Smiraglia defines a distinctive title as

> "1. A title proper for a work that does not consist of the name of a type of composition, or of one or more names of types of composition and a connector ('and,' etc.) (e.g., Lincoln portrait); 2. A title proper for a musical work that consists of a type of composition modified by an adjective (e.g., Little suite)."[1]

Some examples of types of composition are:

Musical form or genre		Tempo indications	
concerto	rondo	adagio	allegro
trio sonata	suite	andantino	lento
symphony	sonata	moderato	presto

Terms commonly used		Medium of performance	
nocturne	piece	duet	quintet
movement	elegy	trio	sextet
music	prelude	quartet	septet

Some examples of commonly used distinctive titles that are often mistaken for types of composition are:

alleluia	double concerto	orientale	setting
antiphon	lament	ostinato	sketch
cantilena	miniature	poem	sonata da camera
canto	novelette	prologue	triple concerto

The Music Library Association's Working Group on Types of Compositions compiled a list of types of composition and distinctive titles often mistakenly considered to be generic. This list, *Types of Compositions for Use in Music Uniform Titles: A Manual for Use with AACR2 Chapter 25* is online at http://www.library.yale.edu/cataloging/music/types.htm.

Determining the Composer's Original Title (25.27A)

The uniform title is based on the composer's original title in the original language, if that can be determined. The first edition title is used to create the uniform title when it is not different from the composer's original title in wording or language. Not all publications of a work bear the composer's original title, and research may be required to determine it.

In his book *Describing Music Materials*, Smiraglia recommends consulting thematic indexes and lists of works in encyclopedias for works composed before 1800 and for works by prolific composers. Standard encyclopedias in the composer's language will suffice for works composed after 1800. For contemporary works, the work in hand may be the only publication, and the title on the item may be used as the uniform title. Smiraglia adds that title should "appear to be formulated in the composer's language or in the language of the country of the composer's principal residence or activity." It is not uncommon, however, for a composer to give a work a title in a language other than that of the country in which he or she lives or publishes.

The process of searching for a composer's original title provides the opportunity to find other information that may be needed to establish the uniform title. Such information could include how many works the composer wrote with that title or in that form, or elements that may be used in the uniform title, such as medium of performance, key, identifying numbers, etc.

The composer's original title is not always used as the uniform title. When another title in the same language is better known, that title is used. Smiraglia suggests checking at least three standard music encyclopedias in that language to determine if another title is better known. Only if the same form of the title is found in all the sources can that title be considered better known. This is generally more research than needs to be done, or indeed, more research than most catalogers have time to do, for most uniform titles.

When the composer's original title is very long, a shortened form may be used as the uniform title. A shorter form found in standard reference sources is preferred. Lacking citations in reference sources, the cataloger may formulate a brief form of the title.

Isolating the Initial Title Element (25.28)

Once the composer's original title is known, the initial title element needs to be isolated. To isolate the name or term from other title information that is commonly found on publications, remove the following information from the title proper:

• medium of performance
• key
• identifying numbers (i.e., numbers that are not an integral part of the title) as well as quantifying numbers
• date of composition.

If, after this type of information is excluded, what remains is the name of one or more type(s) of composition, the title is generic. If what remains is other than that, the title is distinctive.

Medium of Performance

The instrumentation may be stated explicitly ("Sonata for piano," "Orchestral suite") or implied ("Reed trio"). The manner in which the instrumentation is indicated may be unclear, such as "Sonata a cinque." A phrase such as "a due" or "a cinque" is considered to be a statement of medium of performance for a pre-twentieth-century work, and is removed from the initial title element (LCRI 25.28). (When used in the title of a post-nineteenth-century work, such a phrase is part of the initial title element and the title is distinctive. This is explained in Chapter 10, "Distinctive Titles.")

Key

Key may be stated with the mode indicated or merely as a tonal center of the work. It is important to know the names of the keys in French, German, Italian, and Spanish, as well as other languages in which music is published. A chart of the names of the keys in English, French, German, Italian, and Spanish is found in Chapter 8.

Sonate **Es-Dur**	Sonata in **A minor**	Concerto in **E flat**
Sonata **h-Moll**	Sonata en **re mayor**	Sonata in **D**

When the pitch of an instrument is indicated, this should not be considered to be the key of the work itself:

Sonata for trumpet in C & piano

Identifying Numbers

Identifying numbers differ from numbers that are an integral part of the title. Serial, opus, and thematic index numbers are all identifying numbers. They may appear in numeric or alphabetic format.

Serial Numbers

Serial numbers may be cardinal (e.g., 1, 2, 3) or ordinal (e.g., 1st, 2nd, 3rd) and appear in roman or arabic form, or spelled out in full or abbreviated, and may or may not have a term or symbol (e.g., "no.," "Nr.," "#," etc.) preceding them.

2te Sonate	**1ère** sonate	**Erste** Sonate	**First** sonata
1. Sonate	**1st** sonata	**I.** sonata	Sonata **#1**
Sonate **no. VII**	Sonate **Nr. 7**	Sonate **7**	Sonata **n.** 7

A number appearing in a title may be a quantifying number (indicating how many individual works are included) rather than an identifying number. It may be difficult to distinguish between the two when the title is in a language other than English.

Indicates serial number	Indicates the number of sonatas in the item
III. sonata	III sonates
6. Sonate	6 sonate

Opus and Thematic Index Numbers

Opus numbers may appear in arabic or roman form. The word "opus" may be in another language ("œuvre," "soch.," etc.), may be abbreviated ("op.," "œuv.," etc.), or may be another word meaning with the same meaning ("Werk").

Sonata **soch.** 57	Sonata **TWV 43:G10**	Sonate **Opus 13**
Sonata **opus** 1	Sonata **op.** 1	Sonate **op. X/4**
Sonate **55tes Werk**	Sonate **œuvre 55**	Sonate **œuvre XIe**
Sonates **op. I e II**	Sonatas **opp. 1, 14, 28, 29**	

Both opus or thematic index number and serial number may appear in a title proper:

Sonata **op. 1 n. 1**	Sonata **no 1 soch. 3/121**
Sonata **op. 3 Nr. IV**	Sonata **op. 5/1**

Date of Composition

The date of composition can be a single date or a range of dates and may include a revision date.

Sonata **(1828)** in B flat major
Suite for piano **1923-4**
1st symphony **(1965/rev. 1999)**

Examples of the Process of
Isolating the Initial Title Element

Title:
1st string quartet in D major for 2 violins, viola, & violoncello, opus 11 (1902)
• Remove the instrumentation:
    1st **string** quartet in D major ~~for 2 violins, viola, & violoncello~~, opus 11 (1902)
• Remove the key:
    1st ~~string~~ quartet **in D major** ~~for 2 violins, viola, & violoncello~~, opus 11 (1902)
• Remove identifying numbers:
    ~~1st~~ string quartet ~~in D major for 2 violins, viola, & violoncello, opus 11~~ (1902)
• Remove date of composition:
    ~~1st~~ string quartet ~~in D major for 2 violins, viola, & violoncello, opus 11 (1902)~~
• What remains is "quartet," a type of composition.

Title:
Little suite no. III for brass band op. 131 in D major
• Remove the instrumentation:
    Little suite no. III **for brass band** op. 131 in D major
• Remove the key:
    Little suite no. III ~~for brass band~~ op. 131 **in D major**
• Remove identifying numbers:
    Little suite **no. III for brass band op. 131 in D major**
• What remains is "Little suite," which is distinctive. Even though "suite" is a type of composition, the adjective "little" makes the title distinctive.

It is not always easy to isolate other title information. In this example, "unawd" is Welsh for "solo" and "telyn" is Welsh for "harp."

Title:
Diddanwch unawd telyn for solo harp
• Remove the instrumentation:
   Diddanwch ~~unawd telyn for solo harp~~
• What remains is "Diddanwch," which is the Welsh word for
entertainment or amusements, and is thus not a type of composition.

Determining Whether the Initial Title Element Is Generic or Distinctive (25.29A)

Once the initial title element has been isolated from the rest of the title,
there are a number of resources to use to determine whether or not it is a
type of composition. One such resource, mentioned above, is *Types of
Compositions for Use in Music Uniform Titles: A Manual for Use with
AACR2 Chapter 25*. This document includes the names of types of
composition and scope notes to guide in the application of AACR2
Chapter 25. Certain distinctive titles often thought to be types of
composition are also included. The list must be used in conjunction with
AACR2 and the LCRIs, and with the caveat that it is not exhaustive and
is being updated regularly.

  If a term is not found in the list of types, consult a music dictionary or
encyclopedia to determine whether the term is the name of a form or
genre, a generic term commonly used by composers, a tempo designation,
or a medium of performance. If it is not found in a music dictionary or
encyclopedia, searching the term in bibliographic records in OCLC may
reveal how other composers have used the term and whether the term fits
the definition of a type of composition.

  When the name of a type of composition is used for title of a work that
is not in that form, the title is considered to be distinctive (LCRI 25.27A1,
footnote 10). For example, Liszt's *Les Préludes* for orchestra is a
symphonic poem, not a set of preludes. Therefore, it is treated as a
distinctive title.

Liszt, Franz, ‡d 1811-1886. ‡t Préludes
not
Liszt, Franz, ‡d 1811-1886. ‡t Preludes, ‡m orchestra

The *Requiem for Solo Violoncello* by Sculthorpe is not a Requiem, and should be treated as a distinctive title.

Sculthorpe, Peter, ‡d 1929- ‡t Requiem
not
Sculthorpe, Peter, ‡d 1929- ‡t Requiem, ‡m violoncello

Because "song" is a type of composition only when a vocal work, the following uniform title is distinctive.

Golub, Peter. ‡t Song
not
Golub, Peter. ‡t Song, ‡m piano, clarinet, strings

Treatment of Titles Naming
More Than One Type of Composition

When the initial title element includes the names of two or more types of composition, its treatment as generic or distinctive will depend on whether there is a connecting word between the names of the types and what that word is. Whether or not a connecting word is used, it is important to determine if all of the types are actually present in the work or whether one of the names is used to modify the name of the other type.

Treat two or more names of types of composition, connected by a word or not, when each type is individually present in the work, as generic.

Theme with variations	Praeludium und Fuge
Scherzo, intermezzo, toccata	Arietta con variazioni
Introduction, thème & variations	Songs or ayres
Scherzo, Gigue, Romanze und Fughette	Studi o soli

When the initial title element with two or more types with a connecting word also includes an initial or internal number not integral to the title, treat it as generic, and omit the numbers from the uniform title.

Title proper	Initial title element
Thème et 3 variations	Thème et variations
Thème et trois doubles	Thème et doubles
Six valses et un galop	Valses et galop
An overture and six pieces	Overture and pieces

Titles in which two types of composition are named, but only one is actually present in the work, are distinctive. For example, the title "Sonate alla fuga" is distinctive. The adjectival phrase "alla fuga" defines the style of the sonata; there is no fugue in the work.

When two or more names of types of composition are used together, with no connecting word, and one of the types functions as an adjective, consider it to be distinctive.

Fantasy sonata   Symphonic prelude

There are two exceptions:

1. When together the two terms name another type of composition, the resulting title is generic. There are two instances of this exception·

Chorale prelude   Trio sonata

2. When the title of a pre-twentieth-century work is a medium of performance (e.g., "duet," "trio," "quartet"), qualified by an adjective or epithet such as "concertant(s)" or "concertante(s)," omit the adjective when formulating the uniform title. When the title is the name of a form (e.g., "fantasie," "nocturne," "rondo"), retain the adjective in the initial title element (LCRI 25.28).

Title includes medium of performance	Initial title element
Trio concertant	Trio(s)
Quartetto concertante	Quartet(s)

Title is the name of a form	Initial title element
Nocturnes concertants	Nocturnes concertants
Fantaisie concertante	Fantaisie concertante(s)

In all other cases, modifiers other than medium of performance or number make the phrase a distinctive title, no matter how generic sounding it is.

Short sonata   Leichte Stücke

When one or more names of types of composition are used together with a term that is distinctive, with or without a connecting word, treat the initial title element as distinctive.

Initial title element: rondo and miniature
Type: rondo
Not a type: miniature
Treatment: distinctive

Initial title element: prélude, esquisse et valse
Type: prélude, valse
Not a type: esquisse
Treatment: distinctive

Treatment of Terms Used in Phrases

Phrases That Include Medium of Performance

Bound Phrases

When a French or Italian title includes "d'," "de," "di," etc., connected to a medium of performance, a bound phrase results. The medium of performance in a bound phrase is retained in the initial title element.

Title proper	Initial title element
Messe d'intavolatura d'organo 1568	Messe d'intavolatura d'organo
Libro primo d'intavolatura di lauto	Intavolatura di lauto
Les pièces d'orgue (premier livre)	Pièces d'orgue
Premier livre de pièces de clavecin	Pièces de clavecin

Titles With Embedded Medium of Performance

The medium of performance is embedded when it is part of a compound word or is given internally in the title with no prepositional phrase to set it off from other words in the title. Even when embedded, the medium of performance is removed when isolating the initial title element—but it may be retained in the uniform title. It is a two-step process: in the application of 25.28A1, remove medium of performance, including statements that are embedded. When all the elements listed in 25.28A are removed, determine whether what remains is a type of composition or is distinctive. If a type of composition remains, apply 25.30B1 (see Chapters 4 and 5) and omit the medium of performance from the initial title element. If a distinctive title remains, 25.30B1 is *not* applied and the medium of performance is retained as it originally appeared in the title.

Title	Six piano pieces
Embedded medium of performance?	no
Remove medium of performance:	Six ~~piano~~ pieces
Remove quantifying number:	~~Six piano~~ pieces
Remaining elements,	pieces
Type or distinctive?	type
Retain medium of performance?	no
Initial title element:	Pieces

Title	Six little pieces for piano
Embedded medium of performance?	no
Remove medium of performance:	Six little pieces ~~for piano~~
Remove quantifying number:	~~Six~~ little pieces ~~for piano~~
Remaining elements:	little pieces
Type or distinctive?	distinctive
Retain medium of performance?	no
Initial title element:	Little pieces

Title	Six little piano pieces
Embedded medium of performance?	yes
Remove medium of performance:	Six little ~~piano~~ pieces
Remove quantifying number:	~~Six~~ little ~~piano~~ pieces
Remaining elements:	Little pieces
Type or distinctive?	distinctive
Retain medium of performance?	yes
Initial title element:	Little piano pieces

Title	Sechs Klavierstücke
Embedded medium of performance?	yes
Remove medium of performance:	Sechs ~~Klavier~~stücke
Remove quantifying number:	~~Sechs~~ ~~Klavier~~stücke
Remaining elements:	Stücke
Type or distinctive?	type
Retain medium of performance?	no
Initial title element:	Stücke

Title	Sechs kleine Klavierstücke
Embedded medium of performance?	yes
Remove medium of performance:	Sechs kleine ~~Klavier~~stücke
Remove quantifying number:	~~Sechs~~ kleine ~~Klavier~~stücke
Remaining elements:	Kleine Stücke
Type or distinctive?	distinctive
Retain medium of performance?	yes
Initial title element:	Kleine Klavierstücke

If the medium of performance includes a prepositional phrase, even when it is an embedded prepositional phrase, it is removed and is not included in the initial title element:

Title	Variations pour flûte et piano sur un thème de Mozart
Embedded medium of performance?	yes
Remove medium of performance:	Variations ~~pour flûte et piano~~ sur un thème de Mozart
Remaining elements:	Variations sur un thème de Mozart
Type or distinctive?	distinctive
Retain medium of performance?	no
Initial title element:	Variations sur un thème de Mozart

Works in a Numbered Series with Titles That Include a Phrase With the Name of a Type of Composition

When the title proper of a work that is in a numbered sequence of works of all the same type includes the name of that type as well as other words, treat the title as generic and use the name of the type as the initial title element (LCRI 25.27D1). In these two examples, the name of the type appears in the title proper, and so the initial title element is that type.

The serial number in the subtitle *Concerto No 3* indicates that this work is in a numbered sequence of concertos. Because the word "concerto" appears in the title proper, the uniform title is not "Concerto elegíaco." The uniform title is generic, with the initial title element "Concertos."

Title: **Concerto** elegíaco : **concerto** no 3 pour guitare et orchestre
Initial title element: Concertos

"Symphony no. 21" indicates that this work is in a numbered sequence of symphonies. Because the word "symphony" appears in the title proper, the uniform title is not "Symphony Etchmiadzin." The uniform title is generic, with the initial title element "Symphonies."

Title: **Symphony** Etchmiadzin : (**Symphony** no. 21)
Initial title element: Symphonies

The word "suite" appears in the title proper. The chief source of information does not indicate that this is one of a numbered sequence of numbered suites for orchestra. However, because the title on the cover indicates that the work is in a numbered sequence of suites for orchestra, the uniform title is not "Geharnischte Suite." It is generic, with the initial title element "Suites."

Title: Geharnischte **Suite** : op. 34a : für Orchester
On cover: **Zweite** Orchester-**Suite**
Initial title element: Suites

When the name of the type of composition is *not* present in the title proper, the uniform title is based on the title proper, even if the work is one in a numbered sequence. In these examples, the name of the type appears in the subtitle, but not in the title proper, making the uniform title distinctive.

Title: Circe : symphony no. 18 for orchestra
Initial title element: Circe

Title: Mysterious mountain : (Symphony no. 2, opus 132)
Initial title element: Mysterious mountain

This is an example of information found elsewhere changing the choice of uniform title. The title proper includes the name of a type, but there is no indication on the item that the work appears in a numbered sequence of quintets. However, the source on which the uniform title is ultimately based reveals that the work is one in a numbered sequence. The uniform title is generic, with "Quintets" as the initial title element.

Title: Gran quintetto : do minore : für zwei Violinen,
                               Viola, Violoncello, und Kontrabass
Reference source: **2 quint.** per 2 vl, vla, vcl e cb, **n. 1** Gran quintetto
                               in do min., **n. 2** Gran quintetto in mi min.
Initial title element: Quintets

The Word "Double" or "Triple" in the Initial Title Element

The word "double" or "triple" (or their equivalents in other languages) used in conjunction with the name of a type of composition can have various meanings, which will determine whether the initial title element is generic or distinctive. For example, a double quartet is in reality an octet; thus "Double quartet" is distinctive. A double fugue is still a fugue, and the title in any language is generic and is translated into English.

Even though a "double concerto" or "triple concerto" (or their equivalents in other languages) is still a concerto, the title is distinctive, according to LCRI 25.27A1, footnote 10. This treatment implies that the word "double" is more than an indication of medium of performance (e.g., two soloists) and should be retained in the initial title element.

Note

1. Richard P. Smiraglia, *Describing Music Materials: A Manual for Descriptive Cataloging of Printed and Recorded Music, Music Videos, and Archival Music Collections: For Use with AACR2 and APPM*. 3rd ed. (Lake Crystal, Minn.: Soldier Creek Press, 1997), p. 225-27.

Chapter 3
Formulating the Initial Title Element: Generic Titles (25.29)

Once the initial title element has been isolated and determined to be generic, there are two questions to ask about the title (25.29A1):

1. Did the composer write more than one work of this type?	2. Does the name of the type have cognate forms in English, French, German, and Italian?
• If yes, use the plural form of the name of the type. • If not, use the singular form of the name of the type.	• If yes, use the English spelling of the name of the type. • If not, use the composer's original spelling of the name of the type.

Singular Versus Plural

Rule 25.29A1 instructs the cataloger to give the name of the type in the plural unless the composer wrote only one work of the type. Even when the item being cataloged is the only work of that type for that medium of performance, use the plural form if the composer has written other works of that type for other mediums of performance. For example, use "Sonatas" as the initial title element for a composer's only piano sonata among several sonatas for other instruments.

Determining how many works of a specific type a composer has written may be as easy as noting that the title includes a serial number of "2" or higher— a good indication that there is at least one other work of that type. Many scores and recordings include accompanying notes with biographical details, from which may be gleaned information concerning the composer's other works of a particular type.

When it cannot be ascertained from the item itself, determining if the composer wrote more than one work of a specific type can sometimes consume the majority of the time spent establishing the uniform title. There are several sources that can be consulted quickly:

- A thematic catalog or list of the composer's works
- The authority file: If there is no authority record for a particular work, browse the name/title uniform titles in the authority file for an authority record for another work of that type by that composer
- Bibliographic records in OCLC for other works of that type by the composer.

Being familiar with the strengths and quirks of print reference sources can save the cataloger time. Knowing which sources are likely to be useful or which sources *not* to consult is valuable. Older reference sources will not help when the composer is very young. Even current reference works may not include works composed within the last few years.

The Internet can provide a wealth of information about obscure and new composers, and, in fact, sometimes may be the first source to search. Most useful are composers' websites and publishers' websites, both of which usually includes work lists. A publisher's website, however, will usually include *only* the works that it has issued. Any information taken from the Internet should be evaluated according to the nature of the website and expertise of the author. The completeness and accuracy of information on the Internet cannot be assumed.

There is one instance in which the plural form is used when the composer has written only one work of that type. This applies to a living composer who assigned a serial number, including "1," to a work. Even lacking evidence of another work of that type, use the plural form of the name of the type, with the assumption that the composer intends to write more works of that type. However, if the composer is deceased and the work is the only one of that type, even when the composer gave it the serial number "1," use the singular form of the name of the type. (The serial number is also omitted from the uniform title.)

Neither rule 25.29 nor its LCRI specifies whether the cataloger should consider only initial title elements consisting solely of the name of one type of composition or all titles that include the name of a type of composition. General practice is to disregard titles that, after the application of rule 25.28, include the name of the type of composition as well as other words. For example, if a composer wrote one sonata, which is for piano, and another work entitled *Sonata Breve*, should the second work be disregarded when considering whether the initial title element for the first work should be singular or plural? LC practice varies on this, as reflected in the authority file. For example, Bloch's *Concerto Symphonique* was considered in the decision to pluralize the initial title element for Bloch's sole work titled "concerto."

Bloch, Ernest, ‡d 1880-1959. ‡t Concerto symphonique
Bloch, Ernest, ‡d 1880-1959. ‡t **Concertos**, ‡m violin, orchestra

In this example found in the authority file, Britten's *Simple Symphony* was disregarded when formulating the initial title element for his Symphony op. 68.

Britten, Benjamin, ‡d 1913-1876. ‡t Simple symphony
Britten, Benjamin, †d 1913-1876. ‡t **Symphony**, ‡m violoncello, orchestra, ‡n op. 68

Lost Works

Rule 25.29A1 is being interpreted strictly (e.g., "give the name of the type in the plural unless the composer *wrote* [emphasis added] only one work of the type"). When there is evidence that more than one work of the type was written, even when all but one are lost, use the plural form of the name of the type. The example below illustrates the uniform title for Lutosławski's piano sonata. Both of Lutosławski's other sonatas are lost.

Lutosławski, Witold, ‡d 1913-1994. ‡t Sonatas, ‡m piano

Language of the Plural Form of the Name of a Type of Composition

The *Types of Compositions for Use in Music Uniform Titles* indicates for most types of composition their singular and plural forms. The language of the plural form may not be in English, even when the name of the type is in English. For example, "divertimenti," not "divertimentos," is the plural form of "divertimento." AACR2 offers no guidance in formulating the plural form, and often names of types with similar endings in the singular have different endings in the plural, such as "inter-mezzo/intermezzi" and "passamezzo/passamezzos." Other similar names of types have different plural forms, such as "scherzetto/scherzetti" and "scherzino/scherzinos." When one single accepted form of a plural cannot be determined, a scope note indicates this and gives instructions on use of the plural form. For example, the two plural forms "ricercars" and "ricercari" are given with a scope note with the instruction to "use the form used by the composer and maintain that form throughout for that composer."[1]

Sacred Music With Liturgical Titles

Sacred music that is not part of a prescribed liturgy is entered under the name of the composer. (Prescribed liturgical works are entered under the heading for the church or denominational body to which it pertains, as per 21.39A1.) Most sacred titles are not used in the plural form even when the composer wrote more than one work with that title (LCRI 25.29A). Examples of sacred titles always used in the singular are Agnus Dei, Credo, Gloria, Kyrie, Miserere, Offertorium, Salve Regina, Sanctus, Stabat Mater, and Te Deum. The two exceptions to the rule are magnificats and requiems, for which the plural forms are used when a composer wrote more than one work with either of these titles.

Cognates

When the name of the type of composition has cognate forms in English, French, German, and Italian, the English form of the name is used in the uniform title. These are examples of types of composition that are cognates. The name of the type is translated into English for the uniform title.

English	French	German	Italian
symphony	symphonie	Sinfonie	sinfonie
sonata	sonate	Sonate	sonata
Mass	Messe	Messe	Mass
rondo	rondeau	Rondo	rondo

These are examples of types of composition that do not have cognates in all four languages. Therefore, the name of the type is not translated into English; the term is used in the composer's original language.

English	French	German	Italian
piece	pièce, morceau	Stück	pezzo
movement	mouvement	Satz	movimento

For example, the initial title element for *Sechs Klavierstücke* will be "Stücke" rather than "Pieces" because the English, French, German, and Italian forms of the word are not cognates.

There are some types of composition with cognate forms that are used in the composer's original form, even though doing so appears to contradict rule 25.29.

English	French	German	Italian
almain(c), alman	allemande	Allemande	—
chorale prelude	prélude de choral	Choralvorspiele	—
corant	courante	—	corrente
etude, study	étude	Etüde, Studie	studio
fantasia, fantasy, phantasy	fantaisie	Fantasie, Phantasy	fantasia

The *Types of Compositions for Use in Music Uniform Titles* indicates whether to use the English form of the name of the type or the name in the original language.

The names of types of composition in Eastern European languages may not have cognates in English, French, German, and Italian, making them difficult to recognize as types of composition. For example, the following words in Hungarian are all types of composition that appear not to be related to their English equivalents:

Hungarian	English
dal	song
darab	piece
induló	march
kettős	duet(s) (may also mean "double")
rőgtőnzés	improvisation
tétel	movement

Additionally, the plural ending of a name of a type of composition may be unfamiliar or difficult to determine. For example, the singular and plural equivalents of "piece" in are "skladba" and "skladby" in Czech, "darab" and "darabok" in Hungarian, "utwór" and "utwóry" in Polish, and "p′esa" and "p′esy" in Russian. The singular and plural equivalents of "movement" are "tétel" and "tételek" in Hungarian and "chast′" and "chasti" in Russian. Foreign-language dictionaries are necessary when working with music materials in Eastern European languages, although general dictionaries may not always give the correct form of a word as it applies to music. Consultation with colleagues with background in these languages is recommended.

Applying 25.29A1 to Titles Naming More Than One Type of Composition

Singular Versus Plural

When the initial title element includes the names of two or more types of composition, with or without a connecting word, and the composer wrote more than one work with that title, the names are given in the plural only when they appear in that form in the source on which the uniform title is based:

Title:	Prelude and fugue no. 2 for piano
Initial title element:	Prelude and fugue

Title:	Three preludes and fugues for piano
Initial title element:	Preludes and fugues

Cognates

An initial title element consisting of the names of two or more types of composition, whether or not connected by a word, should not be translated into English even if all the names of types of composition in the title have cognates in English, French, German, and Italian. The connecting word should also not be translated into English.

Preĺiudĭi i fugi	*not*	Prelude and fugue
Adagio und Fuge	*not*	Adagio and fugue
Variè et morceau	*not*	Variation and piece
Prélude avec danse	*not*	Prelude with dance
Wariacje i fuga	*not*	Variations and fugue

When the connecting word is a character meaning "and," the character is retained and not spelled out.

Theme & variations   *not*   Theme and variations

When the name of a type of composition is qualified by the adjective "concertant," "concertante," or "concertantes" (or their equivalents in other languages) and the adjective is retained in the initial title element as per LCRI 25.28, neither the name of the type nor the word "concertant" is translated into English.

Sérénade concertante	*not*	Serenade concertante
Serenata concertante	*not*	Serenade concertante
Nocturno concertant	*not*	Nocturne concertant
Notturno concertant	*not*	Nocturne concertant
Variazioni concertanti	*not*	Variations concertantes
Variações concertantes	*not*	Variations concertantes
Polonezy concertant	*not*	Polonaises concertantes
Polonesi concertanti	*not*	Polonaises concertantes

Title on the Item Varies From the Composer's Original Title

The title on the item may not be the title originally given to the work by the composer. For example:

Title proper:	Solos for a German flute, a hoboy, or violin with a thorough bass for the harpsichord or bass violin
Composer's title:	Sonatas
Initial title element:	Sonatas

Title proper:	Sonata h-Moll, op. 2, für Flöte (Violin) und Bass continuo
Composer's title:	Solo
Initial title element:	Solo(s)

Title proper:	Concerto a-Moll für 2 Flöten, 2 Violinen, und Basso continuo
Composer's title:	Concerto grosso
Initial title element:	Concerto grosso or Concerti grossi

When the Composer's Original Title Is Not Used

According to 25.29B1, the names of some types of composition are automatically substituted with a prescribed name. Use the term "duet(s)" as the initial title element for a work entitled "duo," "Duett," "duetto," etc. Use the initial title element "trio sonata(s)" for a seventeenth- or eighteenth-century work for two solo instruments and continuo with the title "Sonata," "Sonata a tre," or "Trio," even if the continuo part is realized for a keyboard and bass instrument (25.29C1).

Note

1 "Ricercare/Ricercars/Ricercari" in *Types of Compositions for Use in Music Uniform Titles.*

Chapter 4
Additions to the
Initial Title Element:
Generic Titles (25.30)

Further identifying elements are added to the initial title element of generic titles (under most circumstances) for the purpose of identification of the work and to distinctive titles when needed for the purpose of conflict resolution. These elements are to be added, as appropriate, in the following order:

1. medium of performance (25.30B)
2. numeric identifying elements (25.30C)
3. key (25.30D)
4. other identifying elements (25.30E)

Each of these categories is explained below and discussed in detail in later chapters.

1. Medium of Performance (25.30B)

The statement of medium of performance is defined as "a concise statement of the instrumental and/or vocal medium of performance for which a musical work was originally intended."[1] It is usually added to the uniform title when the initial title element consists solely of the name of a type, or two or more types, of composition. The statement of medium of performance may also be added to break a conflict between titles that would not generally include it, such as liturgical titles and distinctive titles.

A statement of medium of performance is *not* added to generic titles under any of these conditions (25.30B1, 25.30B11):

- The work:
    - consists of a set of compositions for different instrumentation
    - is one in a series of works with the same title, each for a different medium of performance (25.30B1b).
- Stating the medium of performance would be so complex that arranging the title(s) by another identifying element, such as number, would be better (25.20B1d).
- The medium of performance was not designated or clearly defined by the composer or is indeterminate (25.30B1c and 25.20B11).
- The medium is implied by the title. The following list of types of composition fall within this category (25.30B1a).

Title	Implied medium
chorale prelude	organ
mass	voices, with or without accompaniment
overture	orchestra
songs, Lieder, etc.	solo voice(s) with accompaniment for stringed keyboard instrument (e.g., piano, harpsichord, clavichord, virginal)
symphony	orchestra (including chamber orchestra); this also applies to "sinfonietta"

Although AACR2 does not specifically state it, this list is not exhaustive and other types of similar nature may also be assumed to have implied mediums of performance. For example, the implied medium of performance for anthems, motets, psalms, etc., is the same as for masses: voices, with or without accompaniment.

2. Numeric Identifying Elements (25.30C)

Numeric identifying elements are added to generic titles when they can be determined.

Serial Numbers (25.30C2)

Serial numbers apply to a composer's works with the same title and the same medium of performance. Add the serial number to a uniform title when it is present on the item or can be found in standard reference works. A range of numbers may be used when they are consecutive. Serial numbers are usually given before the opus number, when both are used.

Opus and Thematic Index Numbers (25.30C3-25.30C4)

Opus numbers may be used in addition to serial numbers for some composers' works. Generally, opus numbers are assigned by the composer, although a work published before 1800 may have had the opus number assigned by the publisher.

Thematic index numbers are assigned by the person who creates a catalog of a composer's works. A "thematic index" may be arranged by medium of performance, by type of composition, or by some other criterion.

3. Key (25.30D)

The key of a musical work is the tonality of the work or of its principal movements. For works composed before 1900, include the key in the uniform title, even if it is not stated on the item. For works composed from 1900 to the present, the key is given in the uniform title only if it is part of the composer's original title or is in the title of the first edition

4. Other Identifying Elements (25.30E)

Occasionally, the uniform titles for two different works by the same composer will be identical, even after applying the rules outlined above. This is considered to be a conflict, which is resolved by adding these elements, in the following order of preference, to break the conflict:
• year of completion of composition
• year of publication
• any other identifying element such as place of composition or first publisher.

Note

1. AACR2, Appendix D, *Glossary.*

Chapter 5
Medium of Performance: Instrumental Music (25.30B2-B7)

When it is required to state the medium of performance, it follows the initial title element, preceded by a comma, in ‡m. Individual elements within the statement of medium of performance are separated by a comma. Follow 25.30B1 and 25.30B11 to determine when the statement of medium of performance is omitted from a uniform title for an instrumental work (see Chapter 4, Section 1, "Medium of Performance").

Names of Instruments

Rule 25.30B4 prescribes the use of English when naming the instruments. When an instrument is known by more than one name, the rule and its corresponding rule interpretation specify which form to use.

Use this term	Rather than
continuo	basso continuo, figured bass, thorough bass
contrabassoon	double bassoon
double bass	string bass, contrabass
English horn	cor anglais
harpsichord	cembalo, virginal, clavecin
horn	French horn
keyboard instrument	unspecified keyboard instrument
timpani	kettle drums
viola da gamba	bass viol, gamba
violoncello	cello

In addition to using the specific names above, when stating the name of any instrument, omit the following:

1.The key in which instrument is pitched (25.30B4a)

Use	Rather than
clarinet	clarinet in A
horn	F horn

2. The designation of range of instrument (25.30B4b)

Use	Rather than
clarinet	bass clarinet
recorder	treble recorder
trombone	tenor trombone

3. The names of alternative instruments (25.30B4c). For example, use "flute" for a work for flute or violin, not "flute/violin."

The terms used for flute and recorder can be misleading, depending on the country and date of publication. In general, the following terminology was used in French and English publications before 1800.

Use *recorder* when the following terms appear on an item published in England or France before 1800	
common flute	flûte à neuf trous
English flute	flûte d'Angleterre
flauto	flûte douce
flûte	recorder
flûte à bec	
flute (only in English publications of 1673-1800)	
Use *flute* when the following terms appear on an item published in England or France before 1800	
flauto traverso	flûte traversière
flute (in English publications)	German flute
flute/flûte d'Allemagne	traverso

Table 5.1: The Terms Used for Flute and Recorder[1]

Works for One Instrument

A uniform title for a work composed for one instrument identifies that instrument in the statement of medium of performance.

Sonatas, ‡m oboe
Mazurka, ‡m accordion
Impromptu, ‡m viola

Keyboard Instruments

Stating the medium of performance for keyboard instruments requires special instructions. Use "keyboard instrument" for music for an unspecified solo keyboard instrument that can be played on any keyboard instrument.

Rondos, ‡m keyboard instrument

"Keyboard instrument" is also used when a composer's works of a given type are split between a specified keyboard instrument and an unspecified keyboard instrument or between harpsichord or clavichord and piano, and the predominant instrument among these is not apparent. When the predominant instrument can be determined, use the name of that instrument for all works of that type (LCRI 25.30B4).

For named keyboard instruments, use the name of that instrument using an indication of number of hands when there is more than one performer per instrument. The following examples use piano, but the practice applies to all keyboard instruments.

Use	For
piano, 1 hand	1 instrument, 1 hand, either right or left
piano	1 instrument, 2 hands (1 performer)
piano, 3 hands	1 instrument, 3 hands (2 performers)
piano, 4 hands	1 instrument, 4 hands (2 performers)
piano, 6 hands	1 instrument, 6 hands (3 performers)

Percussion Instruments

Individual percussion instruments may be named in the statement of medium of performance.

Etude(s), ‡m snare drum   Suite(s), ‡m marimba

The term "percussion" is used to denote a single percussionist playing two or more percussion instruments.

Etude(s), ‡m percussion   Suite(s), ‡m percussion

Works for Computer, Electronics, Synthesizer, or Tape

Medium of performance for music for computer, electronics, synthesizer, or tape is not addressed in AACR2 or the LCRIs. General practice is to use the term used by the composer.

Title: Two pieces for computer
Uniform title: Pieces, ‡m computer

Title: Study : electronic study
Uniform title: Study, ‡m electronics

Title: Fanfare in 19-note equal tuning
Uniform title: Fanfare, ‡m synthesizer

Title: Three etudes for magnetic tape
Uniform title: Etudes, ‡m tape

Works for More Than One Instrument, One Performer to a Part

Follow rule 25.30B2 when stating the medium of performance for music for more than one performer, one performer to a part. Name the medium in one or more of the following ways, in this order of preference:

1. by standard chamber music combinations
2. by individual instruments
3. by groups of instruments.

Although using standard chamber combinations is the first preference for stating medium of performance, naming individual instruments will be discussed first, followed by standard chamber combinations, and then other groups of instruments.

Individually Named Instruments

Order of Instruments

Follow the guidelines in 25.30B1 for the order of instruments in the statement of medium of performance:
   • voices
   • keyboard instrument when there is more than one non-keyboard instrument
   • other instruments in score order
   • continuo.

Other Instruments in Score Order

The phrase "other instruments in score order" has been interpreted in two ways: as the order in the particular score in hand and as the order in an orchestral score. The generally accepted interpretation is the order of the score in hand. It is important to note that usually the instruments are listed in the title proper in the order in which they appear in the score, but occasionally the order of instruments stated in the title may not be the order of the instruments in the score itself. Score order for an instrumental work on a sound recording can be determined by consulting a reference source or the published score or by checking bibliographic records for the score. When it is not possible to determine score order for instrumental works on sound recordings, the cataloger should use traditional score order.

New Grove Dictionary of Music and Musicians, 2nd ed. defines the conventional score order for an orchestral work as woodwinds, brass, percussion, and strings, with each group subdivided by range, from highest to lowest. Harp, celesta, and piano usually appear between the percussion and strings in an orchestral score. In chamber music, the piano is generally given in the lowest staff of the score. Score order for the standard chamber combinations (piano trio, string trio, piano quartet, string quartet, woodwind quartet, piano quintet, wind quintet) usually does not vary. Instruments in other chamber works may be scored in orchestral order, by family, or by range, from highest to lowest, regardless of instrumental family.[2] This means that, although there may be a standard convention for orchestral music, practice will vary for chamber music, as will the order of instruments in the uniform title.

Additionally, the function of any given instrument determines its place in the score. For example, celesta may function as a percussion instrument or it may play a chordal role. The function of an instrument may have changed through time from being an accompanying instrument in the Baroque era to a solo instrument in the eighteenth and nineteenth centuries. Compositions of the last hundred years may not even follow conventional scoring practices.

Thus, the application of rule 25.30B1 may result in different uniform titles for similar works by different composers. In these examples of quintets by two different composers, the horn part is above the bassoon part in the score for the first work, but below the bassoon part in the score for the second work.

Title: Quintett für Oboe (auch Englisch Horn), Klarinette,
             Horn, Fagott, und Klavier
Uniform title: Quintet(s), ‡m piano, oboe, clarinet, **horn, bassoon**

Title: Quintet for oboe, clarinet, bassoon, horn, and piano
Uniform title: Quintet(s), ‡m piano, oboe, clarinet, **bassoon, horn**

The composer of the first of these two trios scored the violin above the horn, while the composer of the second trio scored the violin below the horn. Thus the order of instruments in the statement of medium of performance differs, even though the works are for the same medium.

Title: Trio for violin, horn, and piano
Uniform title: Trio(s), ‡m piano, **violin, horn**

Title: Trio for horn, violin, and piano
Uniform title: Trio(s), ‡m piano, **horn, violin**

In all of the examples above, even though the keyboard instrument, piano in this case, was scored below the other instruments, it was named first in the statement of medium of performance. This follows the guidelines for keyboard instruments in 25.30B1, which are explained next.

Keyboard Instrument When There Is More Than One Non-keyboard Instrument

The placement of a keyboard instrument in the medium of performance varies according to the number of other instruments included. When there are two instruments, one of which is a keyboard instrument, the keyboard instrument is named second.

‡m violin, piano

Even when the non-keyboard instrument is described as accompaniment, the keyboard instrument is named second.

Title: Sonate pour le piano-forte avec accompagnemt. de flûte
Uniform title: Sonata(s), ‡m flute, piano

When there are three or more instruments, one of which is a keyboard instruments and two or more of which are *not* keyboard instruments, name the keyboard instrument first, followed the rest of the instruments in the order given in 25.30B1.

‡m organ, flute, violin   ‡m harpsichord, oboe, violoncello

The practice is applied to works for two keyboard instruments and two or more other instruments.

Rondo, ‡m pianos (2), trumpet, trombone

The rule does not specifically address works for two keyboard instruments and one other instrument; however, it is being applied to such works.

Preludes, ‡m pianos (2), vibraphone

Two or More of an Individually Named Instrument

When two or more of an instrument are required for performance and that instrument is named in the statement of medium of performance, it may be necessary to indicate the number required. The name of the instrument is given in the plural followed by the number required in parentheses (25.30B1).

pianos (2)   violins (3)

Follow the guidelines in 25.30B1 to determine when to add quantifying numbers when two or more of any named instrument are required for performance. When it can be inferred from the initial title element, do not indicate the number of instruments, but do use the plural form of the name of the instrument. When it cannot be determined from the initial title element, include the number in parentheses following the name of the instrument in its plural form.

When the initial title element is generic and names a medium of performance, the number of performers may be inferred. Examples of a medium of performance as initial title element are "duet," "trio," "quartet," "quintet," "sextet," "septet," "octet," and "nonet," which imply two, three, four, five, six, seven, eight, and nine performers, respectively.

A medium of performance as initial title element is not always straightforward. A work entitled "Solo" may be for a single instrument; however, many seventeenth-century works for solo instrument and continuo were titled "Solo."

Works titled "duet" imply two performers, thus the number of performers is not indicated.

Duet(s), ‡m pianos

Duets may have keyboard accompaniment, requiring three performers. Even when three performers are required, the number of performers is not indicated. However, the provision of 25.30B1 that prescribes naming the keyboard instrument first when there are two or more non-keyboard instruments is applied here. In this uniform title, the keyboard instrument is named first and the number of bassoons is not indicated, because it is assumed that there are two.

Duet(s), ‡m piano, bassoons

"Trio" implies three performers; either three different instruments, two of one instrument and one of another, or three of the same instrument. Because the number of instruments is implied, it is generally unnecessary to indicate the number of any individual instrument.

Only flutes are named in this statement of medium, and since there can be only three flutes, it is unnecessary to indicate the number of flutes.

Trio(s), ‡m flutes   *not*   Trio(s), ‡m flutes (3)

"Flutes" is in the plural and clarinet in the singular, implying that there are two or more flutes and one clarinet. Because the initial title element is "trio," there can be only two flutes and thus the number of flutes is not needed.

Trio(s), ‡m flutes, clarinet   *not*   Trio(s), ‡m flutes (2), clarinet

"Quartet" implies four performers. In the following uniform title, because only one instrument is named, there can be only four of that instrument. It is unnecessary to indicate the number of violins.

Quartet(s), ‡m violins   *not*   Quartet(s), ‡m violins (4)

When the initial title element is the name of a form or genre, a generic term commonly used by composers, or a tempo designation, it is necessary to include the number of individually named instruments, when two or more are required. For example, "suite" does not imply any number of performers; therefore, the number of violins must be indicated.

Suites, ‡m violins (4)

Works for the same medium of performance, but with different initial title elements, may require different statements of medium. In the example below, because each instrument is named in the plural, it can be assumed there is more than one of each; thus the number of instruments can be inferred from the initial title element "sextet." Sextet implies six. Three instruments are named in the plural. There is more than one of each instrument, but there can be only two of each ($3 \times 2 = 6$).

Sextets, ‡m violins, violas, violoncellos

Because "suite" does not imply any number of performers, the number of each instrument must be indicated.

Suites, ‡m violins (2), violas, (2), violoncellos (2)

It is not always necessary to qualify the names of *all* of the instruments with a quantifying number. Qualify only as many instruments as needed to be able to determine the number of the other instrument(s).

"Quintet" implies five. It is not possible to determine from the uniform title below whether there are there two horns and three trumpets or three horns and two trumpets.

Quintets, ‡m horns, trumpets

In the previous title, only the number of horns needs to be indicated. The number of trumpets can then be inferred from the initial title element and should not be included in the state of medium of performance.

Quintets, ‡m horns (3), trumpets
not
Quintets, ‡m horns (3), trumpets (2)

Quintets, ‡m horns (2), trumpets
not
Quintets, ‡m horns (2), trumpets (3)

"Sextet" implies six. In the next example, are there three violins and three violas, or two violins and four violas, or four violins and two violas required for performance?

Sextets, ‡m violins, violas

The number of violins needs to be indicated, which will then imply the number of violas.

Sextets, ‡m violins (4), violas
not
Sextets, ‡m violins (4), violas (2)

There is an unofficial LC practice that is an exception to rule 25.30B1. When more than one instrument is being qualified, all individually named instruments are qualified when there is more than one of each, even when the number of instruments can be inferred from the initial title element.

For example, a nonet for violins, violas, and violoncellos could require one of these combinations for performance:

1. two of one instrument, two of another instrument, five of one instrument (e.g., five violins, two violas, two violoncellos)

2. two of one instrument, three of one instrument, four of one instrument (e.g., four violins, three violas, two violoncellos)

3. three of each instrument (e.g., three violins, three violas, three violoncellos)

The uniform title for the first combination would include the number of violins only, since the plural forms of the name of the other two instruments imply two each.

Nonets, ‡m violins (5), violas, violoncellos

However, the names of all *three* instruments in the second and third combinations are qualified by number. A string nonet with four violins implies that there are three violas and two violoncellos or two violas and three violoncellos, requiring the number of violas to be indicated. Because the name of more than one instrument is being qualified by number, all of the names are then qualified, even though the number of violoncellos can be inferred.

Nonets, ‡m violins (4), violas (3), violoncellos (2)
not
Nonets, ‡m violins (4), violas (3), violoncellos

Nonets, ‡m violins (4), violas (2), violoncellos (3)
not
Nonets, ‡m violins (4), violas (2), violoncellos

A nonet for three violins, three violas, and three violoncellos requires the number of violins and violas to be indicated. Because the name of more than one instrument is being qualified, the number of violoncellos is indicated, even though it can be inferred.

Nonets, ‡m violins (3), violas (3), violoncellos (3)
not
Nonets, ‡m violins (3), violas (3), violoncellos

The statement of medium of performance for a work requiring one or more performers of the same instrument in different groupings includes a range of numbers representing the total number of performers needed, following the name of the instrument in its plural form.

Title: Zwei Studien für ein bis vier Violoncelli
Uniform title: Studien, ‡m violoncellos (1-4)

One Performer on Two or More Instruments

When a work requires one performer to play two or more instruments, the statement of medium of performance will be formulated according to whether or not the performer is required to play the instruments simultaneously. If the performer switches between the instruments, then the singular form of the name of the instrument is used. In this example, the flutist switches between flute, alto flute, and piccolo; "flute" is used in the statement of medium of performance.

Title: Two ballades, flute (piccolo, alto flute) and piano
Uniform title: Ballades, ‡m flute, piano

When the performer is required to play more than one of the same instrument simultaneously the plural form of the name of the instrument, followed by the appropriate number in parentheses, is used. Here, the guitarist plays both guitars simultaneously.

Title: Nocturne for two guitars performed by one player
Uniform title: Nocturne(s), ‡m guitars (2)

Keyboard Instruments

For named keyboard instruments, use the name of the instrument with an indication of number of instruments, and number of hands when applicable, when there are two or more performers on two or more instruments. The following examples use piano, but the practice applies to all keyboard instruments.

Use	For
pianos (2)	2 instruments, 2 hands each (2 performers)
pianos (2), 6 hands	2 instruments (2 performers on one piano; 1 performer on the other piano)
pianos (2), 8 hands	2 instruments, 4 hands each (4 performers, 2 on each piano)
pianos (3)	3 instruments, 3 performers

Give two different solo keyboard instruments in score order.

Ballade, ‡m piano, organ   Duets, ‡m organ, piano

Percussion Instruments

Percussion music or works that include percussion can present problems in formulating the medium of performance. For works requiring two or more performers of the same instrument, name that instrument in the statement of medium of performance, qualified by number of performers if the number cannot be inferred from the initial title element.

Duets, ‡m drums   Etudes, ‡m drums (2)
Suites, ‡m drum sets (3)   Quartets, ‡m marimbas
Suites, ‡m marimbas (4)   Postludes, ‡m marimbas (2), timpani

Even when one performer is using two or more timpani, the number of timpani is not indicated.

Pieces, ‡m timpani

One performer may be required to play two or more percussion instruments, each notated on a separate line of the staff. When the number of percussionists is not indicated on a score and it cannot be inferred from the initial title element, the cataloger must make a decision if all of the parts could be played by one performer. Bibliographic records for a sound recording of the work may give clues to the number of percussionists required for performance.

The term "percussion" is used to denote a group of percussionists, each playing one or more instruments. This can be confusing, since "percussion" is also used to denote a single percussionist playing two or more percussion instruments. The following examples illustrate the former.

Uniform title	Instrumentation
Quartets, ‡m percussion	percussion quartet
Prelude and fugue, ‡m percussion	percussion quartet
Sextet, ‡m pianos (2), percussion	two pianos, percussion quartet
Sonata, ‡m percussion	three percussionists

The order in which the term "percussion" appears in the statement of medium of performance is determined by the number of performers required. In the first uniform title below, the position of the word "percussion" implies that only one percussionist is required. The number of percussionists required for the work represented by the second uniform title cannot be determined from the uniform title. It can be inferred from the third uniform title that four percussionists are required.

Uniform title	Instrumentation
Rondo, ‡m percussion, organ	1 percussionist, organ
Rondo, ‡m organ, percussion	2 or more percussionists, organ
Quintet, ‡m organ, percussion	4 percussionists, organ

Because the term "percussion" is used to describe both a solo percussionist and a group of percussionists, identical uniform titles for two different works by the same composer may occur. LC has used the number of performers in parentheses following the word "percussion" (in the singular) to resolve such a conflict.

Title: Soli for solo percussion
Uniform title: Solos, ‡m percussion (1)

Title: Soli for percussion duo
Uniform title: Solos, ‡m percussion (2)

Works That Include Computer, Electronics, Synthesizer, or Tape

Medium of performance for works that include computer, electronics, synthesizer, or tape is not addressed in AACR2. Generally, the term used by the composer is used in the statement of medium of performance, given in score order.

Title: Studies for trumpet & computer
Uniform title: Studies, ‡m trumpet, computer

Title: Music for flute and electronic sounds
Uniform title: Music, ‡m flute, electronics

Title: Music for synthesizer and six instruments
Uniform title: Music, ‡m synthesizer, instrumental ensemble

Title: Fantasy for horn and tape
Uniform title: Fantasy, ‡m horn, tape

Title: Trio for harp, clarinet, and tape
Uniform title: Trio, ‡m harp, clarinet, tape

The Rule of Three

The rule of three (25.30B1) prohibits the use of more than three elements in the statement of medium of performance except under certain circumstances. The exceptions to the rule will be discussed first.

The Exceptions to the Rule of Three

The exceptions are for trios, quartets, and quintets and for solo instrument(s) with accompanying ensemble. Rule 25.30B3 allows *all* the instruments to be named when the uniform title has the initial element "trio(s)," "quartet(s)," or "quintet(s)." When the initial title element is not one of these, it may be necessary to group instruments by family. This will be discussed later in this chapter in the section titled "Other Groups of Instruments."

In these headings, each instrument can be specified, even though there are more than three elements in the statement of medium of performance.

Initial title element: quartet
Instrumentation: flute, oboe, violin, violoncello
Uniform title: Quartet(s), ‡m flute, oboe, violin, violoncello

Initial title element: quintet
Instrumentation: flute, clarinet, bassoon, violin, viola
Uniform title: Quintet(s), ‡m flute, clarinet, bassoon, violin, viola

Standard Combinations of Instruments

The preference for the statement of medium of performance is using the name of a standard chamber ensemble, such as "string quartet" (two violins, viola, and violoncello), rather than naming each instrument (25.30B2). The seven standard chamber combinations are:

Combination	Instrumentation
string trio	violin, viola, violoncello
woodwind quartet	flute, oboe, clarinet, bassoon
string quartet	2 violins, viola, violoncello
wind quintet	flute, oboe, clarinet, bassoon, horn
piano trio	piano, violin, violoncello
piano quartet	piano, violin, viola, violoncello
piano quintet	piano, 2 violins, viola, violoncello

Only these specific combinations of instruments apply; other combinations are not thought of as standard chamber combinations. For example, the combination of two violins, viola, and violoncello is called a string quartet, but the combination of four violins is not thought of as a string quartet. Other combinations of instruments are often thought of as standard, but for the purposes of AACR2, they do not apply. For example, a "brass quintet" may be standardized as two trumpets, horn, trombone, and tuba—but not always. Thus "brass quintet" is not to be considered a standard chamber combination.

Initial Title Element Is Trio(s), Quartet(s), or Quintet(s)

When the initial title element is "trio(s)," "quartet(s)," or "quintet(s)," follow the instructions in 25.30B3. For the list of standard chamber combinations in the left-hand column, use the phrases in the right-hand column for the uniform title and do not name the individual instruments.

For the following instrumentation	Use this standard combination
violin, viola, violoncello	Trio(s), ‡m strings
2 violins, viola, violoncello	Quartet(s), ‡m strings
flute, oboe, clarinet, bassoon	Quartet(s), ‡m woodwinds
flute, oboe, clarinet, bassoon, horn	Quintet(s), ‡m winds
piano, violin, violoncello	Trio(s), ‡m piano, strings
piano, violin, viola, violoncello	Quartet(s), ‡m piano, strings
piano, 2 violins, viola, violoncello	Quintet(s), ‡m piano, strings

For example, use "Trio(s), ‡m strings" rather than "Trio(s), ‡m violin, viola, violoncello," and "Quartet(s), ‡m strings," not "Quartet(s), ‡m violins, viola, violoncello."

"Quintet(s), ‡m winds" is used even though the combination is known as a "woodwind quintet," because one of the five, the horn, is from the brass family. However, since all five are wind instruments, "winds" is used.

The standard chamber combinations that include piano require a caveat. Usually rules applying to piano may also be applied to other keyboard instruments. The standard chamber combinations, however, apply only to piano. For example, a trio for harpsichord, violin, and violoncello is not considered to be a piano trio, and the uniform title would be "Trio(s), ‡m harpsichord, violin, violoncello," not "Trio(s), ‡m harpsichord, strings."

Initial Title Element Is *Not* Trio(s), Quartet(s), or Quintet(s)

When the initial title element for a work with one of these seven standard chamber ensembles is *other than* "trio(s)," "quartet(s)," or "quintet(s)," follow these guidelines:

1. Use the name of the standard combination from the list below as the medium of performance.

2. Use it in the singular.

3. Use it only when no other instruments, standard combinations, groups of instruments (other than an accompanying ensemble), or voices are named in the statement of medium of performance (LCRI 25.30B3).

For the following instrumentation	Use the name of the standard combination
violin, viola, violoncello	‡m string trio
flute, oboe, clarinet, bassoon	‡m woodwind quartet
2 violins, viola, violoncello	‡m string quartet
flute, oboe, clarinet, bassoon, horn	‡m wind quintet
piano, violin, violoncello	‡m piano trio
piano, violin, viola, violoncello	‡m piano quartet
piano, 2 violins, viola, violoncello	‡m piano quintet

For example, use "‡m string trio" instead of "‡m violin, viola, violoncello."

Examples

Initial title element: canon
Instrumentation: violin, viola, violoncello
Uniform title: Canon(s), ‡m string trio

Initial title element: suite
Instrumentation: piano, two violins, viola, violoncello
Uniform title: Suite(s), ‡m piano quintet

Chamber combinations that do not appear in this list cannot be used in uniform titles.

Rondos, ‡m saxophones (4)
not
Rondos, ‡m saxophone quartet

Capriccio, ‡m brasses
not
Capriccio, ‡m brass quintet

The third guideline in the list applies below: Use the name of a standard combination only when no other instruments, standard combinations, groups of instruments (other than an accompanying ensemble), or voices are named in the statement of medium of performance.

Initial title element:	nocturne
Instrumentation:	clarinet, two violins, viola, violoncello
Uniform title:	Nocturne(s), ‡m clarinet, strings
Not:	Nocturne(s), ‡m clarinet, string quartet

Initial title element:	fantasie
Instrumentation:	flute, oboe, clarinet, bassoon, horn, two violins, viola, violoncello
Uniform title:	Fantasie(s), ‡m woodwinds, horn, strings
Not:	Fantasie(s), ‡m wind quintet, string quartet

The name of a standard combination from the list of standard combinations may also be used to designate:

• the solo group in a work for solo instruments and accompanying ensemble (25.30B7), which is discussed later in this chapter ("Solo Instrument(s) and Accompanying Ensemble").

• the accompanying ensemble in a vocal work with the initial title element "Songs," "Lieder," etc. (25.30B10), when no other instruments, standard combinations, groups of instruments (other than an accompanying ensemble), or voices are also named in the statement of medium of performance (see Chapter 6, "Medium of Performance: Vocal Music").

Other Groups of Instruments

To avoid using more than three elements in the medium of performance, it may be necessary to group instruments by family. When there are four or more diverse instruments, group them by instrument families (25.30B5). Although the rule says to use "[string, wind, etc.] ensemble," the LCRI overrules that by saying, "[d]o not use the phrases 'string ensemble,' 'wind ensemble,' etc., under this rule. For groups of four or more different instruments from a single family, use 'strings,' 'winds,' etc."

The following table names the instrument families. The list of individual instruments within each family is not exhaustive.

Winds	Woodwinds	flute	recorder
		oboe	English horn
		clarinet	saxophone
		bassoon	basset horn
	Brasses	horn	euphonium
		trumpet	trombone
		baritone	tuba
Strings		violin	viola da gamba
		viola	viola d'amore
		violoncello	double bass
Plucked instruments		harp	guitar
		lute	zither
		mandolin	mandola
Percussion instruments		marimba	drum
		timpani	celesta
		xylophone	cymbals
Keyboard instruments		piano	organ
		harpsichord	keyboard instrument
		clavichord	celesta

Table 5.2: Instrumental Families

Celesta may function as either percussion or as a chordal instrument and is placed in the statement of medium of performance accordingly.

Examples of how instruments might be grouped:

Instrumentation	Group name
flute, oboe, clarinet, bassoon	woodwinds (subset of winds)
flute, oboe, horn, trumpet	winds (woodwinds and brasses)
horn, trumpet, trombone, tuba	brasses (subset of winds)
violin, viola, violoncello, double bass	strings
harp, guitar, mandolin	plucked instruments
marimba, xylophone, timpani, drum	percussion

The last statement of 25.30B1 is not applied to the names of instrument families. The number of instruments within each family is not indicated. Only the name of the instrument family should be given, without a number following it.

İdeал

Use	Not
woodwinds	woodwinds (3)
brasses	brasses (5)
strings	strings (4)

When possible, name individual instruments while grouping other instruments by family. This may be done when the number of instruments from one family is greater than the number of instruments from one or more other families and the resulting medium of performance would have no more than three elements.

Instrumentation	Grouped as
flute, oboe, violin, viola, violoncello	flute, oboe, strings
flute, oboe, bassoon, violin, viola	woodwinds, violin, viola
flute, oboe, clarinet, horn, bassoon, violin, viola, violoncello	woodwinds, horn, strings (not "winds, strings")

Examples

Initial title element:	tango
Instrumentation:	flute, clarinet, bassoon, violin, viola
Uniform title:	Tango(s), ‡m woodwinds, violin, viola
Not:	Tango(s), ‡m woodwinds, strings
	This is incorrect because the two string instruments may be named without exceeding the limit of three elements.

Initial title element:	movement
Instrumentation:	oboe, trumpet, violin, viola, violoncello
Uniform title:	Movement(s), ‡m oboe, trumpet, strings

Initial title element:	Caprice
Instrumentation:	oboe, clarinet, trumpet, horn, baritone
Uniform title:	Caprice(s), ‡m oboe, clarinet, brasses

When there is no majority of instruments from one instrument family, do not make an arbitrary decision about which group of instruments to group together and which individual instruments to name. Instead, follow LCRI 25.30B5 and group *all* the instruments into families. For example, for a work for flute, oboe, violin, and viola, when the initial title element is not "Quartet(s)," use "woodwinds, strings," not "flute, oboe, strings" or "woodwinds, violin, viola."

Initial title element:	fugue
Instrumentation:	flute, oboe, violin, viola
Uniform title:	Fugue(s), ‡m woodwinds, strings
Not:	Fugue(s), ‡m flute, oboe, strings
Not:	Fugue(s), ‡m woodwinds, violin, viola

Works for the same medium of performance, but with different initial title elements, may result in different statements of medium. The two examples below are both for flute, oboe, violin, and violoncello. Because the initial title element of the first is "quartet," all four instruments are named in the statement of medium. The title of the second work is generic, but is not "quartet," so the rule of three applies and all four instruments cannot be named. Because two instrument families are involved and neither family predominates, the instruments are all grouped by family.

Initial title element:	quartet
Instrumentation:	flute, oboe, violin, violoncello
Uniform title:	Quartet(s), ‡m flute, oboe, violin, violoncello
Not:	Quartet(s), ‡m woodwinds, strings

Initial title element:	bagatelle
Instrumentation:	flute, oboe, violin, violoncello
Uniform title:	Bagatelle(s), ‡m woodwinds, strings
Not:	Bagatelle(s), ‡m flute, oboe, violin, violoncello

"Winds" (not "woodwinds, brasses") is used for works for both woodwind and brass instruments when it is not possible because of the rule of three to use "woodwinds" or "brasses" together with the names of individual instruments (LCRI 25.30B5).

Examples

For two woodwind instruments and two brass instruments:

Initial title element:	capriccio
Instrumentation:	flute, oboe, trumpet, horn
Uniform title:	Capriccio(s), ‡m winds

Not:	Capriccio(s), ǂm woodwinds, brasses
Not:	Capriccio(s), ǂm flute, oboe, brasses
Not:	Capriccio(s), ǂm woodwinds, trumpet, horn

For two different woodwind instruments and three different brass instruments:

Initial title element:	piece
Instrumentation:	flute, oboe, trumpet, horn, trombone
Uniform title:	Piece(s), ǂm flute, oboe, brasses
Not:	Piece(s), ǂm woodwinds, brasses

For two different brass instruments and three different woodwind instruments:

Initial title element:	dance
Instrumentation:	flute, oboe, clarinet, trumpet, horn
Uniform title:	Dance(s), ǂm woodwinds, trumpet, horn
Not:	Dance(s), ǂm woodwinds, brasses

For two different woodwind instruments, two different brass instruments, and one other instrument or group of instruments:

Initial title element:	adagio
Instrumentation:	oboe, clarinet, trumpet, trombone, percussion
Uniform title:	Adagio(s), ǂm winds, percussion
Not:	Adagio(s), ǂm woodwinds, brasses, percussion

For two different woodwind instruments, one brass instrument, and one other instrument or group of instruments:

Initial title element:	octet
Instrumentation:	flute, oboe, clarinet, horn, two violins, viola, violoncello
Uniform title:	Octet(s), ǂm woodwinds, horn, strings
Not:	Octet(s), ǂm winds, strings
	This is incorrect because it is possible to name the single brass instrument (horn) while grouping the other instruments into two families.
Not:	Octet(s), ǂm winds (4), strings
	This is incorrect because only the names of individual instruments are qualified.

For two different woodwind instruments, two of the same brass instrument, and one other instrument or group of instruments:

Initial title element:	nonet
Instrumentation:	flute, oboe, clarinet, two horns, two violins, viola, violoncello
Uniform title:	Nonet(s), ‡m woodwinds, horns (2), strings
Not:	Nonet(s), ‡m woodwinds, horns, strings

   This is incorrect because it cannot be inferred from the rest of the statement of medium how many horns are required. Since "horn" is an individually named instrument, the number of horns required is given, enclosed in parentheses.

 The phrase "instrumental ensemble" is used for a group of four or more diverse instruments that cannot be grouped into families resulting in three or fewer elements in the medium of performance (LCRI 25.30B5). "Instrumental ensemble," "jazz ensemble," "wind ensemble," etc., may be used as the statement of medium.

Initial title element:	sextet
Instrumentation:	flute, clarinet, percussion, piano, violin, violoncello
Uniform title:	Sextet(s), ‡m instrumental ensemble
Not:	Sextet(s), ‡m piano, woodwinds, percussion, strings

Initial title element:	bossa nova
Instrumentation:	jazz group: four saxophones, three trumpets, two trombones, three violins, viola, violoncello, double bass, celesta, guitar, and percussion (timpani and snare drum)
Uniform title:	Bossa nova(s), ‡m jazz ensemble

Works for Large Ensembles, Two or More Performers to a Part

Rule 25.30B6 lists the terms to be used for music for large ensembles, generally with more than one performer to a part. Use "orchestra" for full or chamber orchestra and "string orchestra" for string orchestra, even when it includes continuo, keyboard instruments, stringed or not, or percussion. The absence of wind instrument parts is the defining factor in determining if it is a string orchestra.

AACR2 does not address the medium of performance for works requiring two or more orchestras.

Initial title element: Sinfonia concertante
Instrumentation: two orchestras
Uniform title: Sinfonie concertanti, ‡m orchestras (2)

Initial title element: Cassation
Instrumentation: three orchestras
Uniform title: Cassation(s), ‡m orchestras (3)

Use "band" for music for large wind ensemble. AACR2 offers no guidance concerning the use of "band" versus "wind ensemble." Unofficial LC policy is that unless the composer specifies one player on a part, "band" should be used, regardless of the terminology on the item.

Instrumental Choirs

A fairly common instrumental combination that AACR2 does not address is the "choir," that is, a group of two or more of the same instrument, possibly in different ranges, two or more to a part. The statement of medium of performance uses the name of the instrument, regardless of the ranges used in the work, in the singular, followed by the word "choir."

Initial title element: preludio y tango
Instrumentation: piccolo, 7 flutes, alto flute, and bass flute
Uniform title: Preludio y tango, ‡m flute choir

Initial title element: Toccata and fugue
Instrumentation: trombone choir and organ
Uniform title: Toccata and fugue, ‡m organ, trombone choir

Solo Instrument(s) and Accompanying Ensemble

For a work for two or more solo instruments and accompanying ensemble, name the solo instrument(s) as instructed in 25.30B1-25.30B6. Follow with the name of the accompanying ensemble (25.30B7).

Use "instrumental ensemble," "jazz ensemble," "wind ensemble," etc., when the accompanying ensemble requires only one performer to a part (LCRI 25.30B7). (When the same ensemble of non-doubled instruments does not play an accompanying role, follow LCRI 25.30B5 and use only the name of an instrument family such as "winds," "strings," etc., without "ensemble.") For an accompanying ensemble of plucked instruments, use "plucked instrument orchestra."

An accompanying ensemble does not count toward the limit of three elements in the medium of performance and may be added following the names of up to three individual instruments, the name of a standard chamber combination, or the name of an instrument family.

Examples

Initial title element: concerto
Instrumentation: solo violin and chamber orchestra
Uniform title: Concerto(s), ǂm violin, orchestra
Not: Concerto(s), ǂm violin, chamber orchestra
                        According to rule 25.30B6, "orchestra" is used for full or chamber orchestra.

Initial title element: concerto
Instrumentation: violin, violoncello, piano accompanied by orchestra
Uniform title: Concerto(s), ǂm piano trio, orchestra
Not: Concerto(s), ǂm piano, violin, violoncello, orchestra
                        This is incorrect because solo instruments are named according to rules 25.30B1-25.30B6. Rule 25.30B2 requires the name of the standard chamber combination "piano trio" to be used for violin, violoncello, and piano and LCRI 25.30B3 allows for the name of a standard chamber combination when the only other element is an accompanying ensemble.

Initial title element: rondo
Instrumentation: two violins, viola, violoncello, string orchestra
Uniform title: Rondo(s), ǂm string quartet, string orchestra

Initial title element: Concerto grosso
Instrumentation: Doppelorchester mit Klavier
Uniform title: Concerto grosso, ‡m piano, orchestras (2)

Initial title element: concerto
Instrumentation: trumpet accompanied by piano and woodwind quintet
Uniform title: Concerto(s), ‡m trumpet, instrumental ensemble
Not: Concerto(s), ‡m trumpet, piano, wind quintet
     This is incorrect because rule 25.30B7 does not allow the name of a standard chamber combination to be used as an accompanying ensemble for instrumental solos.

Initial title element: variations
Instrumentation: flute, oboe, clarinet, violin, viola, and violoncello accompanied by string orchestra
Uniform title: Variation(s), ‡m woodwinds, strings, string orchestra

Initial title element: variations
Instrumentation: flute, oboe, clarinet, violin, and violoncello accompanied by string orchestra
Uniform title: Variation(s), ‡m woodwinds, violin, violoncello, string orchestra
Not: Variation(s), ‡m woodwinds, strings, string orchestra

Initial title element: variations
Instrumentation: clarinet, horn, violin, viola, and violoncello accompanied by string orchestra
Uniform title: Variation(s), ‡m clarinet, horn, strings, string orchestra
Not: Variation(s), ‡m winds, strings, string orchestra

Initial title element: andante
Instrumentation: flute accompanied by strings and percussion
Uniform title: Andante(s), ‡m flute, string orchestra
Not: Andante(s), ‡m flute, string orchestra, percussion
Not: Andante(s), ‡m flute, orchestra

                                       This is incorrect because the absence of wind parts means the accompanying group is "string orchestra."

Initial title element:	humoresque
Instrumentation:	English horn accompanied by clarinet sextet
Uniform title:	Humoresque(s), ǂm English horn, clarinet ensemble
Not:	Humoresque(s), ǂm English horn, clarinets (6)

        This is incorrect because it implies that the work is for English horn and six clarinets rather than for solo English horn accompanied by six clarinets. "Clarinet ensemble" implies an accompanying ensemble.

Initial title element:	ode
Instrumentation:	flute, oboe, harpsichord, and string orchestra
Uniform title:	Ode(s), ǂm harpsichord, flute, oboe, string orchestra
Not:	Ode(s), ǂm harpsichord, woodwinds, string orchestra

        This is incorrect because an exception to the rule of three is applied to works for solo instruments with accompanying ensemble.

Initial title element:	march
Instrumentation:	flute, oboe, clarinet, trumpet, and band
Uniform title:	March(es), ǂm woodwinds, trumpet, band
Not:	March(es), ǂm flute, oboe, clarinet, trumpet, band

        This is incorrect because, even though the exception to the rule of three applies to solo instruments with accompanying ensemble, the statement of solo instruments is still limited to three elements.

    There is no official LC policy concerning a work for one performer playing two or more different percussion instruments accompanied by a large ensemble. According to correspondence with LC, the term "percussion" is recommended for the medium of performance in the uniform title.

Concerto(s), ‡m percussion, string orchestra

However, either of these could also be used:

Concerto(s), ‡m marimba, string orchestra
Concerto(s), ‡m marimba, vibraphone, string orchestra

Indeterminate or Unspecified Medium of Performance

Indeterminate Medium of Performance

According to 25.30B11, consider the following to be indeterminate mediums of performance to be omitted from the uniform title:
• a work intended for performance by voices and/or instruments (most common for works from the Renaissance period)
• an instrumental chamber work for which the precise medium is not clearly defined.
When needed to break a conflict, use "voices" to designate both vocal and instrumental parts as the medium of performance and record the number of parts or voices.

Fantasies, ‡m voices (4)   Fantasies, ‡m voices (5)

Unspecified Medium of Performance

Rule 25.30B11 is not applied when an instrument is indicated but not specified. Rather, when one or more "instrument," "melody instrument," "soprano instrument," etc., is called for, it falls under the third category of 25.30B1, "other instruments in score order." Use "unspecified instrument(s)" to indicate the instrument(s).

Initial title element: sonata
Instrumentation: solo instrument
Uniform title: Sonata(s), ‡m unspecified instrument

Initial title element: cavatina
Instrumentation: melody instrument and piano
Uniform title: Cavatina(s), ǂm unspecified instrument, piano

Initial title element: duet
Instrumentation: two soprano instruments
Uniform title: Duet(s), ǂm unspecified instruments

Initial title element: invention
Instrumentation: two soprano instruments
Uniform title: Invention(s), ǂm unspecified instruments (2)

Initial title element: piece
Instrumentation: treble instrument, keyboard
Uniform title: Piece(s), ǂm unspecified instrument, keyboard
                        instrument

Initial title element: fanfare
Instrumentation: four equal instruments
Uniform title: Fanfare(s), ǂm unspecified instruments (4)

Initial title element: fugue
Instrumentation: organ and two instruments
Uniform title: Fugue(s), ǂm organ, unspecified instruments (2)

Initial title element: trio
Instrumentation: soprano instrument, bass instrument, harpsichord
Uniform title: Trio(s), ǂm harpsichord, unspecified instruments

Initial title element: quintet
Instrumentation: flute, oboe, clarinet, tenor instrument, bassoon
Uniform title: Quintet(s), ǂm flute, oboe, clarinet, unspecified
                        instrument, bassoon

General practice is to not apply this rule when one unspecified bass instrument is indicated.

Initial title element:	sonata
Instrumentation:	two clarinets, two horns, bass instrument
Uniform title:	Sonata(s), ǂm clarinets (2), horns (2), bass instrument

Initial title element:	minuet
Instrumentation:	zwei Violine und Bass
Uniform title:	Minuet(s), ǂm vlolins (2), bass instrument

Initial title element:	sonata
Instrumentation·	flute and cello; the holograph does not indicate specific bass instrument
Uniform title:	Sonata(s), ǂm flute, bass instrument

Notes

1. David Lasocki. "When Is a Flute Not a Flute?" (unpublished data, 1997)

2. *New Grove*, 2nd ed

Chapter 6
Medium of Performance:
Vocal Music (25.30B8-B10)

The statement of medium of performance in a uniform title for a vocal work follows the initial title element, preceded by a comma, in ‡m. Individual elements within the statement of medium of performance are separated by a comma. Follow 25.30B1 and 25.30B11 to determine when the statement of medium of performance is omitted from a uniform title for a vocal work (see Section 1, "Medium of Performance," in Chapter 4).

When the vocal part is indicated in the statement of medium of performance, only vocal range (e.g., high voice, medium voice, low voice) is specified in certain uniform titles, while the specific voice type is indicated in other uniform titles. These voice types are soprano, tenor, and countertenor (all in the high voice range), mezzo-soprano and baritone (in the medium voice range), and alto (not "contralto") and bass (in the low voice range).

The range of each vocal type is not given AACR2. General practice is to follow the *Subject Cataloging Manual: Subject Headings* section H 1917.5, which bases vocal range in subject headings on the verbal indication on the item. If no vocal range is indicated, the instruction for subject headings is to use the ranges specified in *New Harvard Dictionary of Music* (Table 6.1).

Soprano	Mezzo soprano	Alto
Tenor	Baritone	Bass
High voice	Medium voice	Low voice

Table 6.1: Vocal Ranges[1]

When a vocal line extends above or below a voice range, the category that the vocal line most closely follows is used. When an alternate voice is indicated, use the voice name first in the title.

Rule 25.30B8 lists the vocal types (soprano, mezzo-soprano, alto, tenor, baritone, and bass). AACR2 does not directly address the common practice of specifying a vocal type falling within the ranges of two of these vocal types, such "bass-baritone." The rule does allow the use of "other terms . . . as appropriate," and gives "high voice" and "countertenor" as examples. This sentence of the rule does not explicitly authorize the use of "bass-baritone" in the statement of medium of performances, but it does not disallow its use. Another common practice is to designate a span of vocal ranges, e.g., "medium-high voice." Again, the rule does not prohibit its use in the statement of medium of performance. General practice, however, is to not designate vocal range at all, and to use "voice."

Other terms used to indicate vocal range are "cantus," "altus," "tenor," and "bassus." According to *New Grove*, cantus is a word used before 1660 to indicate the melody or highest voice in a polyphonic composition. "Superius" and "discantus" were also used to indicate this same line. The altus line fell below the cantus line and overlapped with the tenor line, the line around which the rest of the composition was structured. "Quintus" and "sextus" were terms used to indicate the fifth and sixth parts. These parts were not in fixed ranges, but were placed closest to the line with the most similar range. All of these terms were also applied to instrumental works.

Works for One Solo Voice

Initial Title Element Is "Song" or Its Equivalent

When the initial title element is "song(s)" (or its equivalent in other languages (e.g., "canción," "canzone," "chanson," "dal," "Gesang," "Lied," "melodie," "pesnia"), the implied medium of performance is solo voice and keyboard stringed instrument. The statement of medium of performance is omitted from the uniform title unless it differs from the implied medium (25.30B1a). When the accompaniment is other than keyboard stringed instrument, add the name(s) of the accompanying instrument(s) or ensemble followed by the abbreviation "acc." If the work

is not accompanied, the statement of medium of performance consists of
the abbreviation "unacc." (25.30B10).

Examples

Initial title element: Lied
Medium of performance: voice and piano
Uniform title: Lied(er)

Initial title element: song
Medium of performance: alto and organ
Uniform title: Song(s), ‡m organ acc.
        Organ is not a stringed keyboard instrument,
        and therefore is not the implied accompani-
        ment for songs.

Initial title element: dal
Medium of performance: soprano and orchestra
Uniform title: Dal(ok), ‡m orchestra acc.

Initial title element: song
Medium of performance: unaccompanied mezzo-soprano
Uniform title: Song(s), ‡m unacc.

Accompaniment for Two Instruments

When the accompaniment is for two instruments, both can be named,
following the order given in 25.30B1.

Initial title element: song
Medium of performance: soprano, clarinet, and viola
Uniform title: Song(s), ‡m clarinet, viola acc.

Initial title element: song
Medium of performance: high voice, lute, and viol
Uniform title: Song(s), ‡m lute, viol acc.

Initial title element: song
Medium of performance: voice, flute, and electronic processor
Uniform title: Song(s), ‡m flute, electronics acc.

When one of the instruments is a keyboard instrument, it is named after the non-keyboard instrument.

Initial title element:	song
Medium of performance:	alto, piano, and violoncello
Uniform title:	Song(s), ‡m violoncello, piano acc.

Accompaniment for Three or More Instruments

When the accompaniment is for three or more instruments, name then according to the guidelines in 25.30B.

Initial title element:	song
Medium of performance:	alto with clarinet, viola, and violoncello
Uniform title:	Song(s), ‡m clarinet, viola, violoncello acc.

Initial title element:	song
Medium of performance:	high voice and quartet of viols
Uniform title:	Song(s), ‡m viols (4) acc.

Initial title element:	Lied
Medium of performance:	low voice with two clarinets, violin, and violoncello
Uniform title:	Lied(er), ‡m clarinets (2), violin, violoncello acc.

When one of the instruments is a keyboard instrument, it is named before the non-keyboard instruments, as per 25.30B1.

Initial title element:	Gesänge
Medium of performance:	alto with clarinet, bassoon, and piano
Uniform title:	Gesänge, ‡m piano, clarinet, bassoon acc.

LCRI 25.30B3 allows the use of the name of a standard chamber combination (see "Standard Combination of Instruments" in Chapter 5) to designate the accompanying ensemble in a work with the initial title element "Songs," "Lieder," etc.

Initial title element: song
Medium of performance: voice with piano, violin, and violoncello
                        accompaniment
Uniform title: Song(s), ‡m piano trio acc.

Initial title element: Gesänge
Medium of performance: tenor with two violins, viola, and violoncello
Uniform title: Gesänge, ‡m string quartet acc.

When naming the individual instruments in the accompanying
ensemble results in more than three elements in the statement of medium
of performance, use "instrumental ensemble acc."

Initial title element: song
Medium of performance: soprano with English horn, guitar, two
                        percussionists, and double bass
Uniform title: Song(s), ‡m instrumental ensemble acc.

The solo vocal form "romance" is the subject of ongoing discussion
and currently is treated under two different rules, according to the
language of the work. Apply 25.30B8 and name the type of solo voice
when Romance/Romances (English) is a solo vocal form. When Romans/
Romansy (Russian), Romanza/Romanze (Italian), Romanza/Romanzas
(Spanish), and Romanze/Romanzen (German) are solo vocal forms, they
are to be treated like "song," applying 25.30B1a.

English: 25.30B8 applied and vocal type named:

Initial title element: romance
Medium of performance: soprano, violin, string orchestra
Language: English
Uniform title: Romance(s), ‡m soprano, violin, string
                        orchestra
Not: Romance(s), ‡m violin, string orchestra acc.

Non-English: vocal type not named and accompaniment other than piano
indicated:

Initial title element: Romanze
Medium of performance: soprano, violin, string orchestra

Language:	German
Uniform title:	Romanze(n), ‡m violin, string orchestra acc.
Not:	Romanze(n), ‡m soprano, violin, string orchestra

Initial Title Element Is *Not* "Song" or Its Equivalent

When the initial element is not "song" or an equivalent, the type of voice and accompaniment both may be designated (25.30B8). Lack of accompaniment is not indicated.

Initial title element:	piece
Medium of performance:	alto and piano
Uniform title:	Piece(s), ‡m alto, piano

Initial title element:	lullaby
Medium of performance:	soprano with flute accompaniment
Uniform title:	Lullaby(ies), ‡m soprano, flute

Initial title element:	arietta
Medium of performance:	soprano and guitar
Uniform title:	Arietta(s), ‡m soprano, guitar

Initial title element:	darab
Medium of performance:	unacc. mezzo-soprano
Uniform title:	Darab(ok), ‡m mezzo-soprano

When only a designation of vocal range is given, use that instead of a specific voice type.

Initial title element:	seguidilla
Medium of performance:	low voice and piano
Uniform title:	Seguidilla(s), ‡m low voice, piano

Initial title element:	recitative
Medium of performance:	high voice and orchestra
Uniform title:	Recitative(s), ‡m high voice, orchestra

Initial title element: arietta
Medium of performance: high voice and guitar
Uniform title: Arietta(s), ‡m high voice, guitar

When the voice type or range is unspecified, use "voice."

Initial title element: lullaby
Medium of performance: voice and piano
Uniform title.   Lullaby(ies), ‡m voice, piano

Initial title element: solo
Medium of performance: amplified voice alone
Uniform title: Solo(s), ‡m voice

Initial title element: etude
Medium of performance: voice and tape
Uniform title: Etude(s), ‡m voice, tape

Initial title element: arietta
Medium of performance: voice and guitar
Uniform title: Arietta(s), ‡m voice, guitar

Accompaniment for Two Instruments

When the accompaniment is for two instruments, both can be named, following the order in 25.30B1. When one of the instruments is a keyboard instrument, it is named after the non-keyboard instrument.

Initial title element: invention
Medium of performance: low voice, viola, violoncello
Uniform title: Invention(s), ‡m low voice, viola, violoncello

Initial title element: Fantasie
Medium of performance: soprano with violin and piano
Uniform title: Fantasie(s), ‡m soprano, violin, piano

Initial title element: hymn
Medium of performance: tenor with viola and piano
Uniform title: Hymn(s), ‡m tenor, viola, piano

Initial title element:	psalm
Medium of performance:	soprano with flute and organ
Uniform title:	Psalm(s), ‡m soprano, flute, organ

Initial title element:	prelude
Medium of performance:	voice, saxophone, sarrusophone
Uniform title:	Prelude(s), ‡m voice, saxophone, sarrusophone

Initial title element:	serenade
Medium of performance:	flute, medium voice, and harp
Uniform title:	Serenade(s), ‡m medium voice, flute, harp

Accompaniment for Three or More Instruments

When the accompaniment is for three or more instruments, group them by family according to the rules for instrumental music to avoid more than three elements in the statement of medium of performance. When one of the instruments is a keyboard instrument, it is named before the non-keyboard instruments, as per 25.30B1.

Initial title element:	music
Medium of performance:	alto with clarinet, viola, and violoncello
Uniform title:	Music, ‡m alto, clarinet, strings

Initial title element:	rhapsody
Medium of performance:	alto with clarinet, viola, and piano
Uniform title:	Rhapsody(ies), ‡m alto, instrumental ensemble
Not:	Rhapsody(ies), ‡m alto, piano, clarinet, viola
	This is incorrect because there are four elements in the statement of medium of performance.

Initial title element:	quartet
Medium of performance:	voice, violin, cello, and piano
Uniform title:	Quartet(s), ‡m voice, piano, violin, violoncello

| | Four elements are allowed in this statement of medium of performance because the initial title element is "quartet." |
| *Not:* | Quartet(s), ǂm voice, piano, strings |

Initial title element:	nocturne
Medium of performance:	voice, violin, cello, and piano
Uniform title:	Nocturne(s), ǂm voice, piano, strings
Not:	Nocturne(s), ǂm voice, piano, violin, violoncello
	This is incorrect because there are four elements in the statement of medium of performance.
Not:	Nocturne(s), ǂm voice, piano trio
	This is incorrect because the name of a standard combination cannot be used to designate the accompanying ensemble unless the initial title element is "Songs," "Lieder," etc.

Initial title element:	serenade
Medium of performance:	soprano, two violins, viola, violoncello, and pianoforte
Uniform title:	Serenade(s), ǂm soprano, piano, strings
Not:	Serenade(s), ǂm soprano, piano quintet

Initial title element:	aria
Medium of performance:	unspecified voice and string quartet
Uniform title:	Aria(s), ǂm voice, strings

Initial title element:	movement
Medium of performance:	soprano or mezzo and brass quintet
Uniform title:	Movement(s), ǂm soprano, brasses
Not:	Movement(s), ǂm soprano, brass quintet

Initial title element:	aria
Medium of performance:	soprano, guitar, harp, harpsichord, percussion, and viola
Uniform title:	Aria(s), ǂm soprano, instrumental ensemble

Initial title element: arioso
Medium of performance: soprano and chamber orchestra
Uniform title: Arioso(s), ‡m soprano, orchestra

Initial title element: Thema und Variationen
Medium of performance: soprano, flute obbligato, and string orchestra
Uniform title: Thema und Variationen, ‡m soprano, flute,
                            string orchestra

Two or More Solo Voices

The names of two or more types of solo voices can be included when the
resulting statement of medium of performance has three or fewer
elements. The number of voices is indicated when it cannot be inferred
from the initial title element.

Two Solo Voices of the Same Vocal Type

Initial title element: romance
Medium of performance: two sopranos and orchestra
Uniform title: Romance(s), ‡m sopranos (2), orchestra

    When the number of voices can be inferred from the title, it is not
necessary to include the number.

Initial title element: duet
Medium of performance: two tenors and piano
Uniform title: Duet(s), ‡m tenors, piano

    When the vocal types are not designated, use "voices," qualified by
the number when it cannot be inferred from the initial title element.

Initial title element: ballad
Medium of performance: two voices and piano
Uniform title: Ballad(s), ‡m voices (2), piano

Two Solo Voices of Different Vocal Types

Initial title element:	songs
Medium of performance:	soprano, alto, and piano
Uniform title:	Songs, ‡m soprano, alto, piano

Initial title element:	cantata
Medium of performance:	soprano, countertenor, and basso continuo
Uniform title:	Cantata(s), ‡m soprano, countertenor, continuo

Initial title element:	cantata
Medium of performance:	tenor, bass, and string quartet
Uniform title:	Cantata(s), ‡m tenor, bass, strings

Initial title element:	caprice
Medium of performance:	mezzo-soprano and countertenor, unacc.
Uniform title:	Caprice(s), ‡m mezzo-soprano, countertenor

Initial title element:	arioso
Medium of performance:	soprano, tenor, and string orchestra
Uniform title:	Arioso(s), ‡m soprano, tenor, string orchestra

Three or More Solo Voices of the Same Vocal Type

Initial title element:	Gesänge
Medium of performance:	three sopranos and piano
Uniform title:	Gesänge, ‡m sopranos (3), piano

Three or More Solo Voices of Two Different Vocal Types

Initial title element:	song
Medium of performance:	three sopranos, tenor, and piano
Uniform title:	Song(s), ‡m sopranos (3), tenor, piano

Initial title element:	nocturne
Medium of performance:	two sopranos and bass with accompaniment of two flutes, bass clarinet, and trombone
Uniform title:	Nocturne(s), ‡m sopranos (2), bass, winds

Grouping Vocal Types According to Range of Voice

When more than three elements would be needed in the medium of
performance, group vocal types together according to range of voice,
when appropriate, according to 25.30B8. AACR2 has no provision for
using "solo voices" without an adjective specifying the type of voices.

Use	For
women's solo voices	two or more women's voices (soprano, mezzo-soprano, alto)
men's solo voices	two or more men's voices (countertenor, tenor, baritone, bass)
children's solo voices	two or more children's voices
mixed solo voices	a combination of two or more voices from the categories above

Examples

Initial title element: sextet
Medium of performance: SSATTB
Uniform title: Sextet(s), ǂm mixed solo voices

Initial title element: quartet
Medium of performance: Frauenstimmen mit Klavierbegleitung
Uniform title: Quartet(s), ǂm women's solo voices, piano

Rule 25.30B8 does not provide for indicating the number of voices.
even when it cannot be inferred from the initial title element.

Initial title element: lullaby
Medium of performance: SSATTB
Uniform title: Lullaby(ies), ǂm mixed solo voices

Initial title element: serenade
Medium of performance: soprano, alto, tenor, bass
Uniform title: Serenade(s), ǂm mixed solo voices

Works for Non-Solo Voices

When the initial title element is "Chorus(es)" or when a work with a generic title is for chorus, use the terms in the following list from 25.30B9 to designate the medium of performance for the choral ensemble. Do not include solo voices in the statement of medium of performance for works that include solo voices with chorus.

Use	For
women's voices	two or more women's voices (soprano, mezzo-soprano, alto)
men's voices	two or more men's voices (countertenor, tenor, bass)
children's voices	two or more children's voices
mixed voices	a combination of two or more voices from the categories above
unison voices	all the voices sing the same part
equal voices	the parts are within an equal or nearly equal range

Examples

Initial title element:	chorus
Medium of performance:	SA with piano
Uniform title:	Chorus(es), ǂm women's voices, piano

Initial title element:	chorus
Medium of performance:	SATB
Uniform title:	Chorus(es,) ǂm mixed voices

Initial title element:	chorus
Medium of performance:	TTBB
Uniform title:	Chorus(es), ǂm men's voices

Initial title element:	chorus
Medium of performance:	unaccompanied boys' choir
Uniform title:	Chorus(es), ǂm children's voices

Initial title element: song
Medium of performance: girls' chorus and tape
Uniform title: Song(s), ǂm children's voices, tape

Initial title element: carol
Medium of performance: SSAA, piano
Uniform title: Carol(s), ǂm women's voices, piano

Initial title element: prelude
Medium of performance: SSAA
Uniform title: Prelude(s), ǂm women's voices

Initial title element: Gesänge
Medium of performance: women's choir, two horns, and harp
Uniform title: Gesänge, ǂm women's voices, horns (2), harp

Initial title element: adagio
Medium of performance: chorus in unison
Uniform title: Adagio(s), ǂm unison voices

Initial title element: scherzo
Medium of performance: SSATB
Uniform title: Scherzo(s), ǂm mixed voices

Initial title element: burlesque
Medium of performance: SATB with saxophone
Uniform title: Burlesque(s), ǂm mixed voices, saxophone

Initial title element: cantata
Medium of performance: TTBB with brass quintet
Uniform title: Cantata(s), ǂm men's voices, brasses

Sacred Music With Implied
Medium of Performance

Rule 25.30B1a states the implied medium of performance for masses as voices (i.e., non-solo voices), with or without accompaniment. When a mass is for this medium, it is not normally given in the uniform title.

Although the rule lists only "mass," it is applied to other sacred and liturgical titles as well:

Sacred titles: anthem, hymn, motet, psalm
Liturgical titles: Agnus Dei, Ave Maria, Ave Regina, Credo, Gloria,
                      Introit, Kyrie, Magnificat, Miserere, Offertorium,
                      Requiem, Salve Regina, Regina coeli/caeli, Sanctus,
                      Stabat Mater, Te Deum

Include a statement of medium of performance for a work with one of these titles only when the work is for other than the implied medium of performance, or to distinguish identically named works by the same composer (see Chapter 9, "Other Identifying Elements").

Examples

Initial title element: anthem
Medium of performance: SATB, organ
Uniform title: Anthem(s)

Initial title element: hymn
Medium of performance: SATB, unacc.
Uniform title: Hymn(s)

Initial title element: psalm
Medium of performance: SATB, piano
Uniform title: Psalm(s)

Uniform titles for works with these same initial title elements for *solo* voice *do* include medium of performance.

Initial title element: hymn
Medium of performance: tenor accompanied by viola and piano
Uniform title: Hymn(s), ‡m tenor, viola, piano

Initial title element: anthem
Medium of performance: soprano, continuo
Uniform title: Anthem(s), ‡m soprano, continuo

Initial title element:	psalm
Medium of performance:	soprano accompanied by flute and organ
Uniform title:	Psalm(s), ‡m soprano, flute, organ

The statement of medium of performance may be used to distinguish between two or more works by the same composer (LCRI 25.30B1).

Masses, ‡m voices (4)   Masses, ‡m voices (8)

Indeterminate Medium of Performance

Rule 25.30B11 covers works "especially [those] of the Renaissance period intended for performance by voices and/or instruments." Examples of works to which this rule applies are airs/ayres, balletti, canzonets/canzonettas, madrigals, villancicos, and villanelle. The statement of medium of performance is omitted from the uniform title for a work of one of these types.

Initial title element:	airs
Medium of performance:	two, three, or four voices and continuo
Uniform title:	Airs

Initial title element:	songs or ayres
Medium of performance:	four parts
Uniform title:	Songs or ayres

Initial title element:	balletts
Medium of performance:	five voyces
Uniform title:	Balletts

Initial title element:	balletts and madrigals
Medium of performance:	five voyces, with one to six voyces
Uniform title:	Balletts and madrigals

Statement of medium of performance may be added when needed to distinguish between two or more works by the same composer. The statement will consist of "voices" followed by the number in parentheses.

Initial title element: Music
Medium of performance: a 4, apt for vyols or voyces
Uniform title: Music, ‡m voices (4)

Initial title element: Music
Medium of performance: 5vv, apt for vyols or voyces
Uniform title: Music, ‡m voices (5)

Initial title element: balletti
Medium of performance: 3 vv
Uniform title: Balletti, ‡m voices (3)
Initial title element: balletti
Medium of performance: five voices or instruments
Uniform title: Balletti, ‡m voices (5)

Initial title element: canzonets
Medium of performance: three voyces
Uniform title: Canzonets, †m voices (3)

Initial title element: canzonets
Medium of performance: five and sixe voyces
Uniform title: Canzonets, ‡m voices (5-6)

Works That Include Narrator or Speaker

There is no rule to guide the cataloger in constructing a statement of medium of performance for a work that includes spoken words. It is a matter of cataloger's judgement. Generally, if the narrator's part is a small portion of the music, the voice part can be omitted from the statement of medium of performance.

Title: Symphony no. 3
Medium of performance: reciter, orchestra, mixed chorus, and organ
Uniform title: Symphonies, ‡n no. 3

Title:	Symphony no. 5
Medium of performance:	speaker, violin, oboe, trumpet, tuba, and percussion
Uniform title:	Symphonies, ‡n no. 5

If, however, the title includes the word "narrator," "Sprecherin," "speaker," "reciter," etc., it is possible, but not required, to add the medium "narrator."

Title:	Zwei Balladen für Declamation mit Begleitung des Pianoforte
Medium of performance:	reciter and piano
Uniform title:	Ballades, ‡m narrator, piano

When an instrumental work requires the performers to speak, it is not indicated in the uniform title:

Initial title element:	trio
Medium of performance:	oboe, violoncello, and piano; the players recite texts
Uniform title:	Trio(s), ‡m piano, oboe, violoncello

Note

1. *The New Harvard Dictionary of Music* (Cambridge, Mass.: Belknap Press of Harvard University, 1986); under Voice.

Chapter 7
Numeric Identifying Elements (25.30C)

The two kinds of identifying numbers associated with uniform titles are serial numbers and opus or thematic index numbers, which are added in that order of preference. Numbers are tagged in ‡n, usually with the serial number preceding the thematic index number, when both are used. A range of numbers may be used when they are consecutive.

A number associated with a work generally will appear on the item, and usually will be the number used in some form in the uniform title, if it is required. Searching standard reference works, such as *New Grove* or a composer's thematic index, may be required to verify the number and determine the form in which it will be used in the uniform title.

An identifying number is not always present on publications or recordings of a work and may, in some cases, require research to determine whether the composer assigned one to the work or if one has been assigned in a thematic index. Base the decision to do research on whether the number is needed because the initial title element is generic and the number is required or because the uniform title is distinctive and the number is needed to break a conflict with another title. Also, when most of a composer's works have numbers associated with them, an item lacking a number would warrant research.

Serial Numbers (25.30C2)

Serial numbers are applied to a series of works with the same title for the same medium of performance that have been consecutively numbered by the composer. A serial number may appear in either ordinal or cardinal form, as a number alone or with an associated term or symbol (e.g., "#"). This term could mean "number," either spelled out or abbreviated, or may be a word connoting seriality, such as "book" or "set." Following AACR2

Appendix B, use the English abbreviation "no." when the term means "number," even when it appears in abbreviated form in another language. Keep in mind that the serial number may not appear on the item being cataloged.

Serial numbers are generally straightforward.

Title: 1st caprice for horn solo
Uniform title: Caprices, ǂm horn, ǂn no. 1

Title: Rondeau no 2 pour violin et piano
Uniform title: Rondos, ǂm violin, piano, ǂn no. 2

Title: Piano sonatas nos. 30-32
Uniform title: Sonatas, ǂm piano, ǂn no. 30-32

Title: Madrigals for four voices, book 1
Uniform title: Madrigals, ǂm voices (4), ǂn book 1

Title: First set of madrigals
Uniform title: Madrigals, ǂn 1st set

Not all serial numbers are straightforward, however. For example, if a living composer wrote a trio for trombones and titled it "Trio no. 1 for three trombones," but has not yet written a second trio, assume the composer will write another trio for three trombones. The uniform title will include the serial number.

Title: Trio no. 1 for three trombones
Uniform title: Trios, ǂm trombones, ǂn no. 1

If a composer who is deceased wrote a trio for trombones, but wrote no other trio for trombones, determine if it was the composer's only trio. Use the singular form if it was the composer's only trio. If it was the composer's only trio for trombones, do not include the serial number in the uniform title.

Title: Trio no. 1 for three trombones
Uniform title: Trio(s), ǂm trombones

If a composer who is deceased wrote a series of works with the same title for the same medium of performance, but numbered only the second and subsequent works, include the serial number "1" in the uniform title for the first work.

Title: Sonata for violin and piano
Uniform title: Sonatas, ‡m violin, piano, **‡n no. 1**

Title: 2nd sonata for violin and piano
Uniform title: Sonatas, ‡m violin, piano, **‡n no. 2**

When a living composer wrote a work that becomes the first in a series of numbered works with the same title for the same medium of performance, but did not designate it as the first, the uniform title originally will not include a number. The initial title element may not be plural. Once the second and subsequent works are written, "no. 1" should be added to the uniform title for the first work, even if it is still unnumbered. The initial title element should be pluralized, if not already in that form.

Title: Brass quintet for two trumpets, horn, trombone, and tuba
Uniform title: Quintet(s), ‡m trumpets, horn, trombone, tuba

Title: Brass quintet no. 2 for two trumpets, horn, trombone, and tuba
Uniform title: Quintets, ‡m trumpets, horn, trombone, tuba, ‡n no. 2

Update the uniform title of the first work to:

Quintets, ‡m trumpets, horn, trombone, tuba, **‡n no. 1**

When a composer wrote a work for one medium of performance, assigning it "no. 1," and a second work with the same title for a similar, but different medium of performance, giving it "no. 2," omit the medium of performance from the uniform titles (25.30B1b). Because the three quartets below are for different mediums of performance are numbered consecutively, the serial number is included, but not the medium of performance.

Title: Quartet no. 1 for three clarinets and bass clarinet
Uniform title: Quartets, ‡n no. 1
Not: Quartets, ‡m clarinets, ‡n no. 1

Title: Quartet no. 2 for four saxophones
Uniform title: Quartets, ‡n no. 2
Not: Quartets, ‡m saxophones, ‡n no. 2

Title: Quartet no. 3 for four saxophones
Uniform title: Quartets, ‡n no. 3
Not: Quartets, ‡m saxophones, ‡n no. 3

The rule applies to vocal music as well. The four books of madrigals in the examples below are for various voice groupings. The medium of performance is omitted from the uniform title while the serial number is retained.

Title: First book of madrigals for four voices
Uniform title: Madrigals, ‡n book 1
Not: Madrigals, ‡m voices (4), ‡n book 1

Title: Second book of madrigals for four to six voices
Uniform title: Madrigals, ‡n book 2
Not: Madrigals, ‡m voices (4-6), ‡n book 2

Title: Third book of madrigals for five voices
Uniform title: Madrigals, ‡n book 3
Not: Madrigals, ‡m voices (5), ‡n book 3

Title: 4th book of madrigals for four voices
Uniform title: Madrigals, ‡n book 4
Not: Madrigals, ‡m voices (4), ‡n book 4

Rule 25.30C2 and AACR2 Appendix C.8 and their accompanying LCRIs provide the following guidance for serial numbers. (These guidelines do not apply to numbered parts of a work, which will be discussed in Chapter 11, "Additions to Both Generic and Distinctive Titles.")

Use arabic numbers. Convert numbers appearing as roman numerals or in spelled-out form to arabic numbers. However, retain the type of number (cardinal or ordinal) and the position of the number. Do not change ordinal numbers to cardinal numbers or move the number to either precede or follow any term appearing with the number.

Use the conventional English form of ordinal numbers (e.g., 1st, 2nd, 3rd, etc.). For ordinal numbers in languages other than English, follow LCRI C8 and use 1., 2., 3., etc. Because this policy was not always in effect, constructions such as "1o libro," "1er livre," etc., which were correct at the time the uniform title was formulated, appear in the authority file. When creating uniform titles for a composer's works for which the older construction has been used, follow that form for new headings. For example, because headings for some of Couperin's *Pièces de Clavecin* have been established using the older construction, all future headings should follow that practice.

Existing headings

Couperin, François, ‡d 1668-1733. ‡t Pièces de clavecin, ‡n 1er livre
Couperin, François, ‡d 1668-1733. ‡t Pièces de clavecin, ‡n 2e livre

New headings

Couperin, François, ‡d 1668-1733. ‡t Pièces de clavecin, ‡n **3e** livre
Couperin, François, ‡d 1668-1733. ‡t Pièces de clavecin, ‡n **4e** livre

not

Couperin, François, ‡d 1668-1733. ‡t Pièces de clavecin, ‡n 3. livre
Couperin, François, ‡d 1668-1733. ‡t Pièces de clavecin, ‡n 4. livre

When the form of the numeric designation varies among different works in a consecutively numbered series of works, use one of the forms in the uniform titles for the entire series of works. If a pattern has already been established for that series of works, use the existing form of numbering, even if it varies from the designation on the work being cataloged.

When a pattern of numbers contrary to these guidelines already exists for music uniform titles for a series of works by a composer, follow the existing pattern. If the existing headings need to be changed for another reason, the numbering can be updated to current guidelines and used for all headings in the series of works.

Language of a Term Associated With a Serial Number (25.30C2)

When a term or abbreviation associated with the serial number appears in a language other than English, it may or may not be translated into English in the uniform title. There are two considerations involved: whether the initial title element is in English and whether the term means "number."

Translate the term into English when:
- the initial title element is in English, whether or not the term means "number"
- the initial title element is not in English and the term means "number."

Retain the original language when:
- the initial title element is *not* in English and the term does *not* mean "number."

In either case, when the term does not mean "number," it can be abbreviated only when it is abbreviated in the source on which the uniform title is based.

LCRI 25.30C2	Initial title element is in English		Initial title element is *not* in English	
	Term means number	Term does not mean number	Term means number	Term does not mean number
Use the English term?	Yes	Yes	Yes	No
Abbreviate the term?	Yes	Only when it is abbreviated in the source	Yes	Only when it is abbreviated in the source

Table 7.1: Language of a Term Associated With a Serial Number (LCRI 25.30C2)

The Initial Title Element Is in English and the Term Means "Number"

The term is a non-English word or abbreviation meaning "number" and the initial title element is in English because of 25.29A1, the rule concerning cognates. Use the English form of the term or abbreviation.

Title: Simfonia núm. 1
Uniform title: Symphonies, ‡n **no.** 2

Since "Nr." is the German abbreviation for the equivalent English term "number," use the English abbreviation.

Title: Sonate für Flöte und Klavier Nr. 2
Uniform title: Sonatas, ‡m flute, piano, ‡n **no.** 2

The Initial Title Element Is in English and the Term Does Not Mean "Number"

The term is a non-English word or abbreviation not meaning "number" and the initial title element is translated into English according to 25.29A1. Use the English form of the word or abbreviation as it appears in the source on which the uniform title is based. If the word is abbreviated in the source, use the abbreviation in the uniform title. If the word is spelled out in the source, use that form even if there is an abbreviation for the word in AACR2 Appendix B.

Title: Primo libro di madrigali, quattro voci
Uniform title: Madrigals, ‡m voices (4), ‡n **book 1**

Title: Neuvième livre de duos pour deux flûtes
Uniform title: Duets, ‡m flutes, ‡n **9th book**

The Initial Title Element Is Not in English and the Term Means "Number"

When the term is a non-English word or abbreviation meaning "number" and the initial title element is *not* translated into English following 25.29A1, use the English form of the word or abbreviation.

Title: Pezzo n. 2 per corno e pianoforte
Uniform title: Pezzi, ‡m horn, piano, ‡n **no.** 2

The Initial Title Element Is Not in English and the Term Does Not Mean "Number"

When the term is a non-English word or abbreviation not meaning "number" and the initial title element is *not* translated into English following 25.29A1, use the original language of the term or abbreviation.

Title: Deuxième recueil de pièces pour la flûte traversière
Uniform title: Pièces, ‡m flute, ‡n 2. **recueil**

Title: Il primo libro delle canzoni
Uniform title: Canzoni, ‡n 1. **libro**

Title: 5te. Sammlung der Lieder
Uniform title: Lieder, ‡n 5. **Sammlung**

Use the original language of the term or abbreviation in all other cases. In this example, since the initial title element "études" is not translated into English following rule 25.29A1, the word "série" is not also translated into English, nor is it abbreviated. Even though there is an AACR2-prescribed abbreviation for "série," it is not used here because the word is spelled out in the source on which the uniform title is based.

Title: 5 études pour piano et orchestre, IIème série
Uniform title: Études, ‡m piano, orchestra, ‡n 2. **série**

When a term other than "number," in any language, is abbreviated in the source on which the uniform title is based, use the abbreviated form, whether or not it is a prescribed abbreviation in AACR2 Appendix B.

Title: Pièces pour orgue, IIème sér.
Uniform title: Pièces, ‡m organ, ‡n 2. **sér.**

When no term is associated with the number either on the item or in a reference source, give the number in the uniform title as a cardinal number preceded by the English abbreviation "no."

Title: Sonata I for piano
Uniform title: Sonatas, ‡m piano, ‡n **no.** 1

When, contrary to current rules, an abbreviated form of a term has been used in older headings for a composer's works, use that form when creating new headings for related works by that composer.

Older heading: Madrigals, ‡n **bk.** 1
New heading·   Madrigals, †n **bk.** 2
Not: Madrigals, ‡n book 2

When "book," "livre," or its equivalent is not associated with a number, it is retained in the initial title element (25.28A).

Title: Livre de sonates a violon seul second œuvre avec continuo
Uniform title: Livre de sonates

Title: Booke of ayres with a triplicite of musicke
Uniform title: Booke of ayres

A Range of Consecutive Serial Numbers

When a uniform title includes a sequence of consecutive serial numbers with an associated term or abbreviation, do not pluralize the term or abbreviation associated with the number:

Use	Not
‡n no. 2-5	‡n nos. 2-5
‡n book 1-3	‡n books 1-3
‡n 1st-3rd book	‡n 1st-3rd books
‡n libro 2-5	‡n libros 2-5
‡n 1.-4. livre	‡n 1.-4. livres
‡n 1er-4e livre	‡n 1er-4e livres

The uniform title for a collection of three or more consecutively numbered works will include a range of serial numbers.

Title: Piano sonatas no. 2, 3, 4, and 5
Uniform title: Sonatas, ‡m piano, ‡n no. 2-5

A collection of three or more non-consecutively numbered works falls under the rules for collective titles (see Chapter 12, "Collective Titles").

The uniform title for all work in a numbered series of works does not include the serial numbers.

Title: Piano sonatas nos. 1-5 : the complete piano sonatas
Uniform title: Sonatas, ‡m piano
Not: Sonatas, ‡m piano, ‡n no. 1-5

Opus Numbers (25.30C3)

Opus numbers, according to *New Grove,* were, until 1800, more common in instrumental music than in vocal music and stage works. Both *New Grove* and the *Harvard Dictionary of Music* state that opus numbers are usually not accurate enough to establish the chronology of a composer's work. However, they function well in uniform titles to uniquely identify individual works.

The opus number may not appear on the item being cataloged or may appear only in some editions. Opus numbers may not have been assigned to all the works of a composer. When most of a composer's works have opus numbers, however, an item lacking an opus number would warrant research to determine if the publisher omitted it.

In the uniform title, the opus number is given in arabic form following the abbreviation "op."

Title: Quintet for trumpet and strings (1999) opus 175
Uniform title: Quintet(s), ‡m trumpet, violins, viola, violoncello, ‡n **op. 175**

Title: Deux duos pour flûte et clarinette, op. 225bis
Uniform title: Duets, ‡m flute, clarinet, **‡n op. 225 bis**

Title: String octet in C minor, op. 15a
Uniform title: Octet(s), ‡m violins (4), violas, violoncellos, **‡n op. 15a**

Title: Zongoradarab op. 30b/1
Uniform title: Darabok, ‡m piano, **‡n op. 30b/1**

In the seventeenth and eighteenth centuries, opus numbers frequently were assigned by the publisher at the time of publication. It was not uncommon for different publishers to issue the same work under different opus numbers or to assign the same opus number to different works by the same composer. Add the name of the publisher in parentheses following the opus number used in the heading (25.30C3). The form of the name of each publisher need not be standardized.

These uniform titles are for two different works by the same composer, to which different publishers assigned the same opus number.

Title: Tre divertimenti a violino e viola, op. 6
Published: Paris : Janet & Cotelle
Uniform title: Divertimenti, ‡m violin, viola, ‡n **op. 6 (Janet et Cotelle)**

Title: Tre divertimenti a violino e viola opera 6a
Published: Milano : G. Ricordi
Uniform title: Divertimenti, ‡m violin, viola, ‡n **op. 6 (Ricordi)**

This uniform title is for the same work by one composer, to which the different publishers assigned different opus numbers.

Title: Trios for a German-flute, violin, and violoncello, op. 4
Published: London : J. Bland
Title: Trios pour la flûte traversière, violino, & violoncello œuvre VI
Published: Amsterdam : J. Schmitt
Title: Trios pour flûte, violon et violoncelle œuvre 11me
Published: Offenbach : J. André
Title: Trios pour flûte, violon et violoncel œuvre XI
Published: Paris : Imbault
Uniform title: Trios, ‡m flute, violin, violoncello, ‡n **op. 4 (Bland)**

References are made from the titles with the other publishers' opus numbers (see Chapter 15, "References").

Trios, ‡m flute, violin, violoncello, ‡n **op. 6 (Schmitt)**
Trios, ‡m flute, violin, violoncello, ‡n **op. 11 (Imbault)**
Trios, ‡m flute, violin, violoncello, ‡n **op. 11 (André)**

When the uniform title has additional elements following the opus number, add the name of the publisher immediately after the opus number and preceding any further elements.

Quintets, ‡m violins, violas, violoncello, ‡n **op. 45 (André)**, ‡r C
    major
Sonatas, ‡m piano, 4 hands, ‡n **op. 9 (Breitkopf & Härtel)**, ‡r B♭
    major

A Range of Consecutive Opus Numbers

Title: Zwei Klavierstücke, op. 33/34
Uniform title: Stücke, ‡m piano, **‡n op. 33/34**

Title: Drei Sonatinen für zwei Violinen op. 96, 97, 98
Uniform title: Sonatinas, ‡m violins (2), **‡n op. 96-98**

Posthumous Opus Numbers

Unofficial LC practice is to consider a posthumous opus number a numberless designation. Thus, "op. posth." should not be regarded as an opus number and should not appear in subfield ‡n. Should it be needed to resolve a conflict, use it as a parenthetical qualifier.

Both Serial and Opus Numbers

When there is also a serial number as well as an opus number, the opus number follows the serial number, in the same ‡n.

Title: Violin concerto no. 3, op. 58
Uniform title: Concertos, ‡m violin, orchestra, **‡n no. 3, op. 58**

Title: Symphony no. 2 for orchestra op. 67
Uniform title: Symphonies, ‡n **no. 2, op. 67**

Individual works within a sequence of works may be identified first by a serial number and then by an opus number, and, when needed, by a serial number within an opus number. Some of these serially numbered piano sonatas are assigned a single opus number, while others are grouped within an opus number.

Sonatas, ‡m piano, ‡n no. 1, op. 2, no. 1 . . .	no. 1, 2, and 3 are
Sonatas, ‡m piano, ‡n no. 2, op. 2, no. 2 . . .	also no. 1, 2, and 3
Sonatas, ‡m piano, ‡n no. 3, op. 2, no. 3 . . .	from op. 2
Sonatas, ‡m piano, ‡n no. 4, op. 7 . . .	
Sonatas, ‡m piano, ‡n no. 5, op. 10, no. 1 . . .	no. 5, 6, and 7 are
Sonatas, ‡m piano, ‡n no. 6, op. 10, no. 2 . . .	also no. 1, 2, and 3
Sonatas, ‡m piano, ‡n no. 7, op. 10, no. 3 . . .	from op. 10
Sonatas, ‡m piano, ‡n no. 8, op. 13 . . .	
Sonatas, ‡m piano, ‡n no. 9, op. 14, no. 1 . .	no. 9 and 10 are also
Sonatas, ‡m piano, ‡n no. 10, op. 14, no. 2 . . .	no. 1 and 2 from op. 14

Omit the serial number from the uniform title for a work in a numbered sequence of works with the same initial title element and for the same medium of performance except for that one work. A reference with the serial number, but without the medium of performance, would be made in the authority record for the title (see Chapter 15, "References").

Concertos, ‡m piano, orchestra, ‡n no. 1, op. 10, ‡r D♭ major
Concertos, ‡m piano, orchestra, ‡n no. 2, op. 16, ‡r G minor
Concertos, ‡m piano, orchestra, ‡n no. 3, op. 26, ‡r C major
Concertos, ‡m piano, orchestra, ‡n no. 5, op. 55, ‡r G major
Concertos, ‡m piano, 1 hand, orchestra, **‡n op. 53**, ‡r B♭ major
not
Concertos, ‡m piano, orchestra, ‡n no. 4, op. 53, ‡r B♭ major

Alternatively, the serial numbering may be retained and the medium of performance omitted. A reference with the medium of performance, but without the serial number, would be made in the authority record for the title (see Chapter 15, "References").

Symphonies, ‡n no. 1, op. 17
Symphonies, ‡n no. 2, op. 132
Symphonies, ‡n no. 3, op. 148
Symphonies, **‡n no. 4**, op. 165
Symphonies, ‡n no. 5, op. 170
Symphonies, ‡n no. 6, op. 173

not
Symphonies, ‡m band, ‡n no. 4, op. 165

Less commonly, individual works not related to each other are assigned serial numbers within a single opus number. In this case, give the opus number first followed by the serial number within the opus number, with a comma separating them. The composer of these works assigned opus 33 to three works, two for violin and piano and one for violin. Each of the works is numbered serially within the opus.

Theme and variations, ‡m violin, ‡n **op. 33, no. 1**
Elegy, ‡m violin, piano, ‡n **op. 33, no. 2**
Toccatas, ‡m violin, piano, ‡n **op. 33, no. 3**

Do not confuse this situation with parts within a larger work assigned a single opus number, which are discussed in Chapter 11, "Additions to Both Generic and Distinctive Titles."

Thematic Index Numbers (25.30C4)

In the absence of, or sometimes in preference to, opus numbers, thematic index numbers may be used. AACR2 defines a thematic index as a "list of a composer's works, usually arranged in chronological order or by categories, with the theme given for each composition or for each section of large compositions." Rule 25.304C specifically mentions "numbers assigned to a work in a *recognized* [emphasis added] thematic index." The idea of a "recognized" thematic index is not clarified; however, it is assumed that when LC uses thematic index numbers, they are from a "recognized" thematic index.

Thematic index numbers are preferred to serial or opus numbers for some composers' works, such as Schubert, Mozart, and Vivaldi. When thematic index numbers have been designated for use in uniform titles for a composer, it is indicated in the 667 field in the authority record for the composer's name. For example:

010   n79021425
100 1b Bach, Johann Sebastian, ‡d 1685-1750
667   Thematic index numbers are those found in Schmieder, e.g.,
          [Sonaten und Partiten, violin, BWV 1001-1006]

When a composer's works are assigned different thematic index
numbers for works of different types or for different mediums of
performance, both the source of the numbers and the works to which they
are applied are indicated in the 667 field of the name authority record for
the composer.

010   n81022281
100 1b Vanhal, Johann Baptist, ‡d 1739-1813
667   **Thematic-index numbers for symphonies** arc those found in
          Bryan, P. The symphonies of Johann Vanhal, e.g., [Symphonies,
          B. C6, C major]. **Thematic-index numbers for other works** are
          those found in Weinmann, A. Themen-Verzeichnis der Komposi-
          tionen von Johann Baptiste Wanhal, e.g., [Sonatinas, piano, W.
          XIII: 46 57], [Masses, W XIX: Es 4, E♭ major]

When thematic index numbers appear on published works but are not
found in a recognized thematic index, LC does not use them. Although
there is a list of works for the composer Stanley Weiner and numbers
from it appear on his published works, LC has chosen not to use the
numbers found there.

100 1b Weiner, Stanley.
240 10 Serenades, ‡m wind quintet
245 00 Serenade für Bläserquintett, für Flöte, Oboe, Klarinette in B,
          Horn in F, Fagott, WeinWV 38

Thematic index numbers generally have an alphabetic prefix in the
form of an initial or acronym. An initial may be first initial of the
compiler's last name. The "K." in Mozart's thematic index number stands
for Ludwig Köchel, the organizer of Mozart's works. When the numbers
are taken from a reference source other than a thematic index, the first
initial of the last name of the author of the article or book may be used.
The thematic index numbers for Michel de Lalande are taken from the
article by Sawkins in *New Grove* and are preceded by the letter "S." Two
letters may represent the first initials of the composer's first and last

names, as is the case with "MH," for Michael Haydn, or multiple authors
of the composer's thematic index, such as "BI," standing for Bianchi and
Inzaghi's index of Alessandro Rolla's works.

A thematic index number may also be an acronym representing the
title of the thematic index. The letters in the thematic index numbers for
J. S. Bach's works, "BWV," stand for *Bach-Werke-Verzeichnis* [Bach
Work List], compiled by Wolfgang Schmieder.

"WoO" is used when most, but not all, of a composer's works have
opus numbers. The works that cannot be identified numerically are
arranged chronologically or by form or genre and assigned numbers
preceded by "WoO." This stands for *Werke ohne Opuszahl*, or "works
without opus numbers." Use WoO numbers for a composer's works when
they appear in a thematic index, in reference sources, or on published
works.

Some thematic index numbers include indication of key, such as those
for Johann Friedrich Fasch or Georg Philipp Telemann. In the following
examples, the "FWV" is taken from the title of the thematic index for
Fasch, *Verzeichnis der Werke von Johann Friedrich Fasch* [List of works
by Johann Friedrich Fasch]. The thematic index is divided into sections
by type of work/medium of performance, with each section assigned a
letter. The letter is given in uppercase in the uniform title. Section L lists
Fasch's concertos. The letter following the colon signifies key, with
uppercase letters for major keys and lowercase letters for minor keys. The
number following the key indicates the position of that work within the
sequence of works in that category and in that key, with numbers assigned
by the compiler of the thematic index.

Thematic index number	Key
FWV L:**D**11	D major
FWV L:**e**1	E minor

The thematic index numbers for Telemann's instrumental music are
from *Telemann-Werkverzeichnis, Instrumentalwerke* [Telemann work list,
instrumental works]. The source is divided into numbered sections.
Section 42 includes works for two instruments and continuo, further
subdivided by key.

Thematic index number	Key
TWV 42:**f**1	F minor
TWV 42:**F**5	F major

When no thematic index exists for a composer, and some or all the works of that composer have been published in a monographic series, the numbering system by which the works have been organized in that source may be used. Work numbers for several early British composers, such as John Bull, William Byrd, Orlando Gibbons, and John Ward, are taken from the series *Musica Britannica*. Work numbers for these composers are preceded by "MB." The number in this uniform title for a work by John Bull is taken from *Musica Britannica* volume 14, which is Bull's keyboard music. The work is number 25 in that volume.

In nomines, ‡m keyboard instrument, **‡n MB 25**, ‡r A minor

A list of thematic index numbers for composers whose works are assigned numbers other than or in addition to opus numbers appears in Appendix A.

Examples of Thematic Index Numbers

Allegretto, ‡m violin, piano, ‡n **TrV 295**
Preludes, ‡m piano, ‡n **A. 86**
Concertinos, ‡m violoncello, piano, ‡n **E. 159**

A Range of Consecutive Thematic Index Numbers

In a range of thematic index numbers, the alphabetic prefix is not repeated.

Quartets, ‡m strings, ‡n **M. D6-8**
not
Quartets, ‡m strings, ‡n M. D6-M. D8

Overtures, ‡m harpsichord, ‡n **TWV 32:11-32:13**
not
Overtures, ‡m harpsichord, ‡n TWV 32:11-TWV 32:13

Symphonies, ‡n **H. I, 88-92**
not
Symphonies, ‡n H. I, 88-H. I, 92

Gesänge, ‡m mixed voices, piano, ‡n **H. XXVb-c**
not
Gesänge, ‡m mixed voices, piano, ‡n H. XXVb-H. XXVc

Symphonies, ‡n **W. C 1a-6a**
not
Symphonies, ‡n W. C 1a-W. C 6a

Trio sonatas, ‡m violin, viola da gamba, continuo, ‡n **BuxWV 259-265**
not
Trio sonatas, ‡m violin, viola da gamba, continuo, ‡n BuxWV 259-BuxWV 265

Other Kinds of Numbers

When a composer uses a non-numeric designation, use that designation in the uniform title.

Quartets, ‡m flute, clarinet, horn, bassoon, ‡n **letter A**
Quartets, ‡m clarinets, horn, bassoon, ‡n **letter B**

Chapter 8
Key (25.30D)

The key of a musical work is the tonality of the entire work or of its principal movements. In a uniform title, the key is given in English in ǂr. Both the flat and sharp signs have specific characters in the ALA character set.

Generic uniform titles for works composed before 1900 include the key, even when it is not stated on the item. Include the key of a post-nineteenth-century work only when it is part of the composer's original title or is in the title of the first edition.

When the key is stated on an item, generally a pitch name and the mode (e.g., major, minor) are given.

Quartets, ǂm strings, ǂn no. 1, op. 1, **ǂr D major**
Symphonies, ǂn no. 5, op. 67, **ǂr C minor**

In post-nineteenth-century works, it is not unusual for only the name of a pitch representing the tonal center of the work to be given. In that case, name the pitch only.

Sonatas, ǂm piano, ǂn no. 2, **ǂr G**
Sonatas, ǂm piano, ǂn no. 2, op. 84, no. 1, **ǂr D♭**

The key or mode may not be stated on the item. When the key of a pre-twentieth-century musical work is not stated on the item or when only a pitch name is given, the cataloger must determine the key. The key can sometimes be ascertained by consulting standard reference works, such as *New Grove* or a composer's thematic index. Failing this, the cataloger must determine the key from the music itself. This is usually done easily, but can be difficult, especially if the work begins in one key and ends in another. AACR2 offers no guidelines to deal with this situation, and LC practice varies. General practice seems to be to use the key of the opening movement of a work, excluding short introductions. Keep in mind that when there are instruments not pitched in C, such as B♭ trumpet, F horn, etc., the line for that instrument will not represent the key the piece is in.

The key may appear on the item in a language other than English. For most keys, it is easily apparent what is meant. Uppercase "A" and lowercase "a" mean "A major" and "A minor," respectively. However, B and B♭ are indicated by the letters "H" and "B" in German publications. Uppercase "B" and lowercase "b" indicate "B♭ major" and "B♭ minor," respectively, and uppercase "H" and lowercase "h" indicate "B major" and "B minor."

The following table gives the foreign equivalents of the names of musical keys.

English	French	German	Italian	Spanish
major	majeur	Dur	maggiore	mayor
minor	mineur	Moll	minore	menor
sharp	dièse	__is	diesis	sostenido
flat	bémol	__es	bemolle	bemol
A flat	la bémol	as	la bemolle	la bemol
A	la	A	la	la
A sharp	la dièse	ais	la diesis	la sostenido
B flat	si bémol	B	si bemolle	si bemol
B	si	H	si	si
C flat	do bémol	ces	do bemolle	do bemol
C	ut/do	C	do	do
C sharp	do dièse	cis	do diesis	do sostenido
D flat	ré bémol	des	re bemolle	re bemol
D	ré	D	re	re
D sharp	ré dièse	dis	re diesis	re sostenido
E flat	mi bémol	es	mi bemolle	mi bemol
E	mi	E	mi	mi
F	fa	F	f	fa
F sharp	fa dièse	fis	fa diesis	fa sostenido
G flat	sol bémol	ges	sol bemolle	sol bemol
G	sol	G	sol	sol
G sharp	sol dièse	gis	sol diesis	sol sostenido

Table 8.1: Foreign Equivalents of Names of Musical Keys

Occasionally, two keys are given. When it is determined that the composer assigned both keys, some catalogers have included both in the uniform title, as in the examples below. Because AACR2 does not address this situation, there is no prescribed punctuation, and different forms are used to separate the names of the two keys involved, a slash in the first uniform title and a hyphen in the second.

Title: Ecossaise for piano in D minor/F major, D158
Uniform title: Ecossaises, ‡m piano, ‡n D. 158, **‡r D minor/F major**

Title: Fuga gis Moll-D Dur für Orgel
Uniform title: Fugues, ‡m organ, **‡r G# minor-D major**

In the case of the following work, the modes were omitted from the uniform title.

Title: Symphony, no. 3, op. 43, in C minor and major
Uniform title: Symphonies, ‡n no. 3, op. 43, **‡r C**

Chapter 9
Other Identifying Elements (25.30E)

Apply rule 25.30E when the uniform titles for two different works by the same composer conflict, even after applying rules 25.29 through 25.30D. Add these elements, in the following order of preference, to break the conflict:

- year of completion of composition
- year of publication
- any other identifying element, such as place of composition or first publisher.

Additional identifying elements are given in parentheses in the same subfield to which they apply, without separately subfielding them. A date used as a qualifier, however, is entered in ‡n when it is not adjacent to a serial, work, or opus number.

Year of Completion of Composition

Give the year of completion of composition or year of publication enclosed in parentheses in ‡n with no punctuation preceding the date.

Exact Year of Composition

Magnificats, ‡r G major **‡n (1763)**

Sonatas, ‡m piano **‡n (1976)**
Sonatas, ‡m piano **‡n (1980)**

Sonatas, ‡m viola, piano, ‡r D **‡n (1953)**
Sonatas, ‡m viola, piano, ‡r D **‡n (1958)**

When the date is used to qualify numeric identifying elements given in ‡n, enter the date in parentheses following the number, with no punctuation preceding it, in the same subfield.

Sonatas, ‡m piano, ‡n no. 5 **(1950)**

Range of Years of Composition

Inclusive dates are given in full as per AACR2 Appendix C.6A.

Romansy **‡n (1895-1896)**
Romansy **‡n (1903-1904)**

Estimated or Guessed Year of Composition

An estimated or guessed year of composition is based on research in a thematic index or encyclopedia. An approximate date is indicated with the abbreviation for "circa," e.g., "c1734" or "ca. 1734."

Quartets, ‡m flute, violin, viola, continuo **‡n (ca. 1752)**
Tantum ergo, ‡r G major **‡n (ca. 1828-1833)**
Solos, ‡m flute, continuo **‡n (1754?)**

The following construction has been used when the date of composition is one of two years.

Tantum ergo **‡n (1848 or 9)**
Tantum ergo **‡n (1854 or 5)**

Year of Composition Is the Same

When the year of composition for two works is the same, add either additional information to the date or another distinguishing element. In the first two uniform titles, the month and day of composition resolve a conflict between two works composed in the same month of the same year; in the second two, letters are added to the date to indicate the order of composition within the year.

Preludes, ǂm organ, ǂr G major ǂn **(1829 Oct. 2)**
Preludes, ǂm organ, ǂr G major ǂn **(1829 Oct. 22)**

Etudes, ǂm clarinet ǂn **(1983a)**
Etudes, ǂm clarinet ǂn **(1983b)**

When more than one additional element is used in a subfield, they are separated from each other with a space-colon-space. In these examples, year of composition and medium of performance are used to resolve the conflict.

Motets ǂn **(1584 : Voices (4))**
Motets ǂn **(1584 : Voices (5))**

Year of Original Publication

Exact Year of Publication

Motets, ǂm voices (4), ǂn book 1 **(1539)**
Motets, ǂm voices (4), ǂn book 1 **(1545)**

Pièces de clavecin ǂn **(1706)**
Pièces de clavecin ǂn **(1724)**

Estimated Year of Publication

Fantasies, ǂm voices (3) ǂn **(ca. 1620)**
Trio sonatas, ǂm flutes, continuo ǂn **(ca. 1730)**
Pièces de clavecin ǂn **(ca. 1729)**

Probable Decade of First Publication

Concertos, ǂm violoncello, string orchestra, ǂr C major ǂn **(176-)**

Any Other Identifying Elements

Other identifying elements are enclosed in parentheses following the last element in the uniform title. They are not separately subfielded. AACR2 does not prescribe the type or order of preference of identifying elements in this category. Suggested elements given in the rule are "place of publication, name of first publisher." The order given here is not meant to be prescriptive.

First Publisher

When year of composition is unknown, the names of the publishers may be used to differentiate between two works with identical titles published by different publishers. The form of the name of each publisher need not be standardized.

Sonatas, ‡m violoncello, continuo, ‡r A major **(Zanibon)**
Solos, ‡m violin, continuo **(Walsh)**
Symphonies, ‡r G major **(Sieber)**

Carol preludes **(Leeds)**
Carol preludes **(Gentry)**

Place of First Publication

Sonatas, ‡m recorder, continuo, ‡n op. 5 **(Rome)**

Edition

Concerti grossi, ‡n op. 3. ‡n No. 4 **(1st ed.)**

Text on Which a Vocal Work Is Based

Magnificats, ‡m voices (5) **(Alma real)**
Magnificats, ‡m voices (5) **(Mort et fortune)**

Author of Text

When there is no other way to distinguish between vocal works, qualify by the last name of the author of the text.

Lieder **(Huch)**
Lieder **(Kaschnitz)**
Lieder **(Sachs)**

Number of Performers

Because the term "percussion" is used to describe both a solo percussionist and a group of percussionists, identical uniform titles for two different works by the same composer may occur. LC has used the number of performers in parentheses following the word "percussion" (in the singular) to resolve such a conflict.

Title: Soli for solo percussion
Uniform title: Solos, ‡m percussion **(1)**

Title: Soli for percussion duo
Uniform title: Solos, ‡m percussion **(2)**

Manuscript Repository and Number

Symphonies, ‡m string orchestra, ‡r G major **(Hessische Landes- und Hochschulbibliothek Darmstadt: Mus. ms. 886/1)**
Symphonies, ‡m string orchestra, ‡r G major **(Bayerische Staats-bibliothek: Mus. ms. 1482)**

Order in Which the Work Appears in a Collection of Several Composers' Works

The qualifier here is "(No. __ in Canzoni per sonare, 1608)." The number assigned to each work refers to the order in which the work appeared in the publication titled *Canzoni per Sonare*, published in 1608.

Canzonas, ‡m voices (5) **(No. 19 in Canzoni per sonare, 1608)**
Canzonas, ‡m voices (8) **(No. 24 in Canzoni per sonare, 1608)**

The qualifier in this uniform title identifies the work as the fourth item in the *Fitzwilliam Virginal Book*, a collection of anonymous works and works by various composers. This work is one of two pavans by the composer Ferdinando Richardson. Both pavans appear in the *Fitzwilliam Virginal Book*. The number within the book is required to distinguish between the two pavans.

Pavans, ǂm keyboard instrument **(Fitzwilliam virginal book, 4)**

These sonatas are qualified by indication of their place in an entry in *Répertoire International des Sources Musicales* (RISM).

Sonatas, ǂm recorders (2), ǂr F major **(RISM 1698⁸, no. 13)**
Sonatas, ǂm recorders (2), ǂr G minor **(RISM 1698⁸, no. 14)**

The examples below are for sonatas by Scarlatti that appeared in a collection of works by various composers titled *24 Concerti del Mano-scritto di Napoli*. Of the seven sonatas by Scarlatti, all are for flute, two violins, and continuo, and two are in A minor. These two are numbers IX and XXI in the collection, numbers assigned by the compiler of the collection and not by Scarlatti. Since both are in A minor and the key is already included in the uniform title, another qualifier must be used to differentiate between the two. The qualifier used here is the number within the collection, but does not include the title of the collection, as in the previous examples. The uniform titles are qualified by the numbers assigned to each sonata by the compiler of the collection, and, because the numbers were not assigned by the composer, each is given at the end of the uniform title as a parenthetical qualifier, rather than as serial numbers in ǂn.

Sonatas, ǂm flute, violins (2), continuo, ǂr A minor **(Sonata IX)**
Sonatas, ǂm flute, violins (2), continuo, ǂr A minor **(Sonata XXI)**

not

Sonatas, ǂm flute, violins (2), continuo, ǂn no. 9, ǂr A minor
Sonatas, ǂm flute, violins (2), continuo, ǂn no. 21, ǂr A minor

Chapter 10
Distinctive Titles (25.3, 25.31A-B)

Formulating the Title

A distinctive title is based on the title given the work by the composer or another, better-known title given to the work later. Rule 25.29A1 concerning singular and plural forms and cognates is not applied to distinctive uniform titles. Nor are rules 25.30B-25.30D applied to distinctive uniform titles unless needed to resolve conflicts.

When formulating a distinctive uniform title, follow the guidelines in rules 25.3 and 25.28 and remove the following from the title: initial articles, subtitles and alternate titles, introductory phrases, and separable statements of responsibility

Initial Articles

Remove an initial article, in any language, from the title. An initial article may include an apostrophe. A list of articles and the languages in which they are used is included in the 2004 update to AACR2 as "*Appendix E: Initial Articles*." The table below lists the definite and indefinite articles in English, French, German, Italian, and Spanish.

English	a, an, d', de, the, ye
French	l', la, le, les, un, une
German	das, dem, den, der, des, die, ein, eine, einem, einen, einer, eines, 's
Italian	gl', gli, i, il, l', la, le, lo, un, un', una, uno
Spanish	el, la, las, lo, los, un, una

Table 10.1: Articles in English, French, German, Italian, and Spanish

Examples

~~The~~ bells of Yale
~~L'~~oiseau blessé d'une flèche
~~Die~~ Zauberflöte

When an initial article is preceded by ellipses, both the ellipses and initial article are removed:

On item: ... ein Schatten auf Erden
Uniform title: Schatten auf Erden
Not: —Schatten auf Erden

Initial articles are removed even when they are grammatically meaningful, as in German language titles. The removal of the initial article may change the meaning of the title or even make it incomprehensible. The initial article "das" in this title does not merely mean "the," but something more on the order of "of the."

~~Das~~ Knaben Wunderhorn

In the latter four languages from the table above, some of the articles are also the word for "one."

Language	Articles that may also mean "one"
French	un, une
German	ein(s)
Italian	uno, una
Spanish	un(o), una

Table 10.2: Articles That May Also Mean "One"

In French, "un(e)" is the word for both "the" and "one." When it appears as the first word of a title, the context in which it is used will determine if it is retained in the uniform title. For example, *Une Journée* means "one day" and "une" is retained in the uniform title. The title *Une Education Manquée* means "an education incomplete." The word "une" functions as an article and is omitted from the uniform title.

It is important also to know that some words that are articles in one language may be other types of words in other languages. For example, "a" is an indefinite article in English, but a preposition in French and Italian. The initial "a" in *A la Manière de—* is retained in the uniform title. "Il" is an article in Italian, but a pronoun in French. *Il Neige* means "it snows;" the initial word is included in the uniform title. "An" is an article in English, but a preposition in German. The initial word in *An die Jugend*, which means "to the youth," is included in the uniform title.

Subtitles and Alternate Titles

Subtitles are removed, as are alternate titles, and, when they appear, a word meaning "or," in any language.

In the beginning : ~~five meditations on texts from the Bhagavad Ghita~~
Occasione fa il ladro, ~~ossia, Il cambio della valigia~~

Introductory Phrases

~~Mel Bay presents~~ Three dimensions
~~Celebrated~~ Dettingen Te Deum

Separable Statements of Responsibility

~~Wagner's~~ Ring of the Nibelung
~~Telemanns~~ fugirende und verändernde Choräle

A distinctive title is created using the form in the composer's original language (but not necessarily the original script) as found on manifestations of the work or in reference sources. Titles in non-roman alphabets are transliterated into the roman alphabet using the *ALA-LC Transliteration Tables*, which are online at http://www.loc.gov/catdir/cpso/roman.html.

According to 25.27B1, when another title in the same language has become better known, it is to be used.

Title: Grandezza d'animo, oder, Arsinoe
Reference source: Arsinoe (La grandezza d'animo, oder, Arsinoe)
Uniform title: Arsinoe

Title:	L'Egisto, overo, Chi soffre speri
Reference source:	Chi soffre speri (L'Egisto; L'Alvida)
Uniform title:	Chi soffre speri

Title:	Prodromus musicalis, ou, Elévations et motets
Reference source:	Elévations et motets à voix seule avec la bc
Uniform title:	Elévations et motets

A very long title may be shortened following the order of preference in 25.27C1:
  • a brief title by which the work is commonly identified in reference sources
  • a brief title formulated by the cataloger.

Composer's title:	Historia des Leidens und Sterbens unsers Herrn und Heylandes Jesu Christi nach dem Evangelisten S. Matheum
First edition title:	Das Leiden unsers Herren Jesu Christi, wie es beschreibet der heilige Evangeliste Matthaeus
Cataloger's title:	St. Matthew Passion
Uniform title:	St. Matthew Passion

Titles With Cardinal Numbers

When a distinctive title includes a cardinal number, whether as the initial word of the title or in an internal position, the cataloger must decide if it is integral to the title. Does the number indicate the number of movements or, in some cases, the number of performers? If removed from the title, does the meaning of the title change?

Initial Cardinal Numbers Integral to the Title

When an initial cardinal number is integral to the title, it is retained in the uniform title.

Title:	The seven deadly sins
Uniform title:	Seven deadly sins

Title:	The fourteen Stations of the Cross
Uniform title:	Fourteen Stations of the Cross

It may not be apparent from a title that an initial ordinal number is integral to the title. An examination of the work may reveal this. The work "*3 Envelopes*" is a one-movement work. Since the number does not indicate the number of movements in the work, it is retained in the uniform title.

Title: 3 envelopes
Uniform title: 3 envelopes

Initial Cardinal Numbers Not Integral to the Title

Initial cardinal numbers are omitted from the uniform title when they are not an integral part of the title. An initial cardinal number is not integral to the title when it indicates seriality or the number of movements in the work, whether or not the movements have distinctive titles. The initial ordinal number in the following examples are not integral to the title and is removed for the uniform title.

Title: Six poems by Emily Dickinson
Uniform title: Poems by Emily Dickinson

Title: 4 morceaux pour 7 musiciens
Uniform title: Morceaux pour 7 musiciens

In certain languages, removing an initial cardinal number changes the case ending of the noun it modifies. For example, in Hungarian, in which the singular form is used after numbers or other expressions of quantity, the plural ending to nouns ending with a vowel is "—k." The ending is preceded by an auxiliary vowel when the word ends in a consonant. When establishing a uniform title for a work with a Hungarian title, consultation with a Hungarian language expert is highly recommended.

Title: Két magyar **tánc**
Number: két = 2
Uniform title: Magyar **táncok**

Title: Három **dal** Radnóti Miklós verseire
Number: Három = 3
Uniform title: **Dalok** Radnóti Miklós verseire

Title: Négy tót **népdal**
Number: Négy = 4
Uniform title: Tót **népdal<u>ok</u>**

Title: Nyolc könnyű **karakterdarab**
Number: Nyolc = 8
Uniform title: Könnyű **karakterdarab<u>ok</u>**

Title: Kilenc **miniatűr**
Number: Kilenc = 9
Uniform title: **Miniatűr<u>ök</u>**

The form of noun in a Russian title beginning with an initial cardinal number is determined by the number. When preceded by 2 (dve), 3 (tri), or 4 (chetyre), the noun is already in the form to be used in the uniform title once the number is removed. When preceded by other numbers (e.g., 5 [piat′], 6 [shest′], 7 [sem′]), the noun is in a declined form that will change when the initial number is removed for the uniform title. Consultation with a colleague with a Russian language expert is highly recommended when working with uniform titles in Russian.

When preceded by 2, (dve), 3 (tri), and 4 (chetyre), the noun is in the form used in the uniform title once the initial number is removed.

Title: Dve starinnye **melodii**
Uniform title: Starinnye **melodii**

Title: Tri kontsertnye **p´esy**
Uniform title: Kontsertnye **p´esy**

Title: Chetyre liricheskikh **fragmenta**
Uniform title: Liricheskikh **fragmenta**

When preceded by the number 5 (piat′), 6 (shest′), 7 (sem′), etc., the form of noun changes when the initial number is removed.

Title: Piat′ **stikhotvorenii̯** K. Bal′monta
Uniform title: **Stikhotvoreni<u>ia</u>** K. Bal′monta

Title: Shest′ **romans<u>ov</u>** na slova Anny Akhmatovoĭ
Uniform title: **Romans<u>y</u>** na slova Anny Akhmatovoĭ

Title: Sem´ armianskikh **pesen**
Uniform title: Armianskie **pesni**

Internal Cardinal Numbers Integral to the Title

Internal cardinal numbers are retained when they are integral to the title.

Title: Psalm 23
Uniform title: Psalm 23

Title: Uvertiura na tri grecheskie temy
Uniform title: Uvertiura na tri grcheskie temy

Title: Introduktion und zwölf Variationen über "Das Blümchen
              wunderhold"
Uniform title: Introduktion und 12 Variationen über "Das Blümchen
              wunderhold"

Title: Prologue et quatre danses
Uniform title: Prologue et quatre danses

Title: Variations on O filii et filiae
Original title: O filii et filiae, avec neuf variations
Uniform title: O filii et filiae, avec neuf variations

It is not always apparent from the title whether the number is integral to the title or indicative of seriality. In the example below, the cataloger must determine if this is the composer's twentieth fanfare or if the number "20" means something else. Further examination of the item reveals that the work was composed for the twentieth annual convention of the National Flute Association; thus the number does not indicate seriality and is integral to the uniform title.

Title: Fanfare 20 for flute choir
Uniform title: Fanfare 20

When a phrase suggesting the number of performers, such as "a due," "zu viert," "pour cinq," etc., appears along with the name of a type of composition in the title of a post-nineteenth-century work, the title is distinctive according to LC practice found in the authority file and the phrase is retained in the uniform title. (For pre-twentieth-century works, such a phrase is considered to be a statement of medium of performance and is not retained in the initial title element.)

Title: Sonata for three
Uniform title: Sonata for three

Title: Concerto for three
Original title: Konzert zu dritt
Uniform title: Konzert zu dritt

Title: Serenade for seven
Uniform title: Serenade for seven

This treatment is being applied when a phrase indicates the number of movements or other parts, as well.

Title: String quartet in four movements
Uniform title: String quartet in four movements

Title: Musik in 3 Sätzen
Uniform title: Musik in 3 Sätzen

Title: Suite in three movements
Original title: Suite em três movimentos
Uniform title: Suite em três movimentos

Title: Suite of eight dances
Uniform title: Suite of eight dances

Internal Cardinal Numbers Not Integral to the Title

An internal cardinal number is omitted when it is not integral to the title. In the examples below, the number refers to one of a sequence of consecutively numbered works with the same title. The number is added to the uniform title in ǂn to distinguish it from other works in the sequence. Following LCRI 25.30C2, use the English abbreviation "no." whether or not it appears on the item and regardless of how the word appears on the item when it is present. Give the number in arabic form.

Title: Vertical thoughts **IV**
Uniform title: Vertical thoughts, **‡n no. 4**

Title: Muzyczka **trzy**
Uniform title: Muzyczka, **‡n no. 3**

Title: Contrapunto espacial **III-c**
Uniform title: Contrapunto espacial, **‡n no. 3-c**

Titles With Ordinal Numbers

When an ordinal number appears in a distinctive title, the cataloger must decide if it is integral to the title. Does the number indicate seriality? If removed from the title, does the meaning of the title change?

Initial Ordinal Numbers Integral to the Title

In these titles, the initial ordinal number does not imply seriality and are integral to the titles, and thus are retained in the uniform title.

Title: Quinta stagione
Uniform title: Quinta stagione

Title: Fourth autumn
Uniform title: Fourth autumn

Title: Fifth continent
Uniform title: Fifth continent

Initial Ordinal Numbers Not Integral to the Title

The initial ordinal number in these titles indicate that these works are in a numbered series of works with the same title. The ordinal number is removed from the initial title element and added as a serial number in ‡n. Follow LCRI 25.30C2 and use the English abbreviation "no." Give the number in arabic form.

Title: **1.** moderne Suite
Uniform title: Moderne Suite, **‡n no. 1**

Title: **Third** fanfare for the uncommon woman
Uniform title: Fanfare for the uncommon woman, ‡n no. 3

Internal Ordinal Numbers Integral to the Title

In these titles, the internal ordinal number does not imply seriality and are integral to the titles, and thus are retained in the uniform title.

Title: Henry the Fifth
Uniform title: Henry the Fifth

Title: And on the seventh day ...
Uniform title: And on the seventh day—

Title: Fanfare for the third millennium
Uniform title: Fanfare for the third millennium

Internal Ordinal Numbers Not Integral to the Title

Internal ordinal numbers are omitted when they are not integral. In the titles below, the numbers refer to one of a sequence of consecutively numbered works with the same title. The number is added to the uniform title as a serial number in ‡n to distinguish it from other works in the sequence. Following LCRI 25.30C2, use the English abbreviation "no." whether or not it appears on the item and regardless of how the word appears on the item when it is present. Give the number in arabic form.

Title: Paganiana **2a**
Uniform title: Paganiana, ‡n no. 2

Title: Episode **4ème**
Uniform title: Episode, ‡n no. 4

When removing an ordinal number from a Latin title, the case of the remaining title words must change from genitive to nominative. When establishing a uniform title for a work with a Latin title, consultation with a Latin language expert is highly recommended.

Title: Sacror<u>um</u> concentu<u>um</u>, **pars prima**
Uniform title: Sacr<u>i</u> concent<u>us</u>, ‡n **pars 1**

Title: Lamentation<u>um</u> **liber secondus**
Uniform title: Lamentation<u>es</u>, ‡n **liber 2**

Title: **Tomus primus** music<u>i</u> op<u>eris</u>
Uniform title: Music<u>um</u> op<u>us</u>, ‡n **1. tomus**

Singular Versus Plural

Rule 25.29A1 is not applied to distinctive uniform titles. They are not given in the plural, even when the composer wrote more than one work with that title, unless the composer gave the title in the plural form.

Title: Monologue II
Uniform title: Monologue, ‡n no. 2
Not: Monologues, ‡n no. 2

Titles Consisting Solely of a Statement of Medium of Performance

Some contemporary composers, such as Morton Feldman and Steve Reich, use the medium of performance as the title for many of their works. These titles are distinctive and are used as they appear for the uniform title, retaining initial and internal numbers.

Six pianos	Eleven instruments
Piano three hands	Cello and orchestra

Additions to Distinctive Titles to Resolve Conflicts (25.31B1)

The application of the rules for formulating distinctive titles may result in identical distinctive uniform titles for two or more different works by the same composer. To resolve such a conflict, follow 25.31A-B1 and LCRI 25.31B1.

The first preference is to add either a statement of medium of performance or a descriptive term or phrase to distinguish the works. The choice is based on whether it is possible to state the medium of performance for all works involved. If it is not possible to state the medium, a word or phrase that describes each work is used. The form used should be parallel, either a statement of medium of performance or a word or phrase.

If neither of these is sufficient to uniquely identify the works, add elements as outlined for additions to generic titles:

- numeric identifying elements
- key
- other identifying elements.

Note that as many identifying elements as can be determined are added to generic uniform titles; only as many elements as needed to uniquely distinguish otherwise identical distinctive uniform titles should be used.

Medium of Performance

When it is possible to state the medium of performance easily, follow 25.30B, the same rules used for generic uniform titles. The statement of medium follows the initial title element in ‡m, preceded by a comma. When the title ends with an exclamation point or a question mark, a comma is not added before the statement of medium of performance (see "Ending Punctuation" in Chapter 1).

Fantasiestücke, ‡m piano
Fantasiestücke, ‡m clarinet, orchestra

Magyar népdalok, ‡m mixed voices
Magyar népdalok, ‡m violin, piano

Česká rapsódie, ‡m baritone, mixed voices, orchestra
Česká rapsódie, ‡m violin, piano

Descriptive Term or Phrase

When the statement of the medium of performance for one or more of the works involved is not possible to formulate or is too diverse to state concisely, use a descriptive term or phrase. The descriptive term or phrase can indicate types of composition (e.g., air, ballet, cantata, chorale prelude, duet, opera, song, symphony) or medium of performance (piano work, vocal trio); designate differing versions (1st version, 2nd setting);

or indicate date of composition or publication. The term or phrase follows the initial title element, enclosed in parentheses. When a date is used, it is tagged in ‡n; in all other cases, no subfield tag precedes the term or phrase.

In the example below, a descriptive term or phrase is applied rather than the medium of performance. Although it is possible to name the medium of performance for the piano work, it is not possible to succinctly state a medium of performance for an opera. The use of a descriptive term for the first title and medium of performance for the second does not result in a parallel construction.

Parallel construction	Not a parallel construction
Goyescas **(Opera)**	Goyescas (Opera)
Goyescas **(Piano work)**	Goyescas, ‡m piano

Other Examples of a Descriptive Term or Phrase

Morgenstern **(Duet)**
Morgenstern **(Song)**

Naturgenuss **(Song)**
Naturgenuss **(Vocal quartet)**

Golem **(Computer work)**
Golem **(Opera)**

Canta in prato **(Introduction)**
Canta in prato **(Motet)**

Gamlet **(Incidental music)**
Gamlet **(Motion picture music)**

Rosenkavalier **(Opera)**
Rosenkavalier **(Silent film music)**

Giul'sara **(Music drama)**
Giul'sara **(Opera)**

Brass larynx **(Literary work)**
Brass larynx **(Musical work)**

When Medium of Performance or a Descriptive Term or Phrase Is Not
Used

There are two situations in which the medium of performance or
descriptive term or phrase is not used to resolve a conflict. The first
occurs when the statement of medium of performance is the same for all
the works involved. One or more of the additional elements explained
below and given in order of preference. For example, the two works
below are both for organ, therefore including the statement of medium of
performance will not distinguish the two works. Another element is
needed to make these titles unique. Medium of performance would not be
included, since it is not a distinguishing feature of the two works.

Concertstück, ‡m organ
Concertstück, ‡m organ

A descriptive term is insufficient to resolve the conflict between these
two cantatas by Bach. Because both are cantatas, and there are no other
works with this title by Bach, some other element should be used to make
the titles unique.

Sie werden euch in den Bann tun (Cantata)
Sie werden euch in den Bann tun (Cantata)

The second situation in which the use of medium of performance or
descriptive term or phrase is deferred occurs when using serial numbers
associated with the works will result in a better file arrangement. AACR2
provides no guidance as to what constitutes a "better file arrangement,"
and so it is left to individual cataloger judgment. Examples of this will
follow the explanation of numeric identifying elements below.

Numeric Identifying Elements

Numeric identifying elements are added when the medium of performance
or a descriptive term or phrase is insufficient to resolve a conflict. As with
numeric identifying elements in generic titles, follow 25.30C and add a
serial number or an opus or thematic index number, in that order of
preference, in ‡n.

When the works are all for the same medium of performance, omit the medium and use only the number, since only one element is needed to distinguish the works.

Serial Number

Add the serial number to a distinctive uniform title when the number was assigned by the composer. The uniform title is not pluralized unless that is the form given by the composer.

Grand trio concertant, ‡n no. 1
Grand trio concertant, ‡n no. 2

When the composer did not assign serial numbers to works with the same title, some other method of differentiation is preferred to resolve the conflict between the uniform titles.

Opus Number

Opus numbers may be used when the composer did not assign serial numbers. In the example below, the medium of performance is the same for both works. It is therefore insufficient to differentiate between the two works and is omitted from the uniform title. Using the opus numbers is sufficient to distinguish between the two works, and no further elements are needed to resolve the conflict.

Concertstück, ‡n op. 80
Concertstück, ‡n op. 90

not

Concertstück, ‡m organ, ‡n op. 80
Concertstück, ‡m organ, ‡n op. 90

Thematic Index Number

Because the composer wrote only the two works with this title, and both are cantatas, only the thematic index numbers are needed to distinguish between them.

Sie werden euch in den Bann tun, ‡n **BWV 44**
Sie werden euch in den Bann tun, ‡n **BWV 183**

not

Sie werden euch in den Bann tun (Cantata), ‡n BWV 44
Sie werden euch in den Bann tun (Cantata), ‡n BWV 183

Omitting Medium of Performance for a Better File Arrangement

LCRI 25.31B1 permits the use of serial numbers to resolve conflicts with distinctive titles in a numbered sequence even when using the medium of performance would suffice, in order to achieve a better file arrangement. Serial numbers may be used when they appear with the title, in numeric or spelled-out form. Following LCRI 25.30C2, use the English abbreviation "no." whether or not it appears on the item and regardless of how the word appears on the item when it is present. Give the number in arabic form.

Once a pattern has been established, it should be applied to all titles in the sequence. The cataloger who established these titles believed that arrangement by serial number was better than by medium of performance.

Sonata da chiesa, ‡n no. 1
Sonata da chiesa, ‡n no. 2
Sonata da chiesa, ‡n no. 3
Sonata da chiesa, ‡n no. 4
Sonata da chiesa, ‡n no. 5
Sonata da chiesa, ‡n no. 6
Sonata da chiesa, ‡n no. 7
Sonata da chiesa, ‡n no. 8
Sonata da chiesa, ‡n no. 9
Sonata da chiesa, ‡n no. 10
Sonata da chiesa, ‡n no. 11
Sonata da chiesa, ‡n no. 12

The same titles arranged by medium of performance was considered not to be as good an arrangement as by serial number:

Sonata da chiesa, ‡m clarinet, organ	[no. 10]
Sonata da chiesa, ‡m flute, organ	[no. 5]
Sonata da chiesa, ‡m horn, organ	[no. 11]
Sonata da chiesa, ‡m oboe, organ	[no. 2]
Sonata da chiesa, ‡m organ, trumpet, trombone	[no. 6]
Sonata da chiesa, ‡m organ, trumpets (2)	[no. 3]
Sonata da chiesa, ‡m organ, trumpets (3), trombones (2)	[no. 12]
Sonata da chiesa, ‡m organ, violin, violoncello	[no. 9]
Sonata da chiesa, †m trombone, organ	[no. 1]
Sonata da chiesa, ‡m trumpet, organ	[no. 4]
Sonata da chiesa, ‡m violin, organ	[no. 8]
Sonata da chiesa, †m violoncello, organ	[no. 7]

Key

When no other element will sufficiently distinguish otherwise identical uniform titles in which key would not normally be included, the key may be used to resolve a conflict.

Missa pastoralis, ‡r **C major**
Missa pastoralis, ‡r **D major**

Both of these works are for violoncello and piano.

Légende, ‡r **B minor**
Légende, ‡r **G minor**

Other Identifying Elements

Year of Completion of Composition

When no numeric identifying elements exist to distinguish among identical titles, year of composition can be used. It is given in ‡n, in parentheses with no other punctuation separating the date from the title.

Fidelio ‡n **(1805)**
Fidelio ‡n **(1806)**
Fidelio ‡n **(1814)**

When the year of composition is the same, add another distinguishing element. The month of composition is used in these examples, in which medium of performance is also needed to resolve conflicts.

Zwölftonspiel, ‡m piano, 4 hands ‡n **(1955 Apr.)**
Zwölftonspiel, ‡m piano, 4 hands ‡n **(1955 May)**
Zwölftonspiel, ‡m piano, 4 hands ‡n **(1955 Oct.)**

Guessed Year of Composition

Research is required when guessing the year of composition. Sources that can be used are thematic indexes, work lists, biographies, library catalogs, etc.

I will magnify thee ‡n **(1726?)**

Range of Years of Composition

Inclusive dates are given in full as per AACR2 Appendix C.6A. Again, in this example, medium of performance is also needed.

Portraits, ‡m piano ‡n **(1948-1953)**

More Than One Method of Differentiation

When the addition of one of the elements discussed above does not resolve a conflict, additional elements are to be added as needed, following 25.31B-25.31C:
  • numeric identifying elements
  • key
  • other identifying elements.

Medium of Performance and Opus Number

Medium of performance is not enough to distinguish among these four works. The opus numbers are added to the titles for the piano works only, since the titles for the other two works, for clarinet and for piano trio, do not conflict.

Fantasiestücke, ‡m **clarinet, piano**
Fantasiestücke, ‡m **piano, ‡n op. 12**
Fantasiestücke, ‡m **piano, ‡n op. 111**
Fantasiestücke, ‡m **piano trio**

Descriptive Term or Phrase and Thematic Index Number

A descriptive term does not resolve the conflict with these titles. The term
"(Cantata)" is sufficient to distinguish the first title; the other titles require
further differentiation. Thematic index numbers are added only to those
titles that still conflict.

Christ lag in Todesbanden **(Cantata)**
Christ lag in Todesbanden **(Chorale), ‡n BWV 277**
Christ lag in Todesbanden **(Chorale), ‡n BWV 278**
Christ lag in Todesbanden **(Chorale), ‡n BWV 279**
Christ lag in Todesbanden **(Chorale prelude), ‡n BWV 695**
Christ lag in Todesbanden **(Chorale prelude), ‡n BWV 718**

Descriptive Term or Phrase and Year of Composition

When no numeric identifying elements exist, as is frequently the case with
large-scale stage works, date of publication can be added following the
descriptive term or phrase. The work *Pskovitianka*, written as incidental
music, needs no further elements to distinguish it from the operas. The
three operas with the same title need the date of publication to distinguish
them from each other. Note that when both a descriptive term and date are
used, they are enclosed in the same set of parentheses, separated by a
space-colon-space.

Pskovitiãnka **(Incidental music)**
Pskovitiãnka **(Opera : 1872)**
Pskovitiãnka **(Opera : 1877)**
Pskovitiãnka **(Opera : 1892)**

Thematic Index Number and Year of Composition

It is rare to encounter two different works with the same title and thematic
index number, but it does happen. In the following uniform titles, date of

composition is used to distinguish between them. The range of dates in
the first title does not follow the practice for inclusive dates given in
AACR2 Appendix C.6A.

As pants the hart, ‡n **HWV 251c (1720/22)**
As pants the hart, ‡n **HWV 251c (1738)**

*Medium of Performance and Placement in a Collection of Several
Composers' Works*

The date comes from *Recueils Imprimés XVIe-XVIIe Siècles* (RISM B1),
which is a chronological listing of collections printed in the sixteenth and
seventeenth centuries. These works appeared as numbers 22 and 25 in a
collection titled *Der Erst Teil Hundert und Ainundsweintzig Newe Lieder.*
This collection was assigned the number "17" in the sequence of
collections published in 1534 that are listed in RISM B1.

Ich stuend an einem Morgen, ‡m voices (4) ‡n (1534[17], no. 22)
Ich stuend an einem Morgen, ‡m voices (4) ‡n (1534[17], no. 25)

Other Means of Differentiation

These following works have no means of differentiation other than the
number of individual pieces within each work. That number is given in
parentheses following the medium of performance, which is required
because the composer also wrote works with this title for other
instruments. Subfield "n" is not used, since that would suggest serial
numbering.

Title: Six résonances : ‡b pour orchestre
Uniform title: Résonances, ‡m orchestra **(6)**

Title: Huit résonances : ‡b pour orchestra
Uniform title: Résonances, ‡m orchestra **(8)**

Title: 6 short solos : ‡b for classical guitar
Uniform title: Short solos **(6)**

Title: 7 short solos : ‡b for classical guitar
Uniform title: Short solos (7)

Singular and Plural Forms of the Same Distinctive Title

When the only difference between two distinctive titles is that one is singular and the other is plural, they are considered to be identical. To resolve the conflict, add elements as needed following the rules outlined above (LCRI 25.31B1). Do not apply 25.29A1 and do not make both titles plural.

Short **piece**, †m clarinet
Short **pieces**, ‡m piano

Incantation †n (1937)
Incantations ‡n (1936)

Cadenzas

A cadenza is an improvised or composed solo virtuoso passage, usually inserted near the end of a concerto movement, with some thematic connection to the work for which it was written. Whether written by the composer of the work in which it is to be played or by another composer, a cadenza is treated as a related work according to 21.28A, and is entered under the name of the composer of the cadenza. An added entry for the work to which it is related is made.

This cadenza for a specific movement in a concerto is entered under the heading for the composer of the cadenza. The added entry is for the movement of the concerto for which it was written.

100 1♭Doktor, Paul.
245 10Cadenza for final movement, Concerto for viola in B minor by
        Handel-Casadesus . . .
700 1♭Casadesus, Henri Gustave, ‡d 1879-1947. ‡t Concertos,
        ‡m viola, orchestra, ‡r B minor. ‡p Allegro molto.

A set of cadenzas composed for all of a composer's concertos for a specific medium of performance is entered under the heading for the

composer of the cadenzas. The added entry is a collective title for the
concertos created according to the rules for collective titles (see Chapter
12, "Collective Titles").

100 1♭Jones, Roland.
245 10New cadenzas for all the Mozart violin concertos . . .
700 1♭Mozart, Wolfgang Amadeus, ‡d 1756-1791. ‡t Concertos,
      ‡m violin, orchestra.

"Cadenza" may also be a type of composition when a composer has
given that title to an independent work.

Title: Sixty-four cadences or solos for the violin in all the major
           and minor keys, op. 11
Uniform title: Cadenzas, ‡m violin, ‡n op. 11

Chapter 11
Additions to Both Generic and Distinctive Titles (25.32, 25.35)

Additional elements may be added to a uniform title, whether it is generic or distinctive, when a composition being cataloged is one or all of the following:

- part(s) of a larger work
- an arrangement of a work
- a different manifestation of a work
- a translation
- three or more excerpts from one work.

These additions will follow any elements added to the initial title element of a generic title or any elements that might be added to a distinctive title: medium of performance, numeric identifying elements, key, and conflict resolution. Make additions in this order:

Subfield	AACR2 rule	
‡p, ‡n	25.32	Part(s) of a larger work
	25.35B	Sketches (parenthetical qualifier)
‡o	25.35C	Arrangements
‡s	25.35D	Vocal scores, chorus scores
‡s	25.35E	Librettos, song texts
‡l	25.35F	Language, when a translation is involved
‡k	25.34C3	Selections

Parts of a Larger Work (‡p, ‡n) (25.32)

The AACR2 treatment of titles of parts of musical works differs from that for other types of materials. The title of a part of a non-musical work is used as the uniform title. For a separately published part of a musical work, use the uniform title for the whole work, followed by the title or verbal designation and/or the number of the part as instructed below (25.32A1). A period separates the uniform title for the whole work from the title of a part of a work in most cases.

Titled Parts

The title of a part of a larger work is given in ‡p, preceded by a period, except when the title ends with an exclamation point or a question mark (see "Ending Punctuation" in Chapter 1). Follow 25.27A, 25.27B, and 25.28A, but not 25.29A, when selecting the title of a part of a musical work (LCRI 25.32A1):

• Use the composer's original title in the language in which it was presented (25.27A) unless another title in the same language has become better known (25.27B). It may be necessary to consult a thematic index to verify the title of the part.

• Omit medium of performance, key, identifying number, date of composition, adjectives, epithets, and words not part of the original title of the work, and initial articles (25.28A).

• When a generic term is the title of a part of a larger work, it is not treated as it were the initial title element and 25.29A is not applied. Use the title of the part in its original language, even if it is a type of composition and has cognate forms in English, French, German, and Italian. In this example, the English form of the name of the type is not used.

Use: Zauberflöte. ‡p **Ouverture**
Not: Zauberflöte. ‡p Overture

Give the title of the part as it appears in the source on which the uniform title is based. Do not give the title in its plural form, even when it is plural in the title for the larger work and even if the composer wrote other works in the same form as the part of the work in hand. Even though the word "Präludien" is in the plural in the title of the larger work and the composer wrote more than one prelude, the title as it appears *on the part of the work* is "Präludium." This is the form used as the title of the part. Medium of performance, numbering, and key are not included.

Use: Präludien und Fugen, ‡m organ, ‡n op. 37. ‡n Nr. 1. ‡p
    Präludium

Not: Präludien und Fugen, ‡m organ, ‡n op. 37. ‡n Nr. 1. ‡p
         Präludien
Not: Präludien und Fugen, ‡m organ, ‡n op. 37. ‡n Nr. 1. ‡p
         Preludes, ‡m organ

If each of the parts is identified only by a title or other verbal designation, use the title or other verbal designation.

Vesperae solennes de confessore. **‡p Laudate Dominum**
Lieder, ‡m mixed voices, ‡n op. 62. **‡p All meine Herzgedanken**
Masses ‡n (1583). **‡p Missa O quam gloriosum**

Opera Arias

The uniform title for an aria from an opera or other large work is made under the name of the opera followed by the name of the aria. When the aria was not titled by the composer, base the title on the text incipit.

Title: Quintetto de Cosí fan tutte
From the source on which the uniform title is based: "No. 9. Quintetto (e coro); incipit: Di scrivermi ogni giorno"
Uniform title: Cosí fan tutte. ‡p Di scrivermi ogni giorno

When the aria has been titled by the composer, use that title, rather than the text incipit.

Title: Andrey's aria from Mazeppe (Act III) . . .
From the source on which the uniform title is based: "No. 16, Stsena i ariia Andreia; 1st line: V boiu krovavom."
Uniform title: Mazepa. ‡p Stsena i ariia Andreia

When the work in hand includes two consecutive arias from a scene of an opera, one uniform title is made under the title for the first aria when both arias are present. When the second aria appears by itself, it is entered under its own title. In the authority record for this uniform title for an aria from *La Traviata*, a 667 field explains how to construct the uniform title in each instance.

667   Sempre libera is a part of a scena beginning with the recitative È
        strano, continuing with Ah, fors' è lui che l'anima, and ending
        with Sempre libera. When Sempre libera is present alone, enter
        under this title; when it is present with preceding aria, with or
        without the recitative, enter under Ah, fors'..., which covers
        both arias.

Title: Sempre libera
Uniform title: Traviata.‡p Sempre libera

Title: Ah, fors' è lui che l'anima and Sempre libera
Uniform title: Traviata.‡p Ah, fors' è lui che l'anima

Numbered Parts

The number of a part of a larger work is tagged in ‡n. It is preceded by a
period, which indicates that it is a part of the work represented in the
uniform title. The punctuation is important here, because a comma
preceding the number suggests a sequence of numbered works with the
same title. A period preceding the number suggests a sequence of
numbered parts *within an individual work*. When the uniform title for the
work as a whole includes a serial, opus, or thematic index number, the
number of the part is tagged in a second ‡n.

The rule for serial numbers for a work in a sequence of numbered
works with the same title (LCRI 25.30C2) does not apply to serial
numbers for parts of a larger work. The guidelines in LCRI 25.32A1
apply to numbered parts of a larger work.

Numbered Parts Without Titles

When a part of a larger work is identified only by a number, the number
is used as the designation in the uniform title. A term associated with the
number is used when it either appears on the work being cataloged or in
the source on which the uniform title is based (e.g., the composer's
thematic index). When no term appears with the number of a part in any
source, use the abbreviation "No." or its equivalent in the language of the
initial title element ("No," "Nr.," "N.," etc.) (LCRI 25.32A1).

Duets, ‡m flutes. ‡n No. 3   *not*   Duets, ‡m flutes. ‡n 3

Follow LCRI C8 for ordinal numbers. Use 1st, 2nd, 3rd, etc., in English and 1., 2., 3., etc., for other languages.

Language of a Term Associated With the Number of a Part

The Term Means "Number"

When the term used with the number of a part of a work means "number," use the abbreviation "No," "Nr.," "N.," etc., whether it appears as an abbreviation or spelled out, in the source on which the uniform title is based (LCRI 25.32A1).

Sonate da camera. ǂn N. 1
Marches militaires. ǂn No 3
Stücke, ǂm piano. ǂn Nr. 2
Marches, ǂm piano, ǂn op. 76. ǂn No. 2
Pezzi, ǂm violoncello, piano, ǂn op. 69. ǂn N. 2
Darabok, ǂm piano, ǂn op. 30b/1. ǂn 7. sz.
Originaltänze. ǂn Nr. 1-6
Slovanské rapsodie. ǂn Čis. 2
Symphonie de Psaumes. ǂn No 1-2

This could result in a non-English abbreviation in the title of the part when the initial title element is in English because of the application of rule 25.29. In the title below, the initial title elements are in English, according to 25.29. The abbreviation for each numbered part ("Nr.") is in German because that is how it appears in the source used as the basis for the uniform title.

Minuets, ǂm woodwinds, horns (2), trumpet, ǂn D. 2D. ǂn **Nr.** 1-2
Fugues, ǂm string quartet, ǂn K. 405. ǂn **Nr.** 4-5

The Term Does Not Mean "Number"

When a term not meaning "number" appears with the number of a part, give it as it appears in the source on which the uniform title is based. Use arabic numerals.

Lieder, ‡n op. 67. **‡n Heft 1**
Lieder ohne Worte. **‡n Heft 1**
Tabulatura nova. **‡n 3. pars**
Méthode complète de guitarre ou lyre. **‡n 1. ptie**
Nouvelle méthode de clarinette. **‡n 1. partie**
Geistliche Harmonien. **‡n 3. Theil**
Weihnachts-Oratorium. **‡n 4. Teil**
Weihnachts-Oratorium. **‡n 1.-3. Teil**
Lorenzaccio. **‡n Atto 1-3**

Individual movements with a number and the term "movement" or its
equivalent are given in ‡n. (Individual movements with a verbal
designation are given in ‡p.)

Quartets, ‡m strings, ‡n no. 3, op. 19. **‡n 2nd movement**
Symphonies, ‡n no. 1, op. 68, ‡r C minor. **‡n Movement 2-4**

This can also result in an English initial title element and a non-
English designation in the title of the part:

Symphonies, ‡n no. 2, ‡r C major. ‡n **1. Satz**

This table presents an overview of 25.32A1 and the language of a term
associated with a serial number of a part of a work.

No term is used	The term means "number"	The term does not mean "number"
Use the abbreviation "No." or its equivalent in the language of the initial title element.	Use the abbreviation for "number," in the language of the source, even if the term is spelled out in the source on which the uniform title is based.	Use the term as it appears in the source, abbreviating only when it appears in that form in the source on which the uniform title is based.

Table 11.1: Language of a Term Associated With a Serial Number of a
Part of a Work (LCRI 25.32A1)

Other Kinds of Numbers

When the source on which the uniform title is based uses a non-numeric designation, use that designation as the number of the part.

Centone di sonate. ‡n Lettera A
Centone di sonate. ‡n Lettera B
Centone di sonate. ‡n Lettera C

Numbered Parts With Titles

If each of the parts is identified by both a number and a title, use the title of the part.

Dichterliebe. ‡p Ich grolle nicht   [also no. 7]
Dichterliebe. ‡p Ich hab im Traum geweinet   [also no. 13]

If each of the parts is identified both by a number and by the same title, use only the number of the part and omit the title (25.32A1c).
Each part has the title "Sonate" as well:

Omit the title of the part	This is incorrect
Sonatas, ‡n op. 5. ‡n No. 1	Sonatas, ‡n op. 5. ‡p Sonate, ‡n no. 1
Sonatas, ‡n op. 5. ‡n No. 2	Sonatas, ‡n op. 5. ‡p Sonate, ‡n no. 2
Sonatas, ‡n op. 5. ‡n No. 3	Sonatas, ‡n op. 5. ‡p Sonate, ‡n no. 3

Consecutively numbered parts are given in a range of numbers.

Sonatas, ‡n op. 5. ‡n No. 4-6

When each of the parts is identified by a number, and *some* of the parts are also identified by a title, the number of each part is included in the uniform title. For any part also given a title, follow the number with the title. The number of the part is tagged in ‡n and the title of the part in ‡p. Because the number and the title both apply to the same part of the work, the subfields are separated by a comma, not a period.

Lieder ohne Worte, ‡m piano, ‡n op. 53. ‡n Nr. 1
Lieder ohne Worte, ‡m piano, ‡n op. 53. ‡n Nr. 2
Lieder ohne Worte, ‡m piano, ‡n op. 53. ‡n Nr. 3
Lieder ohne Worte, ‡m piano, ‡n op. 53. ‡n Nr. 4
Lieder ohne Worte, ‡m piano, ‡n op. 53. ‡n Nr. 5, **‡p Volkslied**
Lieder ohne Worte, ‡m piano, ‡n op. 53. ‡n Nr. 6

More Than One Sequence of Numbered Parts With Titles

Works with more than one numbered sequence of titled parts can be very
confusing. The work *Sinfonie e Concerti Opus 5* consists of two
sequences of titled parts, Concertos no. 1-3 and Sinfonie no. 1-3. The
order within opus 5 alternates between concerto and sinfonia.

op. 5, no. 1: Concerto no. 1
op. 5, no. 2: Sinfonia no. 1
op. 5, no. 3: Concerto no. 2
op. 5, no. 4: Sinfonia no. 2
op. 5, no. 5: Concerto no. 3
op. 5, no. 6: Sinfonia no. 3

The process of formulating the title of each part involves deciding
which designation, numeric or verbal, to include or omit. Leaving off the
titles of the parts would be incorrect, because they do not all have the
same title.

Sinfonie e concerti, ‡n op. 5. ‡n No. 1
Sinfonie e concerti, ‡n op. 5. ‡n No. 2
Sinfonie e concerti, ‡n op. 5. ‡n No. 3
Sinfonie e concerti, ‡n op. 5. ‡n No. 4
Sinfonie e concerti, ‡n op. 5. ‡n No. 5
Sinfonie e concerti, ‡n op. 5. ‡n No. 6

Including the serial numbering with the opus number followed by the
title of the part results in tidy arrangement in the file. However, it is
incorrect. According to 25.32A1c, when each of the parts is identified
both by a number and by a title, only the title of the part is used.

Sinfonie e concerti, ‡n op. 5. ‡n No. 1, ‡p Concerto
Sinfonie e concerti, ‡n op. 5. ‡n No. 2, ‡p Sinfonia
Sinfonie e concerti, ‡n op. 5. ‡n No. 3, ‡p Concerto
Sinfonie e concerti, ‡n op. 5. ‡n No. 4, ‡p Sinfonia
Sinfonie e concerti, ‡n op. 5. ‡n No. 5, ‡p Concerto
Sinfonie e concerti, ‡n op. 5. ‡n No. 6, ‡p Sinfonia

If the serial numbering within the opus is left off, and only the titles remained, this set of uniform titles would remain, which is problematic because there is no way to distinguish between identically named parts.

Sinfonie e concerti, ‡n op. 5. ‡p Concerto
Sinfonie e concerti, ‡n op. 5. ‡p Sinfonia
Sinfonie e concerti, ‡n op. 5. ‡p Concerto
Sinfonie e concerti, ‡n op. 5. ‡p Sinfonia
Sinfonie e concerti, ‡n op. 5. ‡p Concerto
Sinfonie e concerti, ‡n op. 5. ‡p Sinfonia

In order to distinguish among the parts with the same title, it would seem to make sense to add the serial numbering following the title of the part. This, too, would be incorrect, because the serial numbering refers to the placement within the work, but not within the sequence of parts with the same title.

Sinfonie e concerti, ‡n op. 5. ‡p Concerto, ‡n no. 1
Sinfonie e concerti, ‡n op. 5. ‡p Sinfonia, ‡n no. 2
Sinfonie e concerti, ‡n op. 5. ‡p Concerto, ‡n no. 3
Sinfonie e concerti, ‡n op. 5. ‡p Sinfonia, ‡n no. 4
Sinfonie e concerti, ‡n op. 5. ‡p Concerto, ‡n no. 5
Sinfonie e concerti, ‡n op. 5. ‡p Sinfonia, ‡n no. 6

It is misleading. It makes it look as if there are six works entitled "Sinfonia," with the first, third, and fifth left out of the uniform titles.

The only method that resolves the problem is to use the title of each part (because they are not all the same) and include the numbering for each sequence of titled parts.

Uniform title	For
Sinfonie e concerti, ‡n op. 5. ‡p Concerto, ‡n no. 1	op. 5, no. 1
Sinfonie e concerti, ‡n op. 5. ‡p Concerto, ‡n no. 2	op. 5, no. 3
Sinfonie e concerti, ‡n op. 5. ‡p Concerto, ‡n no. 3	op. 5, no. 5
Sinfonie e concerti, ‡n op. 5. ‡p Sinfonia, ‡n no. 1	op. 5, no. 2
Sinfonie e concerti, ‡n op. 5. ‡p Sinfonia, ‡n no. 2	op. 5, no. 4
Sinfonie e concerti, ‡n op. 5. ‡p Sinfonia, ‡n no. 3	op. 5, no. 6

For a collection of consecutively numbered parts all with the same generic title, follow the rules for formulating the title of parts (25.27A-B and 25.28A) and the numbering of parts (25.6B1, 25.32A1). Rule 25.29A (formulation of an initial title element consisting solely of the name of one type of composition) is *not* applied. The title of the parts remains in the original language, even if there is a cognate in English, and is in the singular, even when there are two or more parts with that title in the item being cataloged.

Title: 6 concerts from Concerts et suites
Uniform title: Concerts et suites. ‡p **Concert**, ‡n no. 1-6
Not: Concerts et suites. ‡p Concerts, ‡n no. 1-6

Part of a Part

When the part being cataloged is from an intermediary part with a distinctive title, the title of the intermediary part precedes the title of the smaller part in the uniform title. Each title is tagged in ‡p. Subfield "p" is repeatable and can be used as many times as needed.

Licht. ‡p Dienstag. ‡p Invasion-Explosion mit Abschied Christus.
    ‡p Oratorium in Nativitate Domini. ‡p Angelus Domini

Omit the designation of an intermediary part if it is not distinctive.

Use: Tristan und Isolde. ‡p Isolde! Tristan! Geliebter!
Not: Tristan und Isolde. ‡n 2. Aufzug. ‡p Isolde! Tristan! Geliebter!

Use: Idomeneo. ‡p Idol mio, se ritroso
Not: Idomeneo. ‡n Atto 2o. ‡p Idol mio, se ritroso

However, include the non-distinctive title of an intermediary part when it is necessary to identify the smaller part.

Use: Symphonies, ‡n no. 9, op. 125, ‡r D minor. ‡p Presto.
      ‡p Allegro assai
Not: Symphonies, ‡n no. 9, op. 125, ‡r D minor.‡p Allegro assai

Use: Ring des Nibelungen. ‡p 3. Aufzug. ‡p 3. Szene
Not: Ring des Nibelungen. ‡p 3. Szene

Use: Tristan und Isolde. ‡n 1. Aufzug. ‡p Einleitung
Not: Tristan und Isolde. ‡p Einleitung

Use: Elvira. ‡n Atto 1. ‡p Serenata
Not: Elvira. ‡p Serenata

Titled parts of intermediary numbered, but untitled, parts are tagged in ‡p, preceded by a period. Because the number applies to the larger part, the period indicates that the title following in ‡p applies to a part of the larger part represented in ‡n. A comma would indicate that the number in ‡n and the title in ‡p both apply to the *same part* of the work. That would be incorrect in these examples.

Versuch über die wahre Art das Clavier zu spielen. **‡p** Sonaten.
    ‡n Nr. 6. **‡p** Allegro di molto
Präludium und Fugen, ‡m organ, ‡n op. 37. **‡n** Nr. 1. **‡p** Präludium

Resolving Conflicts in Titles of Parts

Identical uniform titles can result after the addition of the name of a part. Add elements as needed to distinguish between the different titles in the order specified in 25.30-25.31:
- statement of medium of performance or a descriptive term or phrase
- numeric identifying elements: serial, opus, or thematic index number
- key
- year of completion of composition
- year of original publication
- other identifying element(s) (e.g., place of composition, name of first publisher)

Medium of Performance

Recens fabricatus labor. ‡p Sonata, ‡m **trombones (4), continuo**
Recens fabricatus labor. ‡p Sonata, ‡m **trumpet, trombones (3),
  continuo**
Recens fabricatus labor. ‡p Sonata, ‡m **violins (2), trombone,
  continuo**

Descriptive Term or Phrase

Zauberflöte. ‡p O Isis und Osiris **(Aria and chorus)**
Zauberflöte. ‡p O Isis und Osiris **(Chorus of priests)**

Numeric Identifying Elements

Divertimenti, ‡n K. 334, ‡r D major. ‡p Menuetto **(3rd movement)**
Divertimenti, ‡n K. 334, ‡r D major. ‡p Menuetto **(5th movement)**

Chandos anthems. ‡p I will magnify Thee, ‡n **HWV 250a**
Chandos anthems. ‡p I will magnify Thee, ‡n **HWV 250b**

Choräle von verschiedener Art, ‡n BWV 651-668. ‡p Nun komm, der
  Heiden Heiland, ‡n **BWV 659**
Choräle von verschiedener Art, ‡n BWV 651-668. ‡p Nun komm, der
  Heiden Heiland, ‡n **BWV 661**

Two of the three duets for soprano, alto, and piano in opus 20 are titled *Weg der Liebe I* and *Weg der Liebe II*. Because the composer numbered them, the serial numbers may be used in the uniform titles to distinguish between them.

Duets, ‡m soprano, alto, piano, ‡n op. 20. ‡p Weg der Liebe, ‡n **no. 1**
Duets, ‡m soprano, alto, piano, ‡n op. 20. ‡p Weg der Liebe, ‡n **no. 2**

*Distinguishing Between Two or More Parts With the Same Title Without
Numeric Identifying Elements*

Use the English abbreviation "no." and the number indicating position of the part within the larger work to distinguish between two or more parts with the same title with no other means to distinguish between them. The number is given in parentheses following the title of the part and is not subfielded.

In the work represented by the uniform titles below, there are two parts with the title *In der Fremde,* the first and eighth parts within opus 39, respectively. It would be misleading to use serial numbers in ‡n, because it suggests that all of the first eight parts from the larger work have the title *In der Fremde,* when, in fact, these are the only two parts with this title. These uniform titles are incorrect.

Liederkreis, ‡n op. 39. ‡p In der Fremde, ‡n no. 1
Liederkreis, ‡n op. 39. ‡p In der Fremde, ‡n no. 8

The composer did not assign serial numbers to the two parts (e.g., *In der Fremde I* and *In der Fremde II*), so they cannot be used in the uniform titles. These uniform titles are also incorrect.

Liederkreis, ‡n op. 39. ‡p In der Fremde, ‡n no. 1
Liederkreis, ‡n op. 39. ‡p In der Fremde, ‡n no. 2

To resolve the conflict, the position of each part within the larger work is indicated by number in parentheses following the title of the part. The English abbreviation "No." is used.

Liederkreis, ‡n op. 39. ‡p In der Fremde **(No. 1)**
Liederkreis, ‡n op. 39. ‡p In der Fremde **(No. 8)**

The uniform title below is for the first of two or more parts with the title "Allegro" in the concerto for mandolin and string orchestra.

Concertos, ‡m mandolin, string orchestra, ‡n RV 425, ‡r C major.
   ‡p Allegro **(No. 1)**

Each of the parts of this work was titled but unnumbered; therefore, only the title is used in the uniform title. To distinguish between the identically titled parts, the number within the larger work is used.

Fantasien, ‡m piano, ‡n op. 116. ‡p Capriccio **(No. 1)**
Fantasien, ‡m piano, ‡n op. 116. ‡p Capriccio **(No. 3)**
Fantasien, ‡m piano, ‡n op. 116. ‡p Capriccio **(No. 7)**
Fantasien, ‡m piano, ‡n op. 116. ‡p Intermezzo **(No. 2)**
Fantasien, ‡m piano, ‡n op. 116. ‡p Intermezzo **(No. 4)**
Fantasien, ‡m piano, ‡n op. 116. ‡p Intermezzo **(No. 5)**
Fantasien, ‡m piano, ‡n op. 116. ‡p Intermezzo **(No. 6)**

Medium of Performance and Position Within the Larger Work

These uniform titles represent two parts of a larger work with the title
Sonate et Canzoni, which includes sonatas for various mediums of
performance, two of which are for three violins and continuo. To
distinguish between the two, their position within the larger work is given:

Sonate et canzoni. ‡p Sonata, **‡m violins (3), continuo (No. 11)**
Sonate et canzoni. ‡p Sonata, **‡m violins (3), continuo (No. 12)**

Key

The title for each canzona would not normally include key; however, the
key is the only means of differentiating between the canzonas.

Sonate d'intavolatura. ‡n Pt. 1. ‡p Canzona, **‡r E minor**
Sonate d'intavolatura. ‡n Pt. 1. ‡p Canzona, **‡r G minor**

Version

Recopilación de sonetos y villancicos. ‡p Lágrimas de mi consuelo
   (1st setting)
Recopilación de sonetos y villancicos. ‡p Lágrimas de mi consuelo
   (2nd setting)

Subtitle of the Part

Pièces, ‡m organ, ‡n op. 5. ‡p Offertoire **(grand chœur)**
Pièces, ‡m organ, ‡n op. 5. ‡p Offertoire **(andante sostenuto)**

Sketches (25.35B)

Add "Sketches" in parentheses at the end of the uniform title for a composer's sketches of a completed musical composition. This element is not separately subfielded.

Quartets, ‡m strings, ‡n no. 2, op. 18, no. 2, ‡r G major **(Sketches)**
Quartets, ‡m strings, ‡n no. 14, op. 131, ‡r C# minor. ‡p Allegro
   (Sketches)
Magnificat **(Sketches)**

   Keep in mind that "Sketch" and its equivalent in other languages ("Skizze," "Eskiz," "Esquisse," etc.) can itself be a distinctive title, when the composer has given that title to a work (e.g., *Skizzen*), or when the word appears in a distinctive title (e.g., *Sketches on American Folksongs*).

Arrangements (‡o) (25.35C)

Rule 25.35C deals with arrangements and transcriptions of musical works. This includes works or parts of works that have been rewritten for a different medium of performance, simplified, or changed harmonically or stylistically, either by the composer or by another person. (Some works that have been revised or changed by the composer are not considered to be arrangements. This is discussed below.) A work that is based on another work, even with new material added, is also considered to be an arrangement. In all cases, an arranged work is entered under the name of the original composer, with an added entry for the arranger, if other than the composer. The uniform title is formulated for the original, unaltered work and "‡o arr." is added, preceded by a semicolon. It is added to the uniform title for all arrangements of the work, regardless of the medium for which it has been arranged.

   This uniform title is for a work originally for string orchestra that has been arranged for several different instrumentations. The same uniform title, reflecting the original medium of performance, is given to each arrangement. A reference for each arrangement will be made in the authority record (references are discussed in Chapter 15, "References").

Title: Adagio et fugue pour quintette à vent KV 546
Uniform title: Adagio und Fuge, ‡m string orchestra, ‡n K. 546, ‡r C
                 minor; ‡o arr.

Title: Adagio & fugue, K. 546 arranged for string quartet.
Uniform title: Adagio und Fuge, ‡m string orchestra, ‡n K. 546, ‡r C
                 minor; ‡o arr.

Title: Adagio and fugue in C minor, K. 546 for two pianos, four
                 hands
Uniform title: Adagio und Fuge, ‡m string orchestra, ‡n K. 546, ‡r C
                 minor; ‡o arr.

Alterations of Musico-Dramatic Works (25.31C1)

Rule 25.31C applies only to the text of a work, *not* to its musical content.
The rule states that "if the text, plot, setting, or other verbal element of a
musical work is adapted or if a new text is supplied, and the title has
changed, use the uniform title of the original work followed in
parentheses by the title of the adaptation." An example of this is Glinka's
Zhizn' za TSaria [A Life for the Tsar]. Composed in 1836 with a libretto
by Rozen, it was originally to have been called *Ivan Susanin*, but was
given the new title by Tsar Nicholas I. After the Russian Revolution, a
new libretto by Sergei Gorodetsky was written with the original title *Ivan
Susanin*; all references to the Tsar were removed.

For work with the	Use the uniform title
original libretto	Zhizn' za tsaria
new libretto	Zhizn' za tsaria (Ivan Susanin)

What Does *Not* Constitute an Arrangement?

LCRI 25.35C outlines the circumstances under which changes to a work
do not constitute an arrangement. A work composed before 1800 for an
early instrument, such as harpsichord, that is edited for or performed on
a contemporary instrument, such as piano, is not considered to be
arranged.

Title: Toccata in D minor for piano, BWV 913
Uniform title: Toccatas, ‡m harpsichord, ‡n BWV 913, ‡r D minor

These sonatas were composed for recorder. The modern edition is edited for either recorder or flute, with no modification of the music.

Title: Drei Sonaten für Blockflöte (Querflöte) und Basso continuo
Uniform title: Sonatas, ‡m recorder, continuo

A continuo part is realized for a keyboard instrument with or without a bass instrument is not considered to be an arrangement. This is true for a continuo part realized for guitar or other instrument.

Title: Sonate G-Dur für Flöte (Oboe, Violine) und Gitarre
Uniform title: Sonatas, ‡m flute, continuo, ‡n H. 564, ‡r G major
Not: Sonatas, ‡m flute, continuo, ‡n H. 564, ‡r G major;
                ‡o arr.

A work for an alternate instrument indicated by the composer is not considered to be an arrangement. The first edition title of this work gives the medium of performance as clarinet or viola and piano; thus, the version for viola and piano is not an arrangement. The uniform title reflects the first-named instrument and does not include "‡o arr." The authority record for this work will include a reference from the title with the alternate medium of performance, as explained in Chapter 15, "References."

Title: Two sonatas for viola and piano, op. 120
Uniform title: Sonatas, ‡m clarinet, piano, ‡n op. 120

When the statement of responsibility clearly indicates that a work was transcribed for a medium other than the original, consider it to be an arrangement. The statement of medium of performance in the uniform title is for the original medium. Include "‡o arr." in the uniform title.

Title: Sonata for piano and violoncello op. 46 / ‡c . . . viola transcription.
Uniform title: Sonatas, ‡m violoncello, piano, ‡n op. 46, ‡r B♭ major;
                ‡o arr.

Added Accompaniments

When an instrumental accompaniment or an additional part is added without changing the original work, it is not an arrangement. In this case, the work is entered under the heading for the original composer with an added entry for the composer of the added accompaniment or additional part. The following work is a selection from Bach's *Wohltemperierte Klavier*. Moscheles added a violoncello part, but did not otherwise change Bach's original work. Even though the work is given an opus number for Moscheles, it is not considered to be his work or an arrangement of Bach's work. It is entered under the heading for Bach's *Wohltemperierte Klavier*.

Title: Fünf melodisch-contrapunktische Studien über Präludien
              aus Johann Sebastian Bachs Wohltemperiertem Klavier :
              ‡b für Violoncello und Orgel oder Klavier aus op. 137 / ‡c
              Ignaz Moscheles.
Composer: Bach, Johann Sebastian, ‡d 1685-1750.
Uniform title: Wohltemperierte Klavier, ‡n 1. T. ‡k Selections
Added entry: Moscheles, Ignaz, ‡d 1794-1870.

not

Composer: Moscheles, Ignaz, ‡d 1794-1870.
Uniform title: Melodisch-kontrapunktische Studien

Rimsky-Korsakov's and Shostakovich's revisions and re-orchestrations of Mussorgsky's opera *Boris Godunov* are not considered to be arrangements, despite the extent of the changes. For these versions of the opera, use the uniform title for the original work, followed by the last name of the reviser in parentheses.

Boris Godunov **(Rimsky-Korsakov)**
Boris Godunov **(Shostakovich)**

Transposed Works

Consider a work that has been transposed or the notation "significantly changed" to be an arrangement. AACR2 provides no guidance about what constitutes a "significant change." An edition of a Renaissance piece in which the clef has been changed or the note values halved will still sound the same, although reading the printed music may be easier for the modern performer. These types of changes are not generally considered to be arrangements.

Transposition may involve rewriting a work into another key to accommodate the range of a medium of performance other than that specified by the composer. An instrumental work transposed for another instrument is considered to be arranged. In this example, the original solo instrument is violin and the original key is C minor.

Title: Sonate d-Moll für Sopranblockflöte und Basso continuo
Uniform title: Sonata(s), ‡m violin, continuo, ‡r C minor; ‡o arr.

The transposition of a vocal work to accommodate another vocal range is *not* considered to be an arrangement, however. The original voice type is soprano.

Title: 4 serious songs / ‡c . . . transposed for alto voice
Uniform title: Serious songs

A work in which the key has been transposed by the composer, keeping the original medium of performance and not extensively revising the music, is not considered an arrangement when it is clear that the new key is the composer's final choice.

Revisions by the Original Composer (LCRI 25.35C)

When a composer changes the title and/or assigns a new opus number for a revised, transcribed, recomposed, reordered, altered, arranged, or adapted version of an earlier work, treat this new version as a new work, not as a part of, or as an arrangement of, the earlier work.

New Work

Stravinsky's *Otche Nash* is an example. Stravinsky composed the work with Slavonic words, in 1926. In 1949, he revised the work, adding Latin words and changing the title to *Pater Noster*. It is considered to be a new work.

Examples

Original work:
Title: Espace I : ‡b for violoncello and piano
Uniform title: Espace, ‡n no. 1

New work:
Title: Espace II : ‡b for violoncello, harp, and oboe ad lib. / ‡c
                . . . revised by the composer from Espace I
Uniform title: Espace, ‡n no. 2
Not: Espace, ‡n no. 1; ‡o arr.

Original work:
Title: Medea : ‡b (original ballet version) : for chamber
                ensemble
Uniform title: Medea

New work:
Title: Medea's meditation and dance of vengeance : ‡b op. 23a
                : from the orchestral suite (1947) from the ballet Medea,
                op. 23 (1946) / ‡c revised and reorchestrated by the
                composer.
Uniform title: Medea's meditation and dance of vengeance
Not: Medea; ‡o arr.

If the new version's title has not been changed and identifying
elements (such as opus number) unique to the new version are lacking, yet
the revision and/or addition of new material by the composer is extensive,
treat the new version as another work, and assign it a uniform title, with
additional elements needed to distinguish it from the previous versions.

Ave Maria **(Instrumental version)**
Ave Maria **(Vocal version)**

Anneau de Salomon **(Chorus and orchestra version)**
Anneau de Salomon **(Orchestra version)**

25 Oktober 1902 **(1st setting)**
25 Oktober 1902 **(2nd setting)**

Quartets, ‡m strings, ‡n no. 3 **(Shortened version)**

The composer of the following work rewrote the accompaniment for his work for chorus and organ. The new work, with orchestral accompaniment, retained the same opus number. The uniform titles for the works include thematic index numbers rather than the opus number.

Title: Messe D-Dur für gemischten Chor, Soli und Orgel oder Orchester, Opus 86 : ‡b Originalfassung mit Orgel
Uniform title: Masses, †n B. 153, ‡r D major

Title: Messe in D op. 86 : ‡b Orchesterfassung . . .
Uniform title: Masses, ‡n B. 175, ‡r D major

When a composer revises a work extensively or adds new material, even if the original title and numbering has been retained, consider it to be a new work. This applies only when the composer makes the changes to the work. In the following example, the composer extensively revised both movements of his 1937 work, but retained the title, medium of performance, and opus number. Since the revisions were extensive, the 1967 version is considered to be a new work:

Title: Prelude and fugue for oboe and bassoon, opus 13
Uniform title: Prelude and fugue, ‡m oboe, bassoon, ‡n op. 13 **(1937)**

Title: Prelude and fugue for oboe (flute) and bassoon, opus 13
Uniform title: Prelude and fugue, ‡m oboe, bassoon, ‡n op. 13 **(1967)**

Same Work

When a composer modifies a work, keeping the original title and opus number and changing the instrumentation only within the same broad medium, but does not extensively revise or expand the work, consider the original and modified works to be the same and use the same uniform title. Neither work is to be considered an arrangement or a new work.

Title: 1. Sinfonie (1947) : ‡b Neufassung für Kammerorchester (1963) = new version for chamber orchestra
Uniform title: Symphonies, ‡n no. 1

A work originally for six percussionists in a version for four percussionists is considered to be within the same broad medium, and is not a new work. Use the same uniform title for both.

Title: Salpêtrière : ‡b für sechs Schlagzeuger . . .
Uniform title: Salpêtrière

Title: Salpêtrière : ‡b Fassung für 4 Schlagzeuger . . .
                  For percussion (4 players); originally for 6 players
Uniform title: Salpêtrière

The concept of "broad medium" is not defined, but is alluded to in 25.25A footnote 9, where the examples "orchestra, instrumental ensemble, [and] band" are given. This is misleading, as a work for orchestra in a version for band would not be considered within the same "broad medium." Likewise, a work for string quartet in a version for string orchestra would also not be considered within the same broad medium, and is treated as an arrangement, as in the example below.

Title: 3. Streichquartett : ‡b Fassung für Streichorchester
Uniform title: Quartets, ‡m strings, ‡n no. 3; ‡o arr.

Adaptations

Related to these cases that are not considered to be arrangements are adaptations, in which a new work is related to another work or part of a work with its own title or designation (21.18C). Adaptations are considered to be new works and are entered under the name of the adaptor, or, if the adaptor is unknown, under title. A name/title added entry is made for the work to which the adaptation is related. Adaptations are defined as:

• A distinct alteration of another work (e.g., a free transcription).

A free transcription by Shchedrin of the two piano tangos by Albéniz:

Composer: Shchedrin, Rodion Konstantinovich, ‡d 1932-
Uniform title: Tango Al'benisa

Added entry: Albéniz, Isaac, ‡d 1860-1909. ‡t Danses espagnoles.
    ‡p Tango.
Added entry: Albéniz, Isaac, ‡d 1860-1909. ‡t España, ‡n op. 165.
    ‡p Tango.

• A paraphrase of various works or of the general style of another
composer. Each of these works is entered under the heading for the
composer of the new work, not the composer of the original work.

The work *Waltz From Faust: Concerto Paraphrase (Gounod)* is
entered under the composer of the paraphrase (Liszt), not the composer
of the original work (Gounod).

Composer: Liszt, Franz, ‡d 1811-1886.
Uniform title: Valse de l'opèra Faust
Added entry: Gounod, Charles, ‡d 1818-1893. ‡t Faust. ‡p Valse.

This is incorrect:

Composer: Gounod, Charles, ‡d 1818-1893.
Uniform title: Faust. ‡p Valse; ‡o arr.

Enter under the heading for the composer of the scherzo (Fritz
Kreisler), not the composer whose style is being imitated (Dittersdorf).

Composer: Kreisler, Fritz, ‡d 1875-1962.
Uniform title: Scherzo in the style of Dittersdorf
Added entry: Dittersdorf, Karl Ditters von, ‡d 1739-1799.

Enter under the heading for the composer of the symphony (Krzysztof
Meyer), not the composer whose style is being imitated (Mozart).

Composer: Meyer, Krzysztof.
Uniform title: Symfonia w stylu Mozarta
Added entry: Mozart, Wolfgang, ‡d 1756-1791.

• A work merely based on other music (e.g., variations on a theme).

Enter under the heading for the composer of the variation (Brahms),
not the composer of the original work (Paganini).

Composer: Brahms, Johannes, 1833-1897.
Uniform title: Variationen über ein Thema von Paganini
Added entry: Paganini, Nicolò, ‡d 1782-1840. ‡t Caprices, ‡m violin,
             ‡n M.S. 25. ‡n No. 24.

For each of these types of adaptations, the name/title added entry for
the work to which the adaptation is related is made *without* the addition
of "‡o arr.," since the work is not actually included in the item being
cataloged nor has it been arranged.

When it cannot be determined whether the work is an arrangement or
an adaptation, treat it as an arrangement.

Vocal Scores and Chorus Scores (‡s) (25.35D)

"Vocal score(s)" and "Chorus score(s)" are tagged in ‡s. When applied
to a single work, use the singular; when applied to a collective title (see
Chapter 12, "Collective Titles"), use the plural.

"Vocal score" is used with works originally for chorus and/or one or
more solo voices, with accompaniment that has either been arranged for
keyboard instrument or omitted. If the work originally has solo voices,
they must also be included in the vocal score. A vocal score is the same
as a "piano-vocal score."

"Chorus score" is used with works originally for chorus and/or one or
more solo voices, with accompaniment that has either been arranged for
keyboard instrument or omitted. A chorus score is distinguished from a
vocal score by the fact that the parts of the work in which the chorus does
not sing are not included in the chorus score.

Examples of Vocal Scores and Chorus Scores

All vocal parts are included; the orchestral parts are arranged for piano.
Note that the phrase "piano-vocal score" is included in the statement of
responsibility, since it implies an arrangement. Even though the reduction
of accompaniment for a keyboard instrument is an arrangement, "‡s
Vocal score" is used here, not "‡o arr."

Title: The second hurricane : ‡b play opera in two acts / ‡c . . .
                    piano-vocal score.
Uniform title: Second hurricane. ‡s **Vocal score**

Title: Voice and piano version of Two songs for voice and string
                    quartet
Uniform title: Songs, ‡m string quartet acc. ‡s **Vocal score**

Title: Sommernacht : ‡b für Sopran und Kammerorchester : op.
                    73 / ‡c . . . Klavierauszug von Komponisten.
Uniform title: Sommernacht. ‡s **Vocal score**

One caveat concerning the use of "vocal score" relates to sound recordings. Obviously, since a recording is not printed music, "‡s Vocal score" would not apply. Use "‡o arr." in the uniform title for a recorded work originally for chorus and/or one or more solo voices, with accompaniment arranged for keyboard instrument or omitted. The following examples are for the same work, an excerpt from an opera, for which the original orchestral accompaniment has reduced for piano. The first uniform title applies to the vocal score; the second applies to the recorded version.

Vocal score: Robin Hood. ‡p Oh, promise me. ‡s **Vocal score**
Sound recording: Robin Hood. ‡p Oh, promise me; ‡o **arr.**

In the next example, only the sections of the work in which the chorus sings are included and the orchestra part has been arranged for piano. The term "Chorpartitur" is given in the statement of medium of presentation, even when the accompaniment has been arranged for a keyboard instrument.

Title: Missa in C, KV 259, Orgelsolo-Messe
                    Chorpartitur.
Uniform title: Missa brevis, ‡n K. 259. ‡s **Chorus score**

Librettos and Song Texts (‡s) (25.35E)

"Libretto" is added in ‡s to the uniform title for a dramatic work such as an opera, oratorio, or similar work when the text is published separately or included separately from the music in a score. The work is entered under the name of the composer when the music is referred to on the item.

Title: Lucrezia Borgia : ‡b melodramma in due atti . . . / ‡c di Felice Romani ; musica e del signor maestro Gaetano Donizetti.

   Enter under composer:

100 1♭Donizetti, Gaetano, ‡d 1797-1848.
240 10Lucrezia Borgia. ‡s **Libretto**

   When a libretto is published as a literary work, i.e., without reference to its musical setting, it is entered under the name of the author rather than under composer (21.28A1, note 7). In the next example, no mention of the Donizetti opera is made, so the work is entered under the author. Do not include a uniform title with "‡s Libretto."

100 1♭Romani, Felice, ‡d 1788-1865.
245 10Lucrezia Borgia : ‡b melodramma in un prologo e due atti / ‡c
       di Felici Romani.

   For a collection of works by the same composer with a collective title (see Chapter 12, "Collective Titles"), use "Librettos."

Musicals. ‡s Librettos

   "Text" is added in ‡s to the uniform title for the texts of individual songs or song cycles published without the music. Regardless of the author of the text, the work is entered under the name of the composer. This term is used in the plural form when a collection of texts for works by the same composer is involved.

100 1♭Strauss, Richard, ‡d 1864-1949.
240 10Songs. ‡s **Texts**
245 14Die Texte der Lieder von Richard Strauss . . .

Language (‡l) (25.35F)

The language is included in uniform titles for vocal works only, and only when a translation of the text is involved. When the text has been translated, the language into which the work has been translated is added to the uniform title in ‡l, preceded by a period. The name of the language is that found in the *MARC Code List for Languages*, maintained by CPSO.

Zauberflöte. ‡l **English**

When the last element of the uniform title ends in an exclamation point or question mark, do not precede ‡l with a period (see "Ending Punctuation" in Chapter 1).

Medjé! ‡l German

When the entire work includes both the original and one translated language, the language of the translation is listed first, followed by an ampersand and the original language. The original language is German.

Zauberflöte. ‡l **English & German**

When the entire work has been translated into two languages and neither is the original, name the languages in alphabetical order of their names in English separated by an ampersand. The original language is German.

Zauberflöte. ‡l **English & Italian**

When the entire work includes three or more languages, regardless of whether one is the original, use "Polyglot" in place of indicating each language.

Zauberflöte. ‡l **Polyglot**

When a part of a larger work has been translated, the language follows the name of the part.

Lieder, ‡m mixed voices, ‡n op. 62. ‡p All meine Herzgedanken. ‡l
English

The text the composer set to music may itself have been translated.
This translation would not be reflected in the uniform title.

Title: Seven choruses from the Alcestis of Euripides / ‡c
                 translated by Gilbert Murray ; set to music by . . .
Uniform title: Choruses from the Alcestis of Euripides

Former practice was to include language for liturgical works whether
or not they were translated. The rule for that practice has been canceled.
Indicate the language of a liturgical work only when it has been translated.

Selections (‡k) (25.34C3)

"Selections" is used in a uniform title, either generic or distinctive, for
three or more excerpts from one work by one composer. (It may also be
a collective title or an addition to collective titles for three or more works
or three or more excerpts from three or more works by one composer.
This will be discussed in Chapter 12, "Collective Titles.") It is usually
added as the last element of the uniform title, in ‡k, preceded by a period,
under the following situations:

• For three or more non-consecutively numbered parts of a larger work
by one composer:

Title: Suites 1, 4, and 7 from op. 1 for harpsichord
Uniform title: Suites, ‡m harpsichord, ‡n op. 1. **‡k Selections**

• For three or more unnumbered parts of one work:

Title: Selected choruses from The Messiah . . .
Uniform title: Messiah. **‡k Selections**

"‡k Selections" is not used for three or more consecutively numbered
parts of one work by one composer. Rule 25.32 concerning parts of a
larger work applies in this case.

"‡k Selections" is not the last element of a uniform title when the work has been arranged. Instead, "‡o arr." is given as the last element, preceded by "‡k Selections."

The entire work has been arranged:

Requiem; **‡o arr.**

Excerpts from the work have been arranged:

Requiem. **‡k Selections; ‡o arr.**

In all other cases, make additions to the uniform title following the order as given in 25.35B-F:

- (Sketches)
- ‡o arr.
- ‡s format
- ‡l language
- ‡k Selections

Examples of Additions to Uniform Titles for Music

Language and selections:

Faust. **‡l Hungarian. ‡k Selections**

Sketches of selections:

Sonatas, ‡m piano, ‡n D. 958-960 **(Sketches). ‡k Selections**

An arrangement of a work that has been translated:

Mass, ‡n op. 36; **‡o arr. ‡l English**

A work that has been arranged and translated; the original language is French:

Cantique de Jean Racine; **‡o arr. ‡l English & French**

A vocal score of a work that has been translated; the original language is Spanish:

Ausencias de Dulcinea. ‡s **Vocal score.** ‡l **French & Spanish**

Selections from a work that have been arranged and translated:

Wer einsam ist, der hat es gut. ‡l **English.** ‡k **Selections;** ‡o **arr.**

Selections from a work that have been arranged and translated; the original language is German:

Lieder nach Rückert. ‡l **English & German.** ‡k **Selections;** ‡o **arr.**

An arrangement of a part of a work that has been translated:

Beatrice di Tenda. ‡p **Come t'adoro;** ‡o **arr.** ‡l **English**
Duets, ‡m soprano, alto, piano, ‡n op. 52. ‡p **Gornyi kliuch;** ‡o **arr.**
    ‡l **English**

Selections from a libretto:

Telemachus. ‡s **Libretto.** ‡k **Selections**

Translated selections from a libretto:

Avventura di Scaramuccia. ‡s **Libretto.** ‡l **English.** ‡k **Selections**

Selected song texts that have been translated; the original language is Catalan:

Songs. ‡s **Texts.** ‡l **French & Catalan.** ‡k **Selections**

Selections from the librettos of a composer's operatic works that include an English translation with the original German or English and German translations from some other original language:

Operas. ‡s **Librettos.** ‡l **English & German.** ‡k **Selections**

Chapter 12
Collective Titles (25.8, 25.34)

Collective titles are used for collections that are, or purport to be, the complete or partial works of an individual composer. In the AACR2 glossary, the third definition under "uniform title" is applicable to this discussion:

> "A conventional collective title used to collocate publications of an author, composer, or corporate body containing several works or extracts, etc., from several works (e.g., complete works, several works in a particular literary or musical form)."[1]

A collection might include:
• complete works: all of a composer's works
• partial collections: three or more works, or three or more excerpts from two or more works, by the same composer in:
  • the *same* form or type for the *same* medium of performance
  • *two or more* forms or types for the *same* medium of performance
  • the *same* form or type for *two or more* mediums of performance or *one broad* medium
  • *two or more* forms or types for *two or more* mediums of performance.

Collective titles are formulated using the rules for uniform titles, but are based on a subject approach rather than the composer's original title. A collective title uses the form or type of composition, or the medium of performance, or a combination of both. Collective titles for arrangements are based on the original medium of performance.

Complete Works

The complete works of a single composer is usually a scholarly or critical edition based on primary sources. Use the collective title "Works" for a publication that contains, or purports to contain, all of the works of a single composer (25.8). (The rule for composers who wrote both musical and literary works [25.10A] is covered at the end of this chapter.) Include the date of publication, or, with a multivolume item, the date of publication of the first volume, in ‡f. These uniform titles are for the two different editions of the complete works of J. S. Bach.

Bach, Johann Sebastian, ‡d 1685-1750. ‡t Works. ‡f 1954
Bach, Johann Sebastian, ‡d 1685-1750. ‡t Works. ‡f 1998

When a composer's entire output is for a single medium of performance, use "Works" as the uniform title for a collection of the complete works. Edward Collard wrote only for the lute. This uniform title is for a collection of his complete works.

Collard, Edward. ‡t Works. ‡f 1979
not
Collard, Edward. ‡t Lute music

Partial Collections

Follow these guidelines for collections of three or more works, or three or more excerpts from two or more works by the same composer.

In the *Same Form or Type* for the *Same* Medium of Performance

Use the name of the type in the plural followed by medium of performance for all of a composer's works of the same type for the same medium of performance. Follow the rules in 25.27A through 25.30B to formulate the collective title.

Title: Piano sonatas no. 1-10, the complete piano sonatas
Uniform title: Sonatas, ‡m piano
Not: Sonatas, ‡m piano, ‡n no. 1-10

Title: The violin concertos
Uniform title: Concertos, ‡m violin, orchestra

Title: The collected songs
Uniform title: Songs

Title: Theatre music
Uniform title: Incidental music

For three or more, but not all, of a composer's works or three or more excerpts from two or more of a composer's works in the same form or type for the same medium of performance, add "‡k Selections" to the collective title.

Title: Drei Sonaten für zwei Flöten
Uniform title: Sonatas, ‡m flutes (2). ‡k Selections

Title: The early songs
Uniform title: Songs. ‡k Selections

Title: Musik zu Egmont und andere Schauspielmusiken
Uniform title: Incidental music. ‡k Selections

Title: The Maltese falcon and other classic film scores
Uniform title: Motion picture music. ‡k Selections

This applies to a collection of three or more non-consecutively numbered works or excerpts from two or more works in the same form or type for the same medium of performance from a consecutively numbered sequence of works.

Title: Violin concertos no. 1, 2, and 4
Uniform title: Concertos, ‡m violin, orchestra. ‡k Selections

Title: Piano sonatas no. 2, 5, 6, and 8
Uniform title: Sonatas, ‡m piano. ‡k Selections

This does *not* apply, however, to a collection of three or more consecutively numbered works in the same form or type for the same medium of performance. Assign a uniform title following the rules for generic uniform titles, with a range of serial numbers (25.30C2).

Title: Piano sonatas no. 2, 3, 4, and 5
Uniform title: Sonatas, ‡m piano, ‡n no. 2-5

In Two or More Forms or Types for the Same Medium of Performance

According to 25.34C1, a "collective title . . . descriptive of [the] medium" is to be used for all of a composer's works, of various types, for the same medium of performance. The collective title is constructed by naming the medium of performance, followed by the word "music."

Title: Obra completa para piano
Uniform title: Piano music

Title: Complete works for violin and piano
Uniform title: Violin, piano music

Title: Richard Baker reads stories with strings
Uniform title: Narrator, string quartet music

Title: Orchesterwerke
Uniform title: Orchestra music

Title: The complete choral music
Uniform title: Choral music

Title: Opere per tastiera
Uniform title: Keyboard music

The collective title for all of a composer's works for two or more of the same instrument uses the collective title for the medium followed by the name of the instrument, qualified by number. The name of the medium and the name of the individual instrument is not preceded by ǂm.

Use	Not
Piano music, 4 hands	Piano music, ǂm 4 hands
Piano music, pianos (2)	Piano music, ǂm pianos (2)
Guitar music, guitars (4)	Guitar music, ǂm guitars (4)

LCRI 25.34C1 allows the use of "Piano music" for collections of all of a composer's works for piano as well as for collections for varying numbers of performers on one or more pianos. The rule also applies to music for harpsichord, organ, and other keyboard instruments, but not to non-keyboard instruments.

Title: The complete music for piano, two hands and four hands
                and piano duet
Uniform title: Piano music

For three or more, but not all, of a collection of a composer's works
in two or more forms or types for the same medium of performance or the
same broad medium, add "‡k Selections" to the collective title.

Title: Complete works for two pianos and piano four and six
                hands
Uniform title: Piano music. ‡k Selections

Title: Early works for violin and piano
Uniform title: Violin, piano music. ‡k Selections

Title: Aires (c. 1700) for 2 alto recorders (flutes) and continuo
Uniform title: Recorders (2), continuo music. ‡k Selections

Title: Tocatas y sonata para órgano o clave
Uniform title: Keyboard music. ‡k Selections

Title: Selected orchestral works
Uniform title: Orchestra music. ‡k Selections

Title: The complete a cappella works
Uniform title: Choral music. ‡k Selections

Orchestral Excerpts, Etc.

For a publication of one instrumental part from one or more works by one
composer, use the same collective title used for the complete publication
of the score or parts (LCRI 25.35). Apply this rule even when the
instrument for which the music has been excerpted is not reflected in the
collective title.

Music From One Work

100 1♭Mozart, Wolfgang Amadeus, ‡d 1756-1791.
240 10 Masses, ‡n K. 257, ‡r C major
245 00 Missa in C . . .

254   Organ part.
not
240 10 Masses, ‡n K. 257, ‡r C major. ‡k Selections

Music From Two or More Works

100 1b Wagner, Richard, ‡d 1813-1883.
240 10 Orchestra music. ‡k Selections
245 00 Orchestral excerpts from symphonic works for cello
not
240 10 Violoncello music. ‡k Selections

100 1b Wagner, Richard, ‡d 1813-1883.
240 10 Selections
245 00 Orchestral excerpts from operas and concert works for viola
not
240 10 Viola music. ‡k Selections

*In the **Same Form or Type** for **Two or More** Mediums of Performance or*
***One Broad** Medium*

Use the name of the type of composition in the plural for all of a composer's works of the same type for various mediums of performance. Follow the rules in 25.27A to formulate the initial title element.

Title: The 3 sonatas for violin, clarinet, and cello
Contents: One sonata is for violin, one is for clarinet, and one is for
              violoncello
Uniform title: Sonatas

For collections of three or more, but not all, of a composer's works in the same form or type for two or more medium of performance, add "‡k Selections" to the collective title.

Sonatas. ‡k Selections

*In **Two or More Forms or Types** for **Two or More** Mediums of Performance*

*Two or More Mediums Within **One Broad** Medium*

For all of a composer's works for two or more mediums of performance within one broad medium, use a word descriptive of the broad medium followed by the word "music."

Title: The instrumental works
Uniform title: Instrumental music

Title: The collected vocal works
Uniform title: Vocal music

Add "‡k Selections" for three or more works, but not all of a composer's works in two or more forms for mediums of performance within one broad medium.

Title: Grand duo concertant : ‡b pour guitare et violon, op. 28 ;
                Trio concertant pour trois guitares, op. 29 ; Trois duo
                concertants pour deux guitares, op. 34
Uniform title: Instrumental music. ‡k Selections

Title: Selected anthems and motets
Uniform title: Vocal music. ‡k Selections

*Two or More **Diverse** Mediums of Performance*

Use "Selections" as the collective title for partial collections of works in two or more forms or types and for two or more diverse mediums of performance. In this use of the word, "Selections" is not an addition to the uniform title, but the uniform title itself. The date of publication is not added to the collective uniform title "Selections" for music (LCRI 25.9).

Title: Symphony no. 4 ; ‡b Liebeslieder waltzes ; Gesang der
                Parzen . . .
Uniform title: Selections

"‡k Selections" cannot be used with the collective titles "Works" or "Selections." Instead, use the appropriate collective title from the other categories:

Title: The complete vocal music
Uniform title: Vocal music
Not: Works. ‡k Selections

"‡o arr." in Collective Titles

The element "‡o arr." cannot be used with the collective title "Works," but can be used with the collective title "Selections."

Selections; ‡o arr.

Both "‡k Selections" and "‡o arr." can be added to all other collective titles.

Sonatas, ‡m piano. **‡k Selections; ‡o arr.**
Violin, piano music. **‡k Selections; ‡o arr.**
Concertos. **‡k Selections; ‡o arr.**

Collections of Numbered Works With the Same Distinctive Title

Apply rules 25.34B, 25.34C1, or 25.34C2 and assign a collective title to a collection of numbered works with the same distinctive title. Assign the most specific uniform title applicable to all the works in the collection and add "‡k Selections" when appropriate.

Use "Selections" as the collective title when the mediums of performance are too diverse to concisely state (e.g., "instrumental music") and the numbered works are not consecutive.

Title: Sound study I : ‡b for flute and oboe ; Sound study IV :
                for soprano and guitar ; Sound study VI : for chamber
                orchestra
Uniform title: Selections
Not: Sound studies. ‡k Selections

Use a collective title indicating a broad medium of performance for a collection of such works when they are not all of the composer's works for that broad medium of performance and the numbered works are not consecutive.

Title: Sonata da chiesa I : ǂb for trombone and organ ; Sonata da chiesa III : for oboe and organ ; Sonata da chiesa VI : for 2 trumpets and organ
Uniform title: Instrumental music. ǂk Selections

Assign a collective title indicating specific medium of performance for a collection of such works when they are all of the composer's works for that medium of performance and the numbered works are not consecutive.

Title: Instruments II ; ǂb Instruments VII ; Instruments XIV : for flute and piano
Uniform title: Flute, piano music

For a consecutively numbered subset of a group of works with the same distinctive title, even with diverse mediums of performance, include the title of the works with the appropriate serial numbering. If the title is in the singular, it remains in the singular in the uniform title.

Title: Untitled III : ǂb for bassoon solo ; Untitled IV : for violin and cello ; Untitled V : for 2 voices and piano
Uniform title: Untitled, ǂn no. 3-5
Not: Untitleds, ǂn no. 3-5

Include the serial numbering in the uniform title even when all of the consecutively numbered works with the same distinctive title are in the item.

Title: Pastel I : ǂb for piano ; Pastel II : for flute ; Pastel III : for violoncello ; Pastel IV : for guitar
Uniform title: Pastel, ǂn no. 1-4
Not: Pastels

Collections of Songs and Excerpts From Musicals and Revues
(LCRIs 25.32B1 and 25.34C2)

When a score or sound recording contains all the music from a composer's musical or revue, the uniform title does not include "‡k Selections," even if the dialogue is not included in the item. If it is unclear or not stated on the item that all the music is included, assume that it is complete.

100 1ʙ Sondheim, Stephen.
240 10 Funny thing happened on the way to the forum
245 00 Original cast recording of A funny thing happened on the way
            to the forum . . .

When it is clear that not all the musical portions are included, add "‡k Selections" to the uniform title.

100 1ʙ Sondheim, Stephen.
240 10 Funny thing happened on the way to the forum. ‡k Selections
245 00 Selections from A funny thing happened on the way to the
            forum . . .

Use "Songs. ‡k Selections" for a collection of songs even when some are taken from theatrical works, such as these by Sondheim and Berlin.

100 1ʙ Sondheim, Stephen.
240 10 Songs. ‡k Selections
245 10 Old friends ‡h [sound recording] : ‡b Geraldine Turner sings
            the songs of Stephen Sondheim.
500   Chiefly excerpts from musicals.

100 1ʙ Berlin, Irving, ‡d 1888-1989.
240 10 Songs. ‡k Selections
245 10 Irving Berlin anthology.

When all the songs in the collection are from larger works of a single type, base the uniform title on the name of that type (LCRI 25.34C2).

100 1ḇSondheim, Stephen.
240 10 Musicals. ‡k Selections
245 14 A little Sondheim music : ‡b songs from musicals by Sondheim.

100 1ḇBerlin, Irving, ‡d 1888-1989.
240 10 Musicals. ‡k Selections
245 00 Broadway songs . . .

Song Texts and Lyrics

The difference between song texts and lyrics can be confusing. Use "Lyrics" as the collective title when a composer wrote texts for both his/her own compositions as well as for songs by other composers. This collective title is also used for texts written by one composer, but set to music by another composer, and for texts written by a lyricist who never set his or her own lyrics to music. This example is for a composer who wrote lyrics for his own songs and for songs by other composers.

100 1ḇLoesser, Frank, ‡d 1910-1969.
240 10 Lyrics
245 04 The complete lyrics of Frank Loesser.

Use "Songs. ‡s Texts" under the name of the composer for a collection of lyrics to that composer's songs, regardless of who wrote the texts (25.35F1).

100 1ḇCoward, Noel, ‡d 1899-1973.
240 10 Songs. ‡s Texts
245 10 Noël Coward : ‡b the complete lyrics . . .

Composers and Authors (25.10A)

Rule 25.10A applies to persons who write both musical and literary works. "Musical works" is used for a collection of works by a person who is primarily a writer.

100 1♭Nietzsche, Friedrich Wilhelm, ‡d 1844-1900.
240 10 Musical works
245 04 The music of Friedrich Nietzsche . . .

"Musical works. ‡k Selections" (not "Selections") is used for collections of works in three or more forms. The rules in 25.34C are applied to collections of three or more works in two or more types or for two or more different mediums of performance.

100 1♭Nietzsche, Friedrich Wilhelm, ‡d 1844-1900.
240 10 Musical works. ‡k Selections
245 00 Musica di Friedrich Nietzsche . . .

Conversely, use "Literary works" and "Literary works. ‡k Selections" (not "Selections") for a collection of literary works by a person who is primarily a composer.

100 1♭Wagner, Richard, ‡d 1813-1883.
240 10 Literary works
245 00 Dichtungen und Schriften . . .

100 1♭Wagner, Richard, ‡d 1813-1883.
240 10 Literary works. ‡k Selections
245 00 Ausgewählte Schriften . . .

Note

1. AACR2, Appendix D, *Glossary.*

Chapter 13
Works of Unknown or Collective Authorship (21.5, 21.6)

Unknown or Uncertain Authorship (21.5)

Individual works of unknown or uncertain personal authorship are entered under title (21.5A). (Titles of works identified by reference sources as probably by a particular composer are entered under the heading for that composer [21.5B], following the rules in 25.25-25.34.)

130 0b Twelve days of Christmas (English folk song)
245 14 The twelve days of Christmas / ‡c anon.

130 0b Shenandoah (Song)
245 14 The wide Missouri . . .

130 0b Schweigt stille, plaudert nicht. ‡l English & German.
245 10 Schweigt stille, plaudert nicht : ‡b (die andere Kaffeekantate) : für Sopran, Tenor, Bass, zwei Violinen, Viola und Basso continuo = Be silent, not a word : (the other Coffee-cantata) : for soprano, tenor, bass, two violins, viola, and basso continuo / ‡c Musik von einem unbekannten Komponisten . . .

In this example, the title proper functions as the uniform title.

245 00 Ave vera caro Christi : ‡b for 4 voices or instruments / ‡c anonymous, c. 1500 . . .

Individual works of unknown authorship that are in the form of a type of composition are entered under a generic uniform title formulated in the same way as for works by a single composer. The exception is that such a uniform title will never be in the plural.

130 0*b* Concerto, ‡m oboes (4), bassoons (2), ‡r A minor.
245 00 Concerto for 4 oboes and 2 bassoons, ca. 1720 / ‡c anonymous.

130 0*b* Sonata, ‡m violins (4), continuo, ‡r D major.
245 00 Four-violin sonata in D / ‡c anonymous.

130 0*b* Concertino, ‡m harpsichords (2), ‡r G major.
245 00 Anonyme Kompositionen des 18. Jahrhunderts für 2 Cembali (Orgeln, Klaviere) . . .
500 0*b* Concertino in G — Sonata in C.
730 0*b* Sonata, ‡m harpsichords (2), ‡r C major.

130 0*b* Sonata, ‡m trombone, continuo, ‡r D minor.
245 00 Sonata trombono solo & basso for alto or tenor trombone & basso continuo / ‡c anonymous (17th century)

130 0*b* Trio sonata, ‡m flute, violin, continuo, ‡r G major.
245 00 Sonata no. 3 in G, BWV 1038 . . .
500 Previously attributed to J.S. Bach; now doubtful.

130 0*b* Alman, ‡m harpsichord (Fitzwilliam virginal book, 14)
245 00 Almand, FWVB 14 / ‡c anonymous . . .

Additions to Resolve Conflicts

Use additional elements when two uniform titles for two different anonymous works conflict. In this example, a descriptive phrase was used.

130 0*b* Nightingale **(Harpsichord work)**
130 0*b* Nightingale **(Folk song)**

Part of a Work of Unknown Authorship

130 0♭Kleine Präludien und Fugen. ‡n Nr. 1.
245 00Prelude and fugue in C major (for organ) / ‡c Bach, Johann
    Sebastian.
500   Anonymous; formerly attributed to J.S. Bach.

130 0♭Guter, seltzamer, und künstreicher teutscher Gesang. ‡p Wein
    Gesang.
245 14Das Wein Gesang : ‡b ein musikalischer "Weinkatalog" aus der
    Renaissance : Lied zu 4 Stimmen aus Guter seltzamer und
    künstreicher teutscher Gesang, Petreius, Nürnberg 1544.

Collective Authorship (21.6)

Works by four or more composers, with no single composer attributed as
the primary composer, are entered under title (21.6C2). In this example,
the title proper functions as the uniform title.

245 02L'éventail de Jeanne : ‡b ballet in one act / ‡c by ten French
    composers . . .

When the composers are named, make a name added entry for the first
or most predominantly named composer.

130 0♭B-la-F.
245 10Quartet on a theme "B-la-F" : ‡b for two violins, viola and cello
    / ‡c Rimsky-Korsakov, Lyadov, Bordon, and Glazunov.
700 1♭Rimsky-Korsakov, Nikolay, ‡d 1844-1908.

Keep in mind rule 21.6B2 regarding works by two or three composers,
which are entered under the heading for the principal or first-named
composer, with name (not name/title) added entries for the other
composer(s).

100 1b Schumann, Robert, ǂd 1810-1856.
240 10 F.A.E.
245 10 F.A.E. Sonate : ǂb für Violine und Pianoforte / ǂc Robert
        Schumann, Albert Dietrich, und Johannes Brahms.
700 1b Brahms, Johannes, ǂd 1833-1897.
700 1b Dietrich, Albert Hermann, ǂd 1829-1908.

Individual movements from a work by two or three composers are also entered under the name of the principal or first-named composer, even if that composer did not write the movement being cataloged. An added entry is made for the composer of the movement.

100 1b Schumann, Robert, ǂd 1810-1856.
240 10 F.A.E. ǂp Allegro (3rd movement)
245 00 Sonata movement : ǂb for violin and piano / ǂc Johannes
        Brahms.
500   The 3rd movement of F.A.E. by Schumann, Brahms, and
        Dietrich.
700 1b Brahms, Johannes, ǂd 1833-1897.

Previously Existing Music by Various Composers Adapted or Arranged Into a Larger Work

Rule 21.19B applies to works consisting of previously existing music by various composers adapted or arranged by another person into a larger work. A well-known example of this type of work is the ballad opera *The Beggar's Opera*. Publications or recordings of this type of work are entered under title, as are selections from such a work. Individual works are entered under the name of the composer or under title, if the composer is unknown.

A ballad opera, with music by several composers, is entered under title.

245 00 Love in a village : ǂb a pasticcio comic opera / ǂc music,
        Thomas Arne and others . . .

When the composer of an individually published work included in the ballad opera is known, the work is entered under the name of the composer. An added entry is made for the title of the ballad opera.

100 1♭Boyce, William, ‡d 1711-1779.
245 10 If ever I'm catch'd : ‡b sung by Mr. Beard in Love in a village /
    ‡c set by Dr. Boyce.
740 0♭Love in a village.

Individually published works with no known composer are entered
under title, with an added entry for the title of the ballad opera.

245 00 There was a jolly miller : ‡b sung by Mr. Beard in Love in a
    village . . .
740 0♭Love in a village.

Chapter 14
Manuscripts (25.13)

Rule 25.13B1 states the order of preference for the uniform title for a work contained in a manuscript, for a manuscript itself, or for a manuscript group:

1. a title that has been assigned to the work subsequent to its creation or compilation;
2. the name of the manuscript(s) if the work is identified only by that name;
3. the heading of the repository followed by "Manuscript" and the repository's designation for the manuscript(s).

It may be difficult to distinguish between a "title" and a "name." LCRI 25.13 suggests that a *name* includes generic words such as "codex," "codice," "manuscript," etc., "with a generic term ordinarily indicative of text." Substituting the word "text" with "a generic term indicative of musical form, genre, or medium of performance" may help distinguish between a title and a name.

A Title Assigned to the Manuscript

130 0♭ Recueil de pièces choisies pour de clavessin, 1702.
245 10 London, British Library, ms Add. 39569, "Babell ms" . . .

130 0♭ Harmonia organica.
245 10 Ochsenhauser Orgelbuch . . .

*A **Name** Given to the Manuscript or the **Name** by Which the Manuscript Is Known*

130 0♭ Fitzwilliam virginal book.
245 14 The Fitzwilliam book . . .

130 0♭Laborde chansonnier.
245 14 Das Chansonnier Laborde . . .

The name of music manuscripts frequently include a person's name or place name followed by the term "book," "notebook," etc.

130 0♭Straloch lute book.
245 14 The Straloch manuscript . . .

130 0♭Rusconi codex.
245 14 Der Gonzaga-Kodex . . .

130 0♭Fayrfax manuscript.
245 14 The Fairfax book . . .

When it is unclear whether a manuscript is named or not, follow LCRI 25.13 and consider it to be named.

The Heading of the Repository

When a manuscript cannot be identified by a title or name, it is entered under the heading for the repository currently in possession of the manuscript. As Maxwell points out, headings such as these function more to indicate the location of the manuscript; thus the emphasis on possession over ownership.[1] The term "Manuscript" follows the name of the repository. Because it is a form heading rather than a title, it is tagged in ‡k rather than in ‡t. Any applicable identifying alpha-numeric designation used by the repository follows in ‡n. The form of the designation should be that used by the repository to identify the item. If this form is not apparent, use the form on the first manuscript received from that repository. That form is then used in all headings for manuscripts from that repository, unless a later form becomes the predominant form.

110 2♭ Bibliothèque nationale (France). ‡k Manuscript. ‡n Réserve 1122.
245 00 Pièces pour virginal 1646-1654 : fac-similé du manuscrit . . .

110 2♭British Library. ‡k Manuscript. ‡n Additional 10444.
245 12 A curious collection for the common flute . . .

110 2b British Library. ‡k Manuscript. ‡n Additional 4911.
245 13 An anonymous Scottish treatise on music from the sixteenth
    century . . .

If a different form of designation later becomes the form
predominantly used by the repository, use that new form and change
earlier headings to conform.
A repository may use a separate alpha-numeric designation for each
group or collection of manuscripts. In this heading for the British Library,
the manuscript is found in the Egerton collection rather than the
Additional collection.

110 2b British Library. ‡k Manuscript. ‡n Egerton 2046.
245 14 Jane Pickeringe's lute book . . .

For a single item within a manuscript, add the foliation, when it can
be determined, using the abbreviation "fol."

110 2b British Library. ‡k Manuscript. ‡n Additional 62132A, fol.
    228-231.
245 14 The fountains fragments . . .

110 2b Universitätsbibliothek Leipzig. ‡k Manuscript. ‡n Rep. III. fol.
    15i.
245 14 Die Musikalischen Albumblätter der Luise Avé-Lallemant zu
    Leipzig . . .

When facing pages in a manuscript are given the same number, use
"v" (verso) for left-side pages and "r" (recto) for right-side pages.

110 2b Biblioteca capitolare di Verona. ‡k Manuscript. ‡n 759, fol.
    50v-51v.
245 00 2 Salve Regina a 3 voci . . .

110 2b British Library. ‡k Manuscript. ‡n Additional 17792-6, fol.
    57v-59r.
245 00 Four pavans a5, VdGS nos. 1611-14 (TrTrTTB) . . .

LC practice is to not add "‡k Selections" to a uniform title for
selections from a manuscript that includes works by two or more

composers or by anonymous composers. Individual works from such a manuscript are represented by headings appropriate to each work (e.g., name/title or uniform title headings). A collection of two or more works, but not all the works from such a manuscript, is entered under the heading appropriate to the group of works.

Note

1. Maxwell, p. 141.

Chapter 15
References (26.1, 26.4)

References are used in authority records to refer from an unused form of a heading to the established heading or from one heading to a related heading. References for uniform titles may be made from uniform titles, name/title headings, and corporate name/form subheading headings.

References for uniform titles are made according to the rules in AACR2 Chapter 26, but are constructed according to AACR2 Chapter 25. The general rule given in LCRI 26.1 is to "construct a reference in the same form in which it would be constructed if chosen as the heading." This means that references are formulated according to the rules in AACR2 Chapter 25, involving selection of and formulation of the initial title element, additions to the initial title element, and other elements needed to make the reference unique. Initial articles are deleted from distinctive titles functioning as references. LCRI 26.1 includes the caveat that references in older authority records may have been constructed to agree with headings formulated according to earlier practices.

Rules 26.1B-C discuss when to make references. "*See*" (or "Search under") references for uniform titles are made **from** a form that "might reasonably be sought" **to** the form used as the heading in the same authority record. The MARC field for "*see*" references is the 4XX field. The tagging and indicators for a 4XX field correspond to those for the 1XX field.

A personal name/title "*see*" reference heading is tagged as 400/‡t.

100 1b Archer, Violet. ‡t Northern landscape
400 1b Archer, Violet. ‡t Paysage du nord

A corporate name/form subheading "*see*" reference is tagged as 410/‡k.

110 2ხ British Library. ‡k Manuscript. ‡n Additional 53723
410 2ხ British Library. ‡k Manuscript. ‡n Loan 35

A title "*see*" reference is tagged as 430.

130 0ხ Fitzwilliam virginal book
430 0ხ Queen Elizabeth's virginal book

"*See also*" (or "Search also under") references are made from one established heading in one authority record to a related established heading in another authority record. The 5XX field is the MARC tag for "*see also*" references. As with the 4XX fields, the tagging for 5XX fields corresponds to that for the 1XX fields.

A personal name/title "*see also*" reference heading is tagged as 500/‡t. In these examples, the established heading in the first is a "*see also*" reference in the second. The established heading in the second example is a "*see also*" reference in the first example.

100 1ხ Bach, Johann Christian, ‡d 1735-1782. ‡t Endimione.
        ‡p Sinfonia
500 1ხ Bach, Johann Christian, ‡d 1735-1782. ‡t Symphonies, ‡n op.
        18. ‡n No. 3

100 1ხ Bach, Johann Christian, ‡d 1735-1782. ‡t Symphonies, ‡n op.
        18. ‡n No. 3
500 1ხ Bach, Johann Christian, ‡d 1735-1782. ‡t Endimione.
        ‡p Sinfonia

A "*see also*" reference may be made from the title proper of an item whose main entry is a collective title that matches an established heading. The 5XX field in the authority record matches the 1XX field in another authority record.

Bibliographic record:
100 1ხ Debussy, Claude, ‡d 1862-1918.
240 10 Vocal music. ‡k Selections
245 13 La damoiselle élue ‡h [sound recording] : ‡b poème lyrique
        pour voix de femmes solo, choeur et orchestre ; Trois ballades
        de François Villon ; Invocation : choeur pour voix d'hommes et

orchestre ; Salut printemps : choeur pour voix de femmes et orchestre / ‡c Claude Debussy . . .

Heading and "*see also*" reference in the authority record for the collective title:

100 1‡Debussy, Claude, ‡d 1862-1918. ‡t Vocal music. ‡k Selections
500 1‡Debussy, Claude, ‡d 1862-1918. ‡t Damoiselle élue

Heading in the authority record for the first work on the sound recording·

100 1‡Debussy, Claude, ‡d 1862-1918. ‡t Damoiselle élue

The references in authority records may be different types of headings than the established heading, and therefore would be tagged differently.

A name/title reference (400/‡t) referring to a uniform title heading (130).

130 0‡Kleine Präludien und Fugen
400 1‡Bach, Johann Sebastian, ‡d 1685-1750. ‡t Preludes and fugues, ‡m organ, ‡n BWV 553-560

A corporate name/form (410/‡k) heading referring to a uniform title heading (130).

130 0‡Straloch lute book
410 2‡National Library of Scotland. ‡k Manuscript. ‡n Advocates' 5.2.18

A uniform title heading (430) referring to a corporate name/form heading (110/‡k).

110 2‡British Library. ‡k Manuscript. ‡n Additional 53723
430 0‡Henry Lawes autograph song manuscript

110 1♭Leipzig (Germany). ‡b Musikbibliothek. ‡k Manuscript. ‡n
        II.6.15
430 ♭0 Lautenbuch des Albert Dlugorai
430 ♭0 Długoraj-Buch

A name/title reference may be made from a name/title heading for a
composer to whom a work was previously attributed. The established
heading will include the name of the composer to whom the work is
currently attributed. The reference for the erroneous attribution is
formulated as if it were the established heading.

100 1♭Pergolesi, Giovanni Battista, ‡d 1710-1736. ‡t Stabat Mater,
        ‡n P. 77, ‡r F minor
400 1♭Bach, Johann Sebastian, ‡d 1685-1750. ‡t 51. Psalm

100 1♭Hasse, Johann Adolf, ‡d 1699-1783. ‡t Concertos, ‡m flute,
        string orchestra, ‡r G major (Münster Mus. 373); ‡o arr.
400 1♭Telemann, Georg Philipp, ‡d 1681-1767. ‡t Concertos,
        ‡m trumpet, string orchestra, ‡n TWV Anh. 51:G1, ‡r G major

LCRI 26.4B allows for additional references made under either the
name of the attributed composer or the erroneous composer, as needed for
the item being cataloged. This example includes references from
name/title headings of the erroneous composer. The MARC coding in the
first 400 field, "‡w nne," means that this heading was previously the
established AACR2-form of the heading. The remaining references
originally referred to the Vivaldi name/title heading.

100 1♭Chédeville, Nicolas, ‡d 1705-1782. ‡t Pastor fido
400 1♭Vivaldi, Antonio, ‡d 1678-1741. ‡t Pastor fido **‡w nne**
400 1♭Vivaldi, Antonio, ‡d 1678-1741. ‡t Sonatas, ‡n F. XVI, 5-10
400 1♭Vivaldi, Antonio, ‡d 1678-1741. ‡t Sonatas, ‡n op. 13
400 1♭Vivaldi, Antonio, ‡d 1678-1741. ‡t Sonatas, ‡m recorder,
        continuo, ‡n op. 13
400 1♭Vivaldi, Antonio, ‡d 1678-1741. ‡t Faithful shepherd

This authority record includes references from both the attributed and
erroneous composers.

100 1b Mozart, Leopold, ‡d 1719-1787. ‡t Missa brevis, ‡r F major
400 1b Mozart, Leopold, ‡d 1719-1787. ‡t O sing for joy
400 1b Mozart, Wolfgang Amadeus, ‡d 1756-1791. ‡t Missa brevis,
    ‡n K. 116, ‡r F major
400 1b Mozart, Wolfgang Amadeus, ‡d 1756-1791. ‡t O sing for joy

Rules Specific to Uniform Titles (26.4)

The general rules for making references in 26.1 apply to all references; rules specific to uniform titles are in 26.4. The most common "*see*" references for uniform titles are made from different or variant forms of the title (26.4B1). These forms may be found on the item being cataloged or in reference sources. This rule applies to references from an entire work as well as from the title of a part of a work. (References from the title of a part of a work are also covered in 26.4B3, which is discussed later in this chapter.)

    An example of a reference from a variant form of the title:

100 1b Bach, Johann Sebastian, ‡d 1685-1750. ‡t Brandenburgische
    Konzerte
400 1b Bach, Johann Sebastian, ‡d 1685-1750. ‡t Brandenburg
    concertos

    An example of distinctive name/title references made to a generic name/title heading:

100 1b Sibelius, Jean, ‡d 1865-1957. ‡t Trios, ‡m piano, strings, †r C
    major
400 1b Sibelius, Jean, ‡d 1865-1957. ‡t Lovisa trio
400 1b Sibelius, Jean, ‡d 1865-1957. ‡t Loviisa

    An example of a generic name/title reference made to a distinctive name/title heading:

100 1b Gruber, Heinz Karl. ‡t Aerial
400 1b Gruber, Heinz Karl. ‡t Concertos, ‡m trumpet, orchestra

References From Generic Uniform Titles

Initial Title Element

Make a reference when the initial title element is a type of composition, and the work is also known as by the name of another type of composition.

100 1♭Telemann, Georg Philipp, ‡d 1681-1767. ‡t **Sonatas,**
    ‡m strings, continuo, ‡n TWV 44:32, ‡r F minor
400 1♭Telemann, Georg Philipp, ‡d 1681-1767. ‡t **Sextets,**
    ‡m strings, continuo, ‡n TWV 44:32, ‡r F minor

100 1♭Müller-Zürich, Paul. ‡t **Praeludium, Aria und Fuge,**
    ‡m winds, strings, ‡n op. 21
400 1♭Müller-Zürich, Paul. ‡t **Nonet,** ‡m winds, strings, ‡n op. 21

100 1♭Brahms, Johannes, ‡d 1833-1897. ‡t **Gesänge,** ‡m women's
    voices, horns (2), harp, ‡n op. 17
400 1♭Brahms, Johannes, ‡d 1833-1897. ‡t **Chants,** ‡m women's
    voices, horns (2), harp, ‡n op. 17
400 1♭Brahms, Johannes, ‡d 1833-1897. ‡t **Partsongs,** ‡m women's
    voices, horns (2), harp, ‡n op. 17

When the initial title element is not translated into English as per 25.29A1, make references from other forms of the name of the type of composition when they also appear on the item or in reference sources. "Morceaux" is not translated into English; "Pieces" and "Stücke" also appear on the item.

100 1♭Bortkiewicz, Sergei, ‡d 1877-1952. ‡t **Morceaux,** ‡m piano,
    ‡n op. 24
400 1♭Bortkiewicz, Sergei, ‡d 1877-1952. ‡t **Pieces,** ‡m piano, ‡n op.
    24
400 1♭Bortkiewicz, Sergei, ‡d 1877-1952. ‡t **Stücke,** ‡m piano,
    ‡n op. 24

When an ampersand or other symbol meaning "and" appears in the initial title element, make a reference with the spelled-out form of the word "and" in the language of the title.

100 1♭Tansman, Alexandre, ‡d 1897-1986. ‡t Introduction **&** fugue,
     ‡m pianos (2)
400 1♭Tansman, Alexandre, ‡d 1897-1986. ‡t Introduction **et** fugue,
     ‡m pianos (2)

100 1♭Weiner, Stanley. ‡t Introduktion **&** Allegro, †m organ, trumpet,
     horn, ‡n op. 185
400 1♭Weiner, Stanley. ‡t Introduktion **und** Allegro, ‡m organ,
     trumpet, horn, ‡n op. 185

Medium of Performance

A reference is made from a name/title heading when alternate instrumentation is involved. Following 25.30B4c, only the first-named instrumentation is included in the uniform title; a name/title reference is made for the alternate instrumentation.

For clarinet or viola and piano:

100 1♭Brahms, Johannes, ‡d 1833-1896. ‡t Sonatas, ‡m **clarinet,**
     piano, ‡n op. 120
400 1♭Brahms, Johannes, ‡d 1833-1896. ‡t Sonatas, ‡m **viola,** piano,
     ‡n op. 120

For four double basses or violoncellos:

100 1♭Glanert, Detlev. ‡t Quartets, ‡m **double basses,** ‡n op. 12
400 1♭Glanert, Detlev. ‡t Quartets, ‡m **violoncellos,** ‡n op. 12

For oboe d'amore or English horn:

100 1♭Carr, Edwin, ‡d 1926-2003. ‡t Prelude and aria, ‡m **oboe
     d'amore,** piano
400 1♭Carr, Edwin, ‡d 1926-2003. ‡t Prelude and aria, ‡m **English
     horn,** piano

For alto or mezzo-soprano and piano:

100 1♭Meyer-Selb, Horst. ‡t Zigeunerlieder, ‡m **alto**, piano
400 1♭Meyer-Selb, Horst. ‡t Zigeunerlieder, ‡m **mezzo-soprano**,
     piano

For children's voices or women's voices:

100 1♭Britten, Benjamin, ‡d 1913-1976. ‡t Songs, ‡m **children's**
     voices
400 1♭Britten, Benjamin, ‡d 1913-1976. ‡t Songs, ‡m **women's**
     voices

Numeric Identifying Elements

When more than one thematic index numbering system has been applied
to a composer's works, references for individual works may be made from
the number(s) not used in the uniform title.

100 1♭Strauss, Richard, ‡d 1864-1949. ‡t Trios, ‡m piano, strings,
     ‡n **TrV 71**, ‡r D major
400 1♭Strauss, Richard, ‡d 1864-1949. ‡t Trios, ‡m piano, strings,
     ‡n **AV 53**, ‡r D major
400 1♭Strauss, Richard, ‡d 1864-1949. ‡t Trios, ‡m piano, strings,
     ‡n **no. 2**, ‡r D major

100 1♭Tartini, Giuseppe, ‡d 1692-1770. ‡t Sonatas, ‡m violin,
     continuo, ‡n **op. 4. ‡n No. 3**
400 1♭Tartini, Giuseppe, ‡d 1692-1770. ‡t Sonatas, ‡m violin,
     continuo, ‡n **B. B 10**, ‡r B♭ major

100 1♭Rosetti, Antonio, ‡d ca. 1750-1792. ‡t Sonatas, ‡m keyboard
     instrument, ‡n **M. D19-24**
400 1♭Rosetti, Antonio, ‡d ca. 1750-1792. ‡t Sonatas, ‡m keyboard
     instrument, ‡n **K. IV, 13**

There may be variant numbers within the same thematic index.

100 1b Mozart, Wolfgang Amadeus, ‡d 1756-1791. ‡t Sonatas,
   ‡m piano, ‡n **K. 279**, ‡r C major
400 1b Mozart, Wolfgang Amadeus, ‡d 1756-1791. ‡t Sonatas,
   ‡m piano, ‡n **K. 189d**, ‡r C major

When a work has been published under different opus numbers by
different publishers, make references with the other opus numbers,
qualifying each by the name of the publisher that assigned the number.
The form of the publisher's name need not be standardized.

100 1b Gyrowetz, Adalbert, ‡d 1763-1850. ‡t Trios, ‡m flute, violin,
   violoncello, ‡n **op. 4 (Bland)**
400 1b Gyrowetz, Adalbert, ‡d 1763-1850 ‡t Trios, ‡m flute, violin,
   violoncello, †n **op. 6 (Schmitt)**
400 1b Gyrowetz, Adalbert, ‡d 1763-1850. ‡t Trios, ‡m flute, violin,
   violoncello, ‡n **op. 11 (Imbault)**
400 1b Gyrowetz, Adalbert, ‡d 1763-1850. ‡t Trios, ‡m flute, violin,
   violoncello, ‡n **op. 11 (André)**

*References for Works in a Numbered Sequence of Works With the Same
Title, for Different Mediums of Performance*

When 25.30B1b is applied to a work in a numbered sequence of works
with the same title but for different mediums of performance, and the
statements of medium of performance are omitted, make a name/title
reference with the medium of performance, but not the serial number.

100 1b Hovhaness, Alan, ‡d 1911-2000. ‡t Symphonies, ‡n **no. 4**, op.
   165
400 1b Hovhaness, Alan, ‡d 1911-2000. ‡t Symphonies, ‡m **band,**
   ‡n op. 165

When the serial number has been omitted from the uniform title for a
work in a numbered sequence of works with the same initial title element
and for the same medium of performance except for that one work, make
a reference that includes the medium of performance used in the uniform
titles for the rest of the works in the sequence as well as the serial number.

100 1b Prokofiev, Sergey, ‡d 1891-1953. ‡t Concertos, ‡m piano, 1
    hand, orchestra, ‡n op. 53, ‡r B♭ major
400 1b Prokofiev, Sergey, ‡d 1891-1953. ‡t Concertos, ‡m **piano,
    orchestra**, ‡n **no. 4**, op. 53, ‡r B♭ major

Arrangements

References are made when a work has been arranged for a medium of
performance other than the original and the uniform title for the original
work includes the medium of performance. A reference is made for each
medium of performance for which the work has been arranged.

100 1b Bajura, K. V. A. ‡t Kyrie and fugue, ‡m mixed voices, ‡r C
    minor; ‡o arr.
400 1b Bajura, K. V. A. ‡t Kyrie and fugue, ‡m **string quartet**, ‡r C
    minor

100 1b Mozart, Wolfgang Amadeus, ‡d 1756-1791. ‡t Adagio und
    Fuge, ‡m string orchestra, ‡n K. 546, ‡r C minor; ‡o arr.
400 1b Mozart, Wolfgang Amadeus, ‡d 1756-1791. ‡t Adagio und
    Fuge, ‡m **wind quintet**, ‡n K. 546, ‡r C minor
400 1b Mozart, Wolfgang Amadeus, ‡d 1756-1791. ‡t Adagio und
    Fuge, ‡m **organ**, ‡n K. 546, ‡r C minor
400 1b Mozart, Wolfgang Amadeus, ‡d 1756-1791. ‡t Adagio und
    Fuge, ‡m **string quartet**, ‡n K. 546, ‡r C minor

When the work has been transposed to accommodate the range of the
arranged medium, include the key of the arrangement, not the work's
original key, in the reference.

100 1b Mozart, Wolfgang Amadeus, ‡d 1756-1791. ‡t Rondos,
    ‡m violin, orchestra, ‡n K. 373, ‡r **C major**; ‡o arr.
400 1b Mozart, Wolfgang Amadeus, ‡d 1756-1791. ‡t Rondos,
    ‡m flute, orchestra, ‡n K. 373, ‡r **D major**

References From Distinctive Uniform Titles

References are made from titles that include alternate forms of words
occurring as one of the first five words of the title, according to LCRI

21.30J. Alternative forms include abbreviations; ampersand or other symbol representing the word "and"; letters, initials, and acronyms; numbers; and other forms of a word that would be filed differently.

Abbreviations

A reference is made from the spelled-out form of a word that appears as one of the first five words in abbreviated form in the uniform title. (This rule does not apply to prescribed abbreviation such as "acc.," "arr.," "no.," "Nr.," "op.," etc., that may appear in a uniform title.) The spelled-out form should be in the language of title.

100 1b Davies, Peter Maxwell, ‡d 1934- ‡t **No.** 11 bus
400 1b Davies, Peter Maxwell, ‡d 1934- ‡t **Number** 11 bus

100 1b Gounod, Charles, ‡d 1818-1893. ‡t Messe solennelle de **Ste.** Cécile
400 1b Gounod, Charles, ‡d 1818-1893. ‡t Messe solennelle de **Sainte** Cécile

100 1b Britten, Benjamin, ‡d 1913-1976. ‡t Hymn to **St.** Cecilia
400 1b Britten, Benjamin, ‡d 1913-1976. ‡t Hymn to **Saint** Cecilia

100 1b Doppler, Franz, ‡d 1821-1883. ‡t Souvenir à **Mme.** Adelina Patti
400 1b Doppler, Franz, ‡d 1821-1883. ‡t Souvenir à **Madame** Adelina Patti

100 1b Offenbach, Jacques, ‡d 1819-1880. ‡t **Mr** Choufleuri restera chez lui le—
400 1b Offenbach, Jacques, ‡d 1819-1880. ‡t **Monsieur** Choufleuri restera chez lui le—

Ampersand or Other Symbol Representing the Word "and"

When a symbol meaning "and" appears as one of the first five words of a title, a reference is made with the spelled-out form of the word, in the language of the title.

100 1♭Rubbra, Edmund, ‡d 1901-1986. ‡t Prelude **&** fugue on a
   theme by Cyril Scott
400 1♭Rubbra, Edmund, ‡d 1901-1986. ‡t Prelude **and** fugue on a
   theme by Cyril Scott

100 1♭Tansman, Alexandre, ‡d 1897-1986. ‡t Prélude **&** quatre
   petites fugues
400 1♭Tansman, Alexandre, ‡d 1897-1986. ‡t Prélude **et** quatre
   petites fugues

When the symbol does *not* mean "and," it should be spelled out as the
word it is intended to mean. In this example, the "+" stands for "plus"
rather than "and."

100 1♭Hidas, Frigyes. ‡t 1 + 5
400 1♭Hidas, Frigyes. ‡t 1 **plus** 5

Other symbols are spelled out in the language of the title.

100 1♭Sierra, Roberto. ‡t 2 **x** 3
400 1♭Sierra, Roberto. ‡t 2 **times** 3

100 1♭Kan-no, Shigeru, ‡d 1959- ‡t Flageolett+Passacaglia=Blues???
400 1♭Kan-no, Shigeru, ‡d 1959- ‡t Flageolett **plus** Passacaglia **gleich**
   Blues???

Letters, Initials, and Acronyms

A title that contains letters, initials, or acronyms with separating
punctuation as one of the first five words requires a reference in which the
punctuation or the space it occupied is omitted from the word. (This does
not apply to letters indicating key.)

100 1♭Pärt, Arvo. ‡t Concerto piccolo über **B-A-C-H**
400 1♭Pärt, Arvo. ‡t Concerto piccolo über **BACH**

100 1♭Dahl, Ingolf, ‡d 1912-1970. ‡t **I.M.C.** fanfare
400 1♭Dahl, Ingolf, ‡d 1912-1970. ‡t **IMC** fanfare

References are *not* made for initialisms or acronyms without separating punctuation or without spacing.

100 1b Sampson, David, ‡d 1951- ‡t Hommage JFK

This reference would *not* be made:

400 1b Sampson, David, ‡d 1951- ‡t Hommage J.F.K

Numbers

Make a reference from a title that includes as one of the first five words an arabic number (excluding dates) with the number spelled out in the language of the title. References from a title with a roman numeral are made with the numeral in arabic form and in spelled-out form. For numbers in English, follow the rules in *The Chicago Manual of Style*; for other languages, follow the preferred style of the language.

For	Use
25	twenty-five
101	one hundred one *and* one hundred and one
125	one hundred twenty-five (*not* one hundred and twenty-five)
1001	one thousand one *and* one thousand and one

When an initial number is retained in the uniform title, make a reference with the number in spelled-out form, in the language of the title.

100 1b Glanville-Hicks, Peggy. ‡t **13** ways of looking at a blackbird
400 1b Glanville-Hicks, Peggy. ‡t **Thirteen** ways of looking at a blackbird

100 1b Grabner, Hermann, ‡d 1886-1969. ‡t **66.** Psalm
400 1b Grabner, Hermann, ‡d 1886-1969. ‡t **Sechsundsechzigste** Psalm

100 1b Bernaola, Carmelo A., ‡d 1929-2002. ‡t **2-2-2-2----80**
400 1b Bernaola, Carmelo A., ‡d 1929-2002. ‡t **Dos-dos-dos-dos---- ochenta**

When an initial roman numeral is retained in the uniform title, make a reference with the arabic form of the number and from the spelled-out form. In this example, the cataloger also thought that a reference without the initial number would be useful, since, at first glance, the number would not seem to be an integral part of the title.

100 1♭Schuman, William, ‡d 1910-1992. ‡t **XXV** opera snatches
400 1♭Schuman, William, ‡d 1910-1992. ‡t **Twenty-five** opera
         snatches
400 1♭Schuman, William, ‡d 1910-1992. ‡t **25** opera snatches
400 1♭Schuman, William, ‡d 1910-1992. ‡t Opera snatches

A reference is made from a distinctive title from which the initial number has been removed. The reference will include the title with the initial cardinal number and, if needed, another reference with the spelled-out form of the number. If the number in the title was originally a roman numeral, make a reference with the arabic form of the number.

100 1♭Adams, Leslie, ‡d 1932- ‡t Dunbar songs
400 1♭Adams, Leslie, ‡d 1932- ‡t **3** Dunbar songs
400 1♭Adams, Leslie, ‡d 1932- ‡t **Three** Dunbar songs

100 1♭Escaich, Thierry, ‡d 1965- ‡t Instants fugitifs
400 1♭Escaich, Thierry, ‡d 1965- ‡t **III** instants fugitifs
400 1♭Escaich, Thierry, ‡d 1965- ‡t **3** instants fugitifs
400 1♭Escaich, Thierry, ‡d 1965- ‡t **Trois** instants fugitifs

When a number indicating seriality has been removed from the uniform title, make a reference from the title with the serial number as it appears on the item, with another reference with the number in spelled-out form. If the number in the title was originally a roman numeral, make a reference with the arabic form of the number.

100 1♭Hirschfeld, C. René ‡q (Caspar René), ‡d 1965- ‡t Sonett,
         ‡n no. 1
400 1♭Hirschfeld, C. René ‡q (Caspar René), ‡d 1965- ‡t Sonett **I**
400 1♭Hirschfeld, C. René ‡q (Caspar René), ‡d 1965- ‡t Sonett **1**
400 1♭Hirschfeld, C. René ‡q (Caspar René), ‡d 1965- ‡t Sonett **ein**

100 1♭Koch, Erland von, ‡d 1910- ‡t Monolog, ‡n no. 2
400 1♭Koch, Erland von, ‡d 1910- ‡t Monolog **2**
400 1♭Koch, Erland von, ‡d 1910- ‡t Monolog **tva**

100 1♭Leistner-Mayer, Roland. ‡t Poem, ‡n no. 4a
400 1♭Leistner-Mayer, Roland. ‡t Poem **IVa**
400 1♭Leistner-Mayer, Roland. †t Poem **4a**
400 1♭Leistner-Mayer, Roland. ‡t Poem **four a**

A reference is made when an internal number is retained in the uniform title.

100 1♭Davies, Peter Maxwell, †d 1934- ‡t No. **11** bus
400 1♭Davies, Peter Maxwell, ‡d 1934- ‡t No. **eleven** bus

100 1♭Eröd, Iván. ‡t Kleine Suite für **20** finger
400 1♭Eröd, Iván. ‡t Kleine Suite für **zwanzig** finger

100 1♭Hurford, Peter. ‡t Fanfare on Old **100th**
400 1♭Hurford, Peter. ‡t Fanfare on Old **hundredth**

100 1♭Christensen, James. ‡t Fanfare **20**
400 1♭Christensen, James. ‡t Fanfare **twenty**

100 1♭Thornton, William. ‡t Psalm **I**
400 1♭Thornton, William. ‡t Psalm **1**
400 1♭Thornton, William. ‡t Psalm **one**

Examples of References With Both Initial and Internal Numbers

100 1♭Jung, Helge, ‡d 1943- ‡t 4 plus 1
400 1♭Jung, Helge, ‡d 1943- ‡t Vier plus eins

100 1♭Hidas, Frigyes. ‡t 1 + 5
400 1♭Hidas, Frigyes. ‡t One plus five
400 1♭Hidas, Frigyes. ‡t One + five
400 1♭Hidas, Frigyes. ‡t 1 plus 5

100 1♭Sierra, Roberto.‡t 2 x 3
400 1♭Sierra, Roberto.‡t 2 times 3
400 1♭Sierra, Roberto.‡t Two x three
400 1♭Sierra, Roberto.‡t Two times three

100 1♭Cage, John. ‡t Waltzes for the five boroughs
400 1♭Cage, John. ‡t 49 waltzes for the 5 boroughs
400 1♭Cage, John. ‡t Forty-nine waltzes for the five boroughs
400 1♭Cage, John. ‡t 49 waltzes for the five boroughs

100 1♭Humble, Keith. ‡t Short pieces in two parts
400 1♭Humble, Keith. ‡t Five short pieces in two parts
400 1♭Humble, Keith. ‡t 5 short pieces in 2 parts

100 1♭Harbison, John. ‡t I, II, III, IV, V
400 1♭Harbison, John. ‡t 1, 2, 3, 4, 5
400 1♭Harbison, John. ‡t One, two, three, four, five

100 1♭Bernaola, Carmelo A., ‡d 1929-2002. ‡t 2-2-2-2----80
400 1♭Bernaola, Carmelo A., ‡d 1929-2002. ‡t Dos-dos-dos-dos----
    ochenta

Dates

References for titles that include a date are made according to rule 21.30J, which concerns added entries for alternate forms of titles that contain numbers (LCRI 26.4B1). When a date appears in roman numerals, make a reference from the date in arabic numbers.

100 1♭Schmitt, Florent, ‡d 1870-1958. ‡t Fonctionnaire **MCMXII**
400 1♭Schmitt, Florent, ‡d 1870-1958. ‡t Fonctionnaire **1912**

According to Rule 21.30J, under *Guidelines for Making Title Added Entries for Permutations Related to Titles Proper,* do not make a reference from a spelled-out form of a date for a single year or span of years that appears in the title in arabic numbers.

100 1♭Delanoff, Robert, ‡d 1942- ‡t Harlekinade 2001

This reference would *not* be made:

400 1♭ Delanoff, Robert, ‡d 1942- Harlekinade Zwei tausend und ein

Alternative Forms of Words or Characters

A reference from the arabic form of a number that appears in spelled-out form in the title is made when the cataloger thinks it might be used to search for the title in the catalog.

100 1♭ Cage, John. ‡t Fifty-eight
400 1♭ Cage, John. ‡t **58**

100 1♭ Forsyth, Malcolm. ‡t Fanfare and three masquerades
400 1♭ Forsyth, Malcolm. ‡t Fanfare and **3** masquerades

100 1♭ Pyras, Olaf, ‡d 1967- ‡t Eins, gleich zwei, gleich drei
400 1♭ Pyras, Olaf, ‡d 1967- ‡t **1**, gleich **2**, gleich **3**

100 1♭ Demantius, Christoph, ‡d 1567-1643. ‡t Hundertsechzehnte Psalm
400 1♭ Demantius, Christoph, ‡d 1567-1643. ‡t **116.** Psalm

100 1♭ Karg-Elert, Sigfrid, ‡d 1877-1933. ‡t Erste Psalm
400 1♭ Karg-Elert, Sigfrid, ‡d 1877-1933. ‡t **1.** Psalm

100 1♭ Tesson, William. ‡t First Psalm
400 1♭ Tesson, William. ‡t **1st** Psalm

Make a reference from an alternate form of a word that would be filed differently.

100 1♭ Buss, Howard J. ‡t Millennium visions
400 1♭ Buss, Howard J. ‡t **Millenium** visions

100 1♭ Cage, John. ‡t 0'00"
400 1♭ Cage, John. ‡t **0 min., 0 sec.**
400 1♭ Cage, John. ‡t **Zero minutes, zero seconds**

References From the Title of a Part of a Work (26.4B3)

Make a name/title reference from the title of a separately published (or performed) part of a work entered under the name/title heading for the whole work. 25.32A1 further qualifies this with "if the part has a distinctive title," but the corresponding LCRI provides for any reference under the title of a part of a work, whether it be distinctive or generic.

Parts With Distinctive Titles

100 1b Dalla Casa, Girolamo. ‡t Vero modo di diminuir. ‡p Oncques
    amour
400 1b Dalla Casa, Girolamo. ‡t **Oncques amour**

100 1b Marais, Marin, ‡d 1656-1728. ‡t Pièces de violes, ‡n 2e livre.
    ‡p Tombeau pour Mr. de Ste. Colombe
400 1b Marais, Marin, ‡d 1656-1728. ‡t **Tombeau pour M. Ste**
    Colombe
400 1b Marais, Marin, ‡d 1656-1728. ‡t Tombeau pour **Monsieur** de
    Sainte Colombe

100 1b Scheidt, Samuel, ‡d 1587-1654. ‡t Geistliche Concerte, ‡n 3.
    T. ‡p Magnificat (No. 13)
400 1b Scheidt, Samuel, ‡d 1587-1654. ‡t **Christmas Magnificat**
400 1b Scheidt, Samuel, ‡d 1587-1654. ‡t **Sing out, my soul**

Parts With Generic Titles

Rules 25.29A and 25.30 are not applied to the generic title of a part of a larger work (see "Titled Parts" in Chapter 11). They *are* applied to references from titled parts of a larger work. These references are formulated as if they were the established heading. In the uniform titles below, the titled parts of the larger works are the names of types of compositions, which were kept in the original language and not pluralized. Medium of performance, identifying numbers, and key were not added to the title of the part. The references, however, use the cognate and plural forms, and the other elements are included, as they would be if they were the established headings.

100 1b Bach, Johann Sebastian, ‡d 1685-1750. ‡t Wohltemperierte
Klavier, ‡n 1. T. ‡n Nr. 1. ‡p **Fuga**
400 1b Bach, Johann Sebastian, ‡d 1685-1750. ‡t **Fugues,**
‡m harpsichord, ‡n BWV 846, ‡r C major

100 1b Bach, Johann Sebastian, ‡d 1685-1750. ‡t Wohltemperierte
Klavier, ‡n 1. T. ‡n Nr. 1. ‡p **Praeludium**
400 1b Bach, Johann Sebastian, ‡d 1685-1750. ‡t **Preludes,**
‡m piano, ‡n BWV 846, ‡r C major

100 1b Mozart, Wolfgang Amadeus, ‡d 1756-1791. ‡t Serenades,
‡n K. 320, ‡r D major. ‡p **Rondeau**
400 1b Mozart, Wolfgang Amadeus, ‡d 1756-1791. ‡t **Rondos,**
‡m orchestra, ‡n K. 320, no. 4, ‡r G major

In most cases, a reference from a part of a larger work will not include
the title of that work preceding the title of the part. Most references are
made from the title of the part. LCRI 25.32A1 allows for a reference to
be made from the name/title heading for the entire work with the variant
title of the part in ‡p.

100 1b Bellini, Vincenzo, ‡d 1801-1835. ‡t Capuleti e i Montecchi.
‡p Sinfonia
400 1b Bellini, Vincenzo, ‡d 1801-1835. ‡t **Capuleti e i Montecchi.**
‡p Ouverture
400 1b Bellini, Vincenzo, ‡d 1801-1835. ‡t **Capuleti e i Montecchi.**
‡p Overture

Translations

In a bibliographic record, the uniform title for a musical work that has
been translated includes the language into which the work has been
translated (see "Language [‡l] [25.35F]" in Chapter 11). In the authority
record for the work, the uniform title generally will not include the
language into which the work has been translated, according to rule
26.4B1. This rule applies to musical works.

For translations of books, an authority record is created for each
language into which the work has been translated, with the translated title

as a reference. The authority records below are for English and German translations of Berlioz's orchestration treatise.

100 1ь Berlioz, Hector, ‡d 1803-1869. ‡t Grand traité
      d'instrumentation et d'orchestration modernes. ‡l **English**
400 1ь Berlioz, Hector, ‡d 1803-1869. ‡t Treatise on modern
      instrumentation and orchestration
400 1ь Berlioz, Hector, ‡d 1803-1869. ‡t Treatise on instrumentation
400 1ь Berlioz, Hector, ‡d 1803-1869. ‡t Berlioz's orchestration
      treatise

100 1ь Berlioz, Hector, ‡d 1803-1869. ‡t Grand traité
      d'instrumentation et d'orchestration modernes. ‡l **German**
400 1ь Berlioz, Hector, ‡d 1803-1869. ‡t Grosse Instrumentationslehre
400 1ь Berlioz, Hector, ‡d 1803-1869. ‡t Instrumentationslehre

   LCRI 26.4B1, however, states that for musical works, the uniform title being referred to generally should not include additions such as language. Thus all translations of a musical work are entered under the heading for the original work. The original language and the language of the translations are not included in either the heading or references. All translated titles are references under the established heading. This authority record includes the titles of the English, French, Spanish, and Italian translations under the heading for the work in its original language.

100 1ь Mozart, Wolfgang Amadeus, ‡d 1756-1791. ‡t Zauberflöte
400 1ь Mozart, Wolfgang Amadeus, ‡d 1756-1791. ‡t Magic flute
400 1ь Mozart, Wolfgang Amadeus, ‡d 1756-1791. ‡t Flûte enchantée
400 1ь Mozart, Wolfgang Amadeus, ‡d 1756-1791. ‡t Flauta mágica
400 1ь Mozart, Wolfgang Amadeus, ‡d 1756-1791. ‡t Flauto magico

Conflicts

What Constitutes a Conflict?

References that would "normalize" to the same form as the heading in the same record or in another record are considered to be conflicts. The process of normalization involves removing, converting, or retaining characters in the heading so that only alpha-numeric and certain other characters remain. The resulting heading is compared against other normalized headings to determine if they are identical, i.e., in conflict with one another. Rules for normalization are found the PCC's NACO website at http://lcweb.loc.gov/catdir/pcc/naco/normrule.html. The following list summarizes the characters most likely to be found in uniform titles for music and how they are to be treated when normalizing the heading:

Delete the following punctuation marks:
    apostrophe   bracket

Replace the following punctuation marks and characters with a blank space:

angle bracket (< and >)	exclamation point	slash (/)
asterisk	parentheses	back slash (\)
colon	question mark	semicolon
comma	quotation mark	

Retain the following punctuation marks and characters:

flat sign ($\flat$)	ampersand (&)
sharp sign (#)	plus sign (+)

Retain dates, numbers, and roman numerals;

Convert superscript and subscript numbers to their non-superscript and non-subscript equivalents;

Delete accents and diacritics, even those that occupy their own space (e.g., the Russian character miagkii znak);

Convert special alphabetical characters to alphabetical characters. Examples of these are:

Convert these characters	To	Convert these characters	To
Æ and æ	ae	Œ and œ	oe
Đ and đ	d	Ð and ð	d
Ł and ł	l	Ø and ø	o

Once a uniform title has been normalized, it is compared against other headings to determine if it conflicts. A uniform title in a 100, 110, and 130 field is compared against possible conflict with a heading in a 100, 110, 111, 130, or 151 field in another authority record.

Conflicts Between References and Headings

The PCC guidelines state that a heading in a 400, 410, 411, 430, or 451 field that normalizes to a heading in a 100, 110, 111, 130, or 151 field is a conflict and one of the two headings is qualified. For musical works, however, LCRI 26.4B1 requires qualifying *both* the heading and the reference.

Conflicts Between References and Generic Uniform Titles

The serial number is insufficient to distinguish between the first heading and the reference for the second heading, so the date of composition is also added.

100 1♭Shostakovich, Dmitriĭ Dmitrievich, ǂd 1906-1975. ǂt Suites, ǂm jazz ensemble, **ǂn no. 2 (1938)**

100 1♭Shostakovich, Dmitriĭ Dmitrievich, ǂd 1906-1975. ǂt Suites, ǂm orchestra, ǂn no. 1
400 1♭Shostakovich, Dmitriĭ Dmitrievich, ǂd 1906-1975. ǂt Suites, ǂm jazz ensemble, **ǂn no. 2 (2001)**

The question of a reference with the name of a type in the singular form and a heading for a different work with the name of the same type in the singular is currently a subject of discussion among music catalogers and at LC. Current practice varies, and, for now, no official policy has been issued.

One practice is to consider a reference with the name of a type of composition when deciding whether the singular or plural form of a type should be used in the uniform title for another work by the same composer. LCRI 26.4B1 alludes to this when it states "make a reference only in the form that the uniform title would take if the title in question had been selected as the basis for the uniform title." As a result, the cataloger would pluralize the form of the name of the type in the heading *and* the reference, even if the composer wrote only one work in that form. For example, Klengel wrote only one work entitled "caprice." Because of the reference from "Caprice" in an authority record for another of Klengel's works, the word "caprice" was pluralized in both.

100 1ḃ Klengel, Julius, ‡d 1859-1933. ‡t **Caprices**, ‡m violoncello,
    piano, ‡n op. 27, ‡r D minor

100 1ḃ Klengel, Julius, ‡d 1859-1933. ‡t Caprice in Form einer
    Chaconne
400 1ḃ Klengel, Julius, ‡d 1859-1933. ‡t **Caprices**, ‡m violoncello,
    ‡n op. 43

The other practice is to not consider a conflict to exist between the
singular form of a name of a type of composition in a reference and the
singular form of the name of the same type in a heading for a different
work. The reasoning behind this position is that, while this situation rarely
occurs, it is allowed because references do not determine the form of a
uniform title. These two examples reflect this practice. "Sonata" is not
pluralized in either the heading or the reference, even though it looks as
if Liszt wrote two sonatas.

100 1ḃ Liszt, Franz, ‡d 1811-1886. ‡t **Sonata**, ‡m piano, ‡r B minor

100 1ḃ Liszt, Franz, ‡d 1811-1886. ‡t Duet, ‡m violin, piano
400 1ḃ Liszt, Franz, ‡d 1811-1886. ‡t **Sonata**, ‡m violin, piano

Conflicts Between References and Distinctive Uniform Titles

When a uniform title for one work is identical to a reference from another
work by the same composer, follow the same rules used to resolve a
conflict between two uniform titles. Apply 25.31B to both the reference
and the uniform title. If the uniform title is new to the catalog, include the
additional element; add the element to the existing reference if not already
included. If the reference is new to the catalog, include the additional
element in the reference, adding it as well to the existing uniform title, if
it is not already included.

The elements to be added are, in the order of preference stated in the
rule: medium of performance or a descriptive term or phrase; one or more
of the following elements in 25.30C-E (numeric identifying element, key,
and other identifying elements).

Medium of Performance

Medium of performance is the first preference of additional elements used to resolve the conflict between the heading for one work and the reference to another work.

100 1♭Eschmann, J. Carl ‡q (Johann Carl), ‡d 1826-1882.
‡t Phantasiestücke, **‡m clarinet, piano**

100 1♭Eschmann, J. Carl ‡q (Johann Carl), ‡d 1826-1882. ‡t Im
   Herbst
400 1♭Eschmann, J. Carl ‡q (Johann Carl), ‡d 1826-1882.
   ‡t Phantasiestücke, **‡m horn, piano**

100 1♭Cherney, Brian. ‡t Miniatures, **‡m oboe, piano**

100 1♭Cherney, Brian. ‡t Miniatures in the form of a mobile
400 1♭Cherney, Brian. ‡t Miniatures, **‡m viola**

Descriptive Term

When medium of performance cannot be stated concisely, a descriptive term or phrase may be used.

100 1♭Bach, Johann Sebastian, ‡d 1685-1750. ‡t Ich lasse dich nicht,
   du segnest mich denn **(Cantata)**

100 1♭Bach, Johann Christoph, ‡d 1642-1703. ‡t Ich lasse dich nicht
400 1♭Bach, Johann Sebastian, ‡d 1685-1750. ‡t Ich lasse dich nicht,
   du segnest mich denn **(Motet)**

Numeric Identifying Elements

Although there is only one work by this composer titled *Vater Unser Im Himmelreich*, a second work by the same composer requires a reference from the same title. Both the uniform title and the reference should include the thematic index number, which resolves the conflict.

100 1ƀ Buxtehude, Dietrich, ‡d 1637-1707. ‡t Vater unser im Himmelreich, ‡n **BuxWV 219**

100 1ƀ Buxtehude, Dietrich, ‡d 1637-1707. ‡t Nimm von uns, Herr, du treuer Gott (Chorale prelude)
400 1ƀ Buxtehude, Dietrich, ‡d 1637-1707. ‡t Vater unser im Himmelreich, ‡n **BuxWV 207**

Year of Completion of Composition

100 1ƀ Rameau, Jean Philippe, ‡d 1683-1764. ‡t Anacréon ‡n **(1756)**

100 1ƀ Rameau, Jean Philippe, ‡d 1683-1764. ‡t Surprises de l'amour. Anacréon
400 1ƀ Rameau, Jean Philippe, ‡d 1683-1764. ‡t Anacréon ‡n **(1757)**

Publisher

When year of composition is unknown, the names of the publishers may be used to resolve a conflict. The form of the name of each publisher need not be standardized. The heading and reference below also require medium of performance.

100 1ƀ Martinů, Bohuslav, ‡d 1890-1959. ‡t Etudes rhythmiques, ‡m violin, piano **(Schott)**

100 1ƀ Martinů, Bohuslav, ‡d 1890-1959. ‡t Arabesques, ‡m violin, piano
400 1ƀ Martinů, Bohuslav, ‡d 1890-1959. ‡t Etudes rhythmiques, ‡m violin, piano **(Deiss)**

Conflicts Between References

According to the PCC rules, headings in a 400, 410, 411, 430, or 451 field are allowed to normalize to the same heading in a 400, 410, 411, 430, or 451 field, in the same or different authority record. This example in the authority file reflects this practice.

Beethoven, Ludwig van, 1770-1827. Pastoral
  See: Beethoven, Ludwig van, 1770-1827. Sonatas, piano, no. 15,
    op. 28, D major
  See: Beethoven, Ludwig van, 1770-1827. Symphonies, no. 6, op.
    68, F major

LCRI 26.4B1, however, considers two identical references referring
to different uniform titles entered under the same composer to be a
conflict. Further identifying elements should be added, following rule
25.30E1. These elements are the year of completion of composition, year
of original publication, and any other identifying elements, such as place
of publication, name of first publisher, etc.

Year of Completion of Composition

100 1ʙMartinů, Bohuslav, ‡d 1890-1959. ‡t Variace na thema
    Rossiniho
400 1ʙMartinů, Bohuslav, ‡d 1890-1959. ‡t Variations,
    ‡m violoncello, piano ‡n **(1942)**

100 1ʙMartinů, Bohuslav, ‡d 1890-1959. ‡t Variace na thema
    slovenské lidové pisně
400 1ʙMartinů, Bohuslav, ‡d 1890-1959. ‡t Variations,
    ‡m violoncello, piano ‡n **(1959)**

Title of Larger Work

100 1ʙOffenbach, Jacques, ‡d 1819-1880. ‡t Orphée aux enfers.
    ‡p Galop infernal
400 1ʙOffenbach, Jacques, ‡d 1819-1880. ‡t **Can can (Orphée aux
    enfers)**

100 1ʙOffenbach, Jacques, ‡d 1819-1880. ‡t Vie parisienne. ‡p Je
    suis brésilien, j'ai de l'or
400 1ʙOffenbach, Jacques, ‡d 1819-1880. ‡t **Can-can (La vie
    parisienne)**

LCRI 26.4B1 allows adding the identifying elements in 25.30E1, but
does not mention adding medium of performance, descriptive term or
phrase, or numeric identifying elements. When the prescribed elements

are insufficient to resolve a conflict, however, these elements may be used.

Medium of Performance

In this example, however, medium of performance is required to resolve a conflict between the two uniform titles as well as between references. Without the qualifier in the references, they would conflict.

100 1ḃFeBland, Jonathan. ‡t Miniatures, †m clarinet, piano
400 1ḃFeBland, Jonathan. ‡t Three miniatures, **‡m clarinet, piano**
400 1ḃFeBland, Jonathan. ‡t 3 miniatures, **‡m clarinet, piano**

100 1ḃFeBland, Jonathan. ‡t Miniatures, ‡m flute, piano
400 1ḃFeBland, Jonathan. ‡t Three miniatures, **‡m flute, piano**
400 1ḃFeBland, Jonathan. ‡t 3 miniatures, **‡m flute, piano**

Descriptive Term

In these examples for works of Schubert, the references in the first record are both qualified by descriptive. The first reference is qualified because it conflicts with the reference in the second authority record. The second reference is qualified because it conflicts with the heading in the second authority record. Both the heading and reference in the second authority record are also qualified.

100 1ḃSchubert, Franz, ‡d 1797-1828. ‡t Quintets, ‡m piano, violin,
        viola, violoncello, double bass, ‡n D. 667, ‡r A major
400 1ḃSchubert, Franz, ‡d 1797-1828. ‡t Trout **(Quintet)**
400 1ḃSchubert, Franz, ‡d 1797-1828. ‡t Forelle **(Quintet)**

100 1ḃSchubert, Franz, ‡d 1797-1828. ‡t Forelle **(Song)**
400 1ḃSchubert, Franz, ‡d 1797-1828. ‡t Trout **(Song)**

Appendix A
Thematic Index Numbers for Composers Whose Works Are Assigned Numbers Other Than or in Addition to Opus Numbers

This chart, to be used in the application of AACR2 25.30C, is a compilation of special instructions given in composers' name authority records, in the 667 field, indicating when to assign numbers other than opus numbers. Such numbers cannot be used until they are authorized by LC in the name authority record for the composer or with LC's permission. For each composer, the numbering system and its source are given. It is indicated when the work number is to be assigned only in specific categories of works. For complete citations for the sources of the work numbers, consult the name authority record for each composer. Keep in mind that the name authority file is dynamic, and so no printed list can ever be assumed to be exhaustive. Also, the thematic index numbering for a composer's works may change, so the name authority record should always be consulted.

These names are not necessarily in their established forms found in the authority file.

Composer	Abbrev.	Source	Comments
Adlgasser, Anton Cajetan	A.	Catanzaro and Rainer	
Albinoni, Tomaso	G.	Giazotto	
Bach, Carl Philipp Emanuel	H.	Helm	
Bach, Johann Christian	W.	Warburton	use for J. C. Bach's works *except* for op. 9 (Hummel), op. 15 (Welcker), and op. 18 (Roullède de la Chevardière), op. 18 (Foster)
Bach, Johann Christoph Friedrich	W.	Wohlfarth	
Bach, Johann Sebastian	BWV	Schmieder	
Bach, Wilhelm Friedemann	F.	Falck	
Beck, Franz Ignaz	C	Callen	use for Beck's symphonies without opus numbers
Beecke, Ignaz von	M	Murray	use for Beecke's symphonies
Beethoven, Ludwig van	WoO	Kinsky	use for Beethoven's works without opus numbers
Beethoven, Ludwig van	H.	Hess	use for Beethoven's works without opus or Kinsky numbers
Benda, Franz	L.	Lee	
Boccherini, Luigi	G.	Gérard	
Bornefeld, Helmut	BoWV	Sarwas	
Brahms, Johannes	WoO	McCorkle	use for Brahms' works without opus numbers
Brunetti, Gaetano	J.	Jenkins	use for Brunetti's overtures, symphonies, and symphonies concertantes
Bull, John	MB	*Musica Britannica*, v. 9, 14, 19	
Buxtehude, Dietrich	BuxWV	Karstadt	
Byrd, William	MB	*Musica Britannica*, v. 27-28	
Cabezón, Antonio de	J.	Jacobs	
Cambini, Giuseppe Maria	T.	Trimpert	use for Cambini's quartets

Composer	Abbrev.	Source	Comments
Cannabich, Christian	W.	Wolf	use for Cannabich's symphonies with neither opus numbers nor sequential numbers assigned by Cannabich
Charpentier, Marc Antoine	H.	Hitchcock	
Chopin, Frédéric	B.	M. J. E. Brown	use for Chopin's works without opus numbers
Clementi, Muzio	T.	Tyson	use for Clementi's works without opus numbers
Colista, Lelio	W-K.	Wessely-Kropik	
Coperario, John	RC	Charteris	
Couperin, Louis	B.	Brunold	
Croubelis, Simoni dall	no.	*The Symphony in Denmark*	use for Croubelis' symphonies
Danzi, Franz	P.	Pechstaedt	use for Danzi's works without opus numbers
Deutschmann, Gerhard	DWV	Deutschmann	
Dittersdorf, Karl Ditters von	K.	Krebs	
Donizetti, Gaetano	In.	Inzaghi	
Dowland, John	P.	Poulton	
Dvořák, Antonín	B.	Burghauser	use for Dvořák's works without opus numbers
Eckhardt-Gramatté, S. C.	E.	Eckhardt	
Erbach, Christian	R.	Rayner	use for Erbach's keyboard works
Eybler, Joseph, Edler von	H.	Hermann	
Fasch, Johann Friedrich	FWV	Pfeiffe	
Ferrabosco, Alfonso	RC	Charteris	
Fiala, Joseph	WV	Reinländer, 2. Aufl.	
Frederick II, King of Prussia	S.	Spitta	
Fux, Johann Joseph	K.	Köchel	
Gabrieli, Giovanni	K.	Kenton	

Composer	Abbrev.	Source	Comments
Galuppi, Baldassare	I.	Illy	use for Galuppi's harpsichord sonatas
Garcia, José Mauricio Nunes	M.	Mattos	
Gassmann, Florian Leopold	H.	Hill	use for Gassmann's instrumental music
Gibbons, Orlando	H.	Hendrie, *Musica Britannica*, v. 20	use for Gibbons' keyboard music
	H.	Harper, *Musica Britannica*, v. 48	use for Gibbons' consort music
Graun, Johann Gottlieb	M.	Mennick	use for Graun's symphonies
Graupner, Christoph	GWV	Bill/Grosspietsch	use for Graupner's instrumental music
Griffes, Charles Tomlinson	A.	Anderson	use for Griffes' works without opus numbers
Handel, George Frideric	HWV	Baselt	
Hartmann, Johann Ernst	no.	*The Symphony in Denmark*	use for Hartmann's symphonies
Haydn, Joseph	H.	Hoboken	
Haydn, Michael	MH	Sherman	
Heinichen, Johann David	S.	Seibel	
Hoffmann, E. T. A.	AV	Allroggen	
Hoffmeister, Franz Anton	H.	Hickman	use for Hoffmeister's symphonies and symphonies concertantes without opus numbers
	no.	Hoffmeister	use for Hoffmeister's solo flute concertos, including those with opus numbers
Ivanschiz, Amandus	P.	Pokorn	use for Ivanschiz's symphonies
Ives, Charles	K.	Kirkpatrick	
Johnson, Robert	S.	Sunderman	use for Johnson's lute music
Kozeluch, Leopold	P.	Postolka	

Composer	Abbrev.	Source	Comments
Kraus, Joseph Martin	VB	von Boer	
Krommer, Franz	FVK	Gillaspie	use for Krommer's wind music without opus numbers
Lalande, Michel Richard de	S.	Sawkins, in *New Grove*, 2nd ed.	
Laube, Antonín	R.	Rutov	use for Laube's symphonies
Maldere, Pierre van	VR	Rompaey	use for Maldere's instrumental works not in sets (by opus number, date, etc.)
Marcello, Benedetto	S.	Selfridge-Field	
Martinů, Bohuslav	H.	Halbreich	use only to resolve conflicts
Molter, Johann Melchior	MWV	Häfner	
Monn, Matthias Georg	F.	Fischer	use for Monn's instrumental works
Mozart, Leopold	S.	Seiffert	use for L. Mozart's works only when practicable
	E.	Eisen	use for L. Mozart's symphonies
Mozart, Wolfgang Amadeus	K.	Köchel, 6th ed.	
Mysliveček, Josef	E.	Evans	use for Mysliveček's instrumental works
Novotny, Ferenc	S.	Somorjay	use for Novotny's symphonies
Oxinaga, Joaquín de	L.	*Oxinaga's Obras Musicales*	
Pachelbel, Johan	P.	Peereault	
Paganini, Nicolò	M.S.	Moretti and Sorento	
Pasquini, Bernardo	H.	Haynes	use for Pasquini's keyboard music
Pergolesi, Giovanni Battista	P.	Paymer	
Pla, José	D.	Dolcet	
Pla, Juan	D.	Dolcet	
Pleyel, Ignaz	B.	Benton	
Pugnani, Gaetano	Z.	Zschinsky-Troxler	
Purcell, Henry	Z.	Zimmerman	

Composer	Abbrev.	Source	Comments
Quantz, Johann Joachim	QV	Augsbach	use for Quantz's trio sonatas (QV2) and compositions for 1-3 flutes with bass (QV3)
	B.	ten Brink	use for Quantz's flute concertos
Rolla, Alessandro	BI	Bianchi and Inzaghi	use for Rolla's works without opus numbers
Roman, Johan Helmich	B.	Bengtsson	
Rosetti, Antonio	M.	Murray	use for Rosetti's instrumental music
Rust, Friedrich Wilhelm	C.	Czach	
Ryba, Jakub Jan	N.	Němeček	
Sammartini, Giovanni Battista	J.	Jenkins	
Scarlatti, Domenico	K.	Kirkpatrick	
Scheidemann, Heinrich	B.	Breig	use for Scheidemann's organ works
Schneider, Franz	F.	Freeman	
Schubert, Franz	D.	Deutsch	
Schütz, Heinrich	SWV	Bittinger	
Seixas, Carlos	K.	Sampayo-Ribeir	use for Seixas' keyboard sonatas
Soler, Antonio	M.	Marvin	use for Soler's keyboard music
Sperger, Johann Matthias	M.	Meier	
Stamitz, Anton	S.	Sandberger	use for A. Stamitz's symphonies
Stamitz, Johann	W.	Wolf	use for J. Stamitz's symphonies and orchestral trios without opus numbers
Štěpán, Josef Antonín	P.	Picton	use for Štěpán's works *except* keyboard music
	Š	Šetkove	use for Štěpán's keyboard music
Stradella, Alessandro	G.	Gianturco	
Strauss, Richard	TrV	Trenner	use for Strauss' works without opus numbers
Sweelinck, Jan Pieterszoon	L.	Leonhardt	use for Sweelinck's keyboard music

Composer	Abbrev.	Source	Comments
Tartini, Giuseppe	D.	Dounias	
Telemann, Georg Philipp	TWV	*Telemann-Werkverzeichnis*	use for Telemann's instrumental music
	TVWV	*Telemann-Vokal-Werkverzeichnis*	use for Telemann's vocal music
Torelli, Giuseppe	G.	Giegling	
Tye, Christopher	W.	Weidner	
Vanhal, Johann Baptist	B.	Bryan	use for Vanhal's symphonies
	W.	Weinmann	use for Vanhal's works *except* symphonies
Viotti, Giovanni Battista	W.	White	use for Viotti's instrumental music
Vivaldi, Antonio	RV	Ryom	
Vogler, Georg Joseph	S.	Schafhäut	use for Vogler's works without opus numbers
Wagenseil, Georg Christoph	WV	Scholz-Michelitsch	
Wagner, Richard	WWV	Deathridge	use for Wagner's works without opus numbers
Ward, John	MB	*Musica Britannica*, v. 25	
	J.	Jähns	use for Ward's instrumental music
Weber, Carl Maria von	K.	Klima	use for Weber's works without opus numbers
Weiss, Silvius Leopold	KO	Kassler and Olleson	
Wesley, Samuel	no.	*The Symphony in Denmark*	
Weyse, Christoph Ernst Friedrich			use for Weyse's symphonies
Zelenka, Johann Dismas	ZWV	Reich	
Zimmermann, Anton	AZ	Múdra	do not use for Zimmermann's sonatas, duos, and quartets with opus numbers

Appendix B
Comparison of Uniform Titles for Music and LC Subject Headings

There is understandable confusion about how uniform titles for music and Library of Congress Subject Headings differ. This chart shows many of the similarities and differences between uniform titles and topical subject headings (tagged in the 650 field). Name/title headings used as subject headings, which are not covered in this chart, follow the same principles of construction as when used as main or added entries and are tagged in the 600 field.

Uniform titles	Subject headings
A uniform title brings together in the catalog all of the manifestations of a specific work under one heading.	A subject heading brings together in the catalog all of the works for that medium of performance or in that form of genre or both.
The uniform title is based on the composer's title, using AACR2 Chapter 25.	The subject heading is formulated by using LCSH and the *Subject Cataloging Manual*.
One work has one unique title representing that work.	One work may require more than one subject heading to completely describe it.
A uniform title is unique to one work; it cannot be assigned to another work by the same composer.	A subject heading may be assigned to as many works as it applies.

Initial Element

Uniform titles	Subject headings
Generic titles: Using the composer's original title, follow AACR2 Chapter 25 and consult the list of types of composition for use in music uniform titles for the term to use in the uniform title; give it in the plural when the composer wrote more than one of that type.	Use the term for the type of composition when it is found in LCSH. It will *usually* be given in the plural form.
Uniform titles beginning with "Trio(s)," "Quartet(s)," "Quintet(s)," etc., are not modified by name of the instrument family.	Subject headings beginning with "Trios," "Quartets," "Quintets," etc., are modified by name of instrument family when applicable.

Choice of Term

The term in the uniform title may or may not be the same term used in the subject heading.

Uniform titles	Subject headings
Symphonies same as ➜	Symphonies.
Canons not the same as ➜	Canons, fugues, etc.
The vocal types "Songs," "Cantatas," "Choruses," etc., are not given designation of secular or sacred use.	The vocal subject headings "Songs," "Solo cantatas," "Cantatas," "Choruses," "Part songs," etc., can be given designation of secular or sacred use.

Some terms used in uniform titles are not used as subject headings

Uniform titles	Subject headings
"Duet(s)" is used when it is the composer's title.	"Duets" is used as a subject heading only for works for unspecified instrument(s) or for vocal duets.

"Sonata(s)" is used when it is the composer's title, regardless of the number of instruments:
Sonata, ‡m piano, oboe, clarinet

"Sonatas" as a subject heading is used for works for one or two instruments only. Works given the title "Sonata" that are for more than two instruments are assigned medium of performance subject headings:
Trios (Piano, clarinet, oboe)

Some terms that are types of composition in uniform titles are not used as subject headings because they do not appear in LCSH:

Uniform titles		Subject headings
Preludes, ‡m piano	→	Piano music.
Fantasies, ‡m flute	→	Flute music.
Nocturne, ‡m oboe	→	Oboe music.

Medium of Performance

Some terms that are types of composition in uniform titles cannot be qualified by instrument as a subject heading:

Uniform titles		Subject headings
Toccatas, ‡m harpsichord	→	Toccatas.
	→	Harpsichord music.

Name of Instrument

Uniform titles	Subject headings
Chamber orchestra is designated as "orchestra."	Chamber orchestra can be specifically named.

The terms "alto," "tenor," "bass," and "contra__" are not given for instruments such as flute, clarinet, bassoon, horn, recorder, saxophone, etc., in uniform titles, but are given in subject headings for works for one or two solo instruments such as flute, clarinet, bassoon, horn, and trombone (but not for recorder, saxophone, and viol). Check the authority file or LCSH to verify when to use "alto," "tenor," "bass," or "contra__" with the name of an instrument in subject headings.

Uniform titles	Subject headings
for alto flute: Pieces, ‡m flute, ‡n op. 59 →	for alto flute: Alto flute music.

For works for three or more instruments, the generic term "flute," "clarinet," "bassoon," etc., is used.

Uniform titles	Subject headings
for flute, alto flute, and bass flute: Pieces, ‡m flutes (3), ‡n op. 7 →	for flute, alto flute, and bass flute: Woodwind trios (Flutes (3))

The terms used may be different.

Uniform titles	Subject headings
Keyboard music →	Keyboard instrument music.

Name of Voice

Uniform titles	Subject headings
Specific vocal types may be named.	Specific vocal types are not used; instead designation of range (high, medium, low) is used.

Order of Instruments

Uniform titles	Subject headings
Add in score order, following 25.30B1: • voices • keyboard instrument, when there is more than one non-keyboard instrument • all other instruments in score order • continuo	Specific vocal types are not used; instead designation of range (high, medium, low) is used. • keyboard instruments • wind instruments • plucked instruments • percussion and other instruments • bowed string instruments (in score order) • unspecified instruments • continuo

Order of instruments when one is a keyboard instrument:

Uniform titles	Subject headings
When the work is for one keyboard instrument and one other instrument, name the solo instrument first.	When the keyboard or plucked instrument plays a chordal role, name the solo instrument first.
When the work is for one keyboard instrument and two or more other instruments, follow the order in 25.30B1.	When the work is for one keyboard instrument and two or more other instruments, follow the prescribed order, as above.

Number of Instruments/Voices

Uniform titles	Subject headings
Indicate the number of individually named instruments when there is more than one only when it cannot be inferred from the uniform title.	Always indicate the number of individually named instruments when each is named and there is more than one.
The number of vocal parts in choruses is not specified.	The number of vocal parts in choruses may be indicated under certain circumstances.

Medium of performance with three or more elements

Uniform titles	Subject headings
The "rule of three" (use only three names of specific instruments or instrument families) applies except when the first word of the title is "Trio(s)," "Quartet(s)," or "Quintet(s)"	Up to nine instruments may be named in headings for specific forms when LCSH allows for the medium to be included or in headings such as "Trios," etc., "Brass trios," etc.
When the initial title element is "Trio(s)," "Quartet(s)," etc., and all the instruments are from the same instrument family, the initial title element is not to be qualified by the name of the instrument family. score order:	When the initial element is "Trios," "Quartets," etc., and all the instruments are from the same instrument family, the initial element can be qualified by the name of the instrument family. alphabetical order:

Trios, ‡m flute, oboe, clarinet	Woodwind trios (Clarinet, flute, oboe)

When the initial title element is other than "Trio(s)," "Quartet(s)," or "Quintet(s)," the rule of three may require grouping instruments by family name:

Each instrument is specified in subject headings for two to nine instruments, with no grouping by instrument family:

Septet, ‡m piano, woodwinds, horn

Septets (Piano, bassoons (2), flute, horn, oboes (2))

Standard Chamber Combinations

When standard chamber combinations are used, individual instruments should not be named.

Uniform titles

There are seven standard chamber combinations used in uniform titles:
• string trio (violin, viola, violoncello)
• string quartet (2 violins, viola, violoncello)
• woodwind quartet (flute, oboe, clarinet, bassoon)
• wind quintet (flute, oboe, clarinet, bassoon, horn)
• piano trio (piano, violin, violoncello)
• piano quartet (piano, violin, viola, violoncello)
• piano quintet (piano, 2 violins, viola, violoncello)

Subject headings

There are five standard chamber combinations used in subject headings:
• string trio (violin, viola, violoncello)
• string quartet (2 violins, viola, violoncello)
• piano trio (piano, violin, violoncello)
• piano quartet (piano, violin, viola, violoncello)
• piano quintet (piano, 2 violins, viola, violoncello)

Note that woodwind quartets and wind quintets are not used as standard chamber combinations in subject headings.

Omit Medium of Performance When It Is Implied

Orchestra is implied for both:

Uniform titles		Subject headings
Symphonies	same as ➔	Symphonies.

Organ is implied for both:

Uniform titles	Subject headings
Chorale preludes same as ➡	Chorale preludes.

Orchestral accompaniment is not implied for uniform titles for concertos and must be indicated. Orchestral accompaniment is implied for subject headings; accompaniment is indicated only when it is for an ensemble other than full orchestra.

Uniform titles	Subject headings
Concertos, violin, orchestra ➡	Concertos (Violin)
Concertos, violin, orchestra ➡	Concertos (Violin with chamber orchestra)
Concertos, violin, string orchestra ➡	Concertos (Violin with string orchestra)

Solo voice with piano accompaniment is implied for songs in uniform titles. Accompaniment is indicated when it is for anything other than piano. Neither is implied for subject headings. Vocal range, if known or when determinable, is indicated in subject headings. Accompaniment must be named in subject headings for single works or works with all the same vocal type and accompaniment.

Uniform titles	Subject headings
Songs ➡	Songs (High voice) with piano.
Songs, ‡m guitar acc. ➡	Songs (High voice) with guitar.
Up to three elements may be included to indicate accompaniment:	When the accompaniment for a song is for two or more non-keyboard instruments, they are not named:
Songs, ‡m piano, flute, violin acc. ➡	Songs (High voice) with instrumental ensemble.

When known, the specific voice type may be designated in uniform titles. Even when the specific voice type is known, only the vocal range is given in subject headings.

Uniform titles	Subject headings
Nocturne, ‡m soprano, orchestra ➡	Songs (High voice) with orchestra.

Arrangements

Uniform titles	Subject headings
The medium of performance in the uniform title is formulated according to the original medium of performance.	The medium of performance in the subject heading is based on its arranged medium of performance.
Designation of arrangement can be added in ǂo to all uniform titles (except for the collective title "Works").	Designation of arrangement can be added to subject headings as the qualifier "Arranged" to headings for instrumental music only.
"Vocal score(s)" may be used in the singular or plural. The medium of accompaniment is not indicated. [Title]. ǂs Vocal score(s)	"Vocal scores" is always given in the plural with indication of accompaniment or lack of accompaniment: Vocal scores with ____. Vocal scores without accompaniment.

Language

Uniform titles	Subject headings
Language is indicated only when a translation of sung or spoken text is involved.	Language may be given in certain vocal music headings, even when there is no translation.

Selections

Uniform titles	Subject headings
"ǂk Selections" is used with three or more unnumbered or non-consecutively numbered parts of one or more works by one composer. It can be added to any applicable uniform title, except the collective title "Selections."	The subdivision "ǂv Excerpts" can be used for one or more parts from one or more works by one or more composers. It is used only with form headings (Sonatas, Symphonies, etc.), but not with medium of performance headings (Trios, Quartets, Flute music, Orchestral music, etc.)

Appendix C
Resources for Authority Work

Cataloging Tools

Koth, Michelle. *Musical Biographical Resources on the Web*. http://www.library. yale.edu/cataloging/music/biograph.htm (accessed January 22, 2008)

————. Program for Cooperative Cataloging, NACO. *Authority File Comparison Rule (NACO Normalization)*. 2001. http://lcweb.loc.gov/catdir/pcc/naco/ normrule.html (accessed January 22, 2008)

Music Library Association. *Music Cataloging Bulletin.* Middleton, Wis.: MLA, 1970- http://www.areditions.com/mcb/MCB_List.html (accessed January 22, 2008)

————. Working Group on Types of Compositions. *Types of Compositions for Use in Music Uniform Titles: A Manual for Use with AACR2 Chapter 25.* 2nd, updated ed. 1997. http://www.library.yale.edu/cataloging/music/types.htm (accessed January 22, 2008)

Music OCLC Users Group, *MOUG Newsletter*. Madison: Music OCLC Users Group, 1977-

OnLine Audiovisual Catalogers. Cataloging Policy Committee. *Authority Tools for Audiovisual and Music Catalogers: An Annotated List of Useful Resources*. 2007. http://ublib.buffalo.edu/libraries/units/cts/olac/capc/auth tools. html (accessed January 22, 2008)

> An annotated bibliography of print and electronic resources covering all audio-visual topics. Topics specific to music include western art music, film music, folk music, and some popular music. This is not an exhaustive list of sources and is updated periodically.

Weidow, Judy. *The Best of MOUG: A List of Library of Congress Name Authority Records for Music Titles of Major Composers.* 7th ed. [S.l.]: Music OCLC Users Group, 2000.

Language Tools

Allen, C.G. *A Manual of European Languages for Librarians.* London: Bowker, 1977.

Cohen, A.I. *International Encyclopedia of Women Composers,* 2nd ed. New York: Books & Music USA, 1987. p. 821. "Music Key Signatures in 25 Languages."

Koth, Michelle. *The Names of Instruments and Voices in English, French, German, Italian, Spanish, and Russian.* http://ww.library.yale.edu/cataloging/music/instname.htm (accessed January 22, 2008)

Library of Congress. Cataloging Policy and Support Office. *ALA-LC Romanization Tables,* 1997. http://lcweb.loc.gov/catdir/cpso/roman.html (accessed January 22, 2008)

————. Network Development and MARC Standards Office. *Initial Definite and Indefinite Articles.* http://www.loc.gov/marc/bibliographic/bdapp-e.html (accessed January 22, 2008)

————. Network Development and MARC Standards Office. *MARC Code List for Languages.* http://www.loc.gov/marc/languages/langhome.html (accessed January 22, 2008)

Terminorum Musicae Index Septem Linguis Redactus = Polyglottes Wörterbuch der Musikalischen Terminologie: Deutsch, Englisch, Französisch, Italienisch, Spanisch, Ungarisch, Russisch = Polyglot Dictionary of Musical Terms: English, German, French, Italian, Spanish, Hungarian, Russian. Budapest: Akadémiai Kiadó, 1978.

A list of musical terms given in English, French, German, Hungarian, Italian, Spanish, and Russian (Cyrillic). Terms generally are entered under their German form, with references from the term in other languages.

Complete Works

"Complete works" refers to a scholarly or critical edition of a single composer's works based on primary sources. A composer's complete works can be used to establish or verify uniform titles when no thematic index has been prepared for the works of that composer. Some composers have had more than one edition of complete works issued, generally reflecting newer material or revisions of existing material.

Thematic Indexes

Brook, Barry S., and Richard Viano. *Thematic Catalogues in Music: An Annotated Bibliography.* 2nd ed. Hillsdale, N.Y.: Pendragon Press, 1997.

Kuyper-Rushing, Lois. *Thematic Indexes Use by the Library of Congress for Formulating Uniform Titles for Music: As Listed in the Music Cataloging Bulletin.* 1996. http://www.music.indiana.edu/tech_s/mla/themlist.96 (accessed January 22, 2008)

Bibliographies and Discographies

Bio-Bibliographies in Music. Westport, Conn.: Greenwood Press, 1984-
> Each volume in this series of bibliographies is devoted to a single composer and includes a classified list of works. Musical incipits are not included.

Garland Composer Resource Manuals; and *Composer Resource Manuals.* New York: Garland, 1983-
> Intended as research guides, each volume covers a single composer. Along with bibliographical citations for writings about the composer, a list of works is included in each volume.

The World's Encyclopedia of Recorded Music. London: Sidgwick & Jackson, 1953-1957.
> Even though it is a very dated source, it is very useful for working with titles of parts of larger works. Excerpts from operas indicate the act from which they are taken.

General Encyclopedias

Baker's Biographical Dictionary of Musicians. Centennial ed. New York: Schirmer, 2001.
> Earlier editions of this source sometimes include persons not covered in the current edition; includes work lists.

Die Musik in Geschichte und Gegenwart. 2. Ausg. Kassel: Bärenreiter, 1994-
> Referred to as MGG, this source is in two parts: *Sachteil* and *Personenteil*; the latter is currently still being issued serially.

Sadie, Stanley, and John Tyrrell, eds. *New Grove Dictionary of Music and Musicians.* 2nd ed. London: Macmillan, 2001.

Internet Resources

Grove Music Online. 2001. http://www.grovemusic.com; requires a subscription (accessed January 22, 2008)

Hofmeister XIX, 2007. http://www.hofmeister.rhul.ac.uk/cocoon/hofmeister/
    index.html (accessed January 22, 2008)
        A searchable database of Hofmeister's monthly lists of music publications
        from the years 1829-1900.
Indiana University School of Music. William and Gayle Cook Music Library.
    Worldwide Internet Music Resources: Composers; Composers Lists. 2002.
    http://library.music.indiana.edu/music_resources/compose.html (accessed
    January 22, 2008)

Resources by Specific Time Period

Twentieth Century

Hermil, Hélène. *Musique: 10,000 Compositeurs du XIIe au XXe Siècle:
    Repertoire Chrono-Ethnique*. Paris: Groupe de Recherches et D'études
    Musicales, 1983.
Morton, Brian, and Pamela Collins, eds. *Contemporary Composers*. Chicago: St.
    James Press, 1992.
        International in scope, but includes only the more well-established
        composers.
Slonimsky, Nicolas. *Baker's Biographical Dictionary of Twentieth-Century
    Classical Musicians*. New York: Schirmer Books, 1997.

Nineteenth Century

Pazdírek, Franz. *Universal-Handbuch der Musikliteratur aller Zeiten und Völker*.
    Wien: Pazdírek, 1904-1910.
        A good source for determining how many works with a given title a
        nineteenth-century composer wrote and for titles of early editions of
        works of that era. Particularly good for less well-known nineteenth-
        century composers.

Seventeenth to Eighteenth Centuries

*Répertoire International des Sources Musicales = International Inventory of
    Musical Sources*. Series A/I, *Einzeldrucke vor 1800*. Kassel: Bärenreiter,
    1971-
        Known as RISM; useful for finding first edition titles.
Sartori, Claudio. *Bibliografia Della Musica Strumentale Italiana Stampata in
    Italia Fino al 1700*. Firenze: L.S. Olschki, 1952-1968.

Before 1600

Brown, Howard Mayer. *Instrumental Music Printed Before 1600: A Bibliography*.
Cambridge, Mass.: Harvard University Press, 1965.
  A good source for individual titles within larger works; organized
  chronologically.

Women Composers

Cohen, Aaron I. *International Encyclopedia of Women Composers*. 2nd ed. New
York: Books & Music, 1987.
Fuller, Sophie. *The Pandora Guide to Women Composers: Britain and the United
States 1629-Present*. London; San Francisco: Pandora, 1994.
Heinrich, Adel. *Organ and Harpsichord Music by Women Composers: An
Annotated Catalog*. New York: Greenwood Press, 1991.
Johnson, Rose-Marie. *Violin Music by Women Composers: A Bio-
Bibliographical Guide*. New York: Greenwood Press, 1989.
Laurence, Anya. *Women of Notes: 1,000 Women Composers Born Before 1900*.
New York: R. Rosen Press, 1978.
LePage, Jane Weiner. *Women Composers, Conductors, and Musicians of the
Twentieth Century: Selected Biographies*. Metuchen, N.J.: Scarecrow Press,
1980-
Marx, Eva, and Gerlinde Haas. *210 Österreichische Komponistinnen Vom 16.
Jahrhundert Bis Zur Gegenwart: Biographie, Werk Bibliographie: Ein
Lexikon*. Salzburg: Residenz Verlag, 2001.
Meggett, Joan M. *Keyboard Music by Women Composers: A Catalog and
Bibliography*. Westport, Conn.: Greenwood Press, 1981.
Olivier, Antje, and Karin Weingartz-Perschel. *Komponistinnen Von A-Z*. 1. Aufl.
Düsseldorf: Tokkata, 1988.
Rieger, Eva, Martina Oster, and Siegrun Schmidt, eds. *Sopran Contra Bass: Die
Komponistin im Musikverlag: Nachschlagewerk Aller Lieferbaren Noten*.
Kassel: Furore-Verlag, 1989.
Sadie, Julie Ann, and Rhain Samuel, eds. *The Norton/Grove Dictionary of Women
Composers*. New York: W.W. Norton, 1994.
  A one-volume work of only 457 pages, it is necessarily limited to better-
  known women composers.

Black Composers

Floyd, Samuel A., ed. *International Dictionary of Black Composers*. Chicago:
Fitzroy Dearborn, 1999.

Horne, Aaron. *Brass Music of Black Composers: A Bibliography*. Westport, Conn.: Greenwood Press, 1996.
    Covers chiefly African-American composers, but also African, Afro-European, and Afro-Latino composers.
————. *Keyboard Music of Black Composers: A Bibliography*. Westport, Conn.: Greenwood Press, 1992.
    Covers chiefly African-American composers, but also African, Afro-European, and Afro-Latino composers.
————. *String Music of Black Composers: A Bibliography*. New York: Greenwood Press, 1991.
    Covers chiefly African-American composers, but also African, Afro-European, and Afro-Latino composers.
Walker-Hill, Helen. *Piano Music by Black Women Composers: A Catalog of Solo and Ensemble Works*. New York: Greenwood Press, 1992.

National Encyclopedias and Books

Encyclopedias that focus on a particular nation usually will contain more in-depth articles about composers of that nationality, but may also include better-known composers not of that nationality and less-known composers of the nationality not found elsewhere.

Argentina

Arízaga, Rodolfo. *Enciclopedia de la Música Argentina*. Buenos Aires: Fondo Nacional de las Artes, 1971.

Australia

Bebbingtton, Warren, ed. *The Oxford Companion to Australian Music*. Melbourne; New York: Oxford University Press, 1997.
Broadstock, Brenton. *Sound Ideas: Australian Composers Born Since 1950: A Guide to Their Music and Ideas*. The Rocks, NSW: Australian Music Centre, 1995.
Saintilan, Nicole, Andrew Schultz, and Paul Stanhope. *Biographical Directory of Australian Composers*. The Rocks, NSW: Australian Music Centre, 1996.

Austria

Lang, Siegfried. *Lexikon Österreichischer U-Musik-Komponisten im 20. Jahrhundert*. Wien: im Auftrag des Österreichischen Komponistenbundes (OKB)/Arbeitskreis U-Musik, 1986.

Lexikon Zeitgenössischer Musik aus Österreich: Komponisten und Komponistinnen des 20. Jahrhunderts. Wien: Music Information Center Austria, 1997.

Flotzinger, Rudolf, ed. *Oesterreichisches Musiklexikon.* Wien: Verlag der Österreichischen Akademie der Wissenschaften, 2002-

Belgium

CeBeDeM et Ses Compositeurs Affiliés: Biographies, Catalogues, Discographie = CeBeDeM en Zijn Aangesloten Componisten: Biografieën, Catalogi, Discografie = CeBeDeM and Its Affiliated Composers: Biographies, Catalogues, Discography. Bruxelles: Centre Belge de Documentation Musicale, 1977-1980.
    Includes only those composers published by CeBeDeM.
Levaux, Thierry. *Dictionnaire Des Compositeurs de Belgique Du Moyen Âge à Nos Jours.* Ohain-Lasne: Éditions Art in Belgium, 200-.

Bolivia

Rivera de Stahlie, Ma. Teresa. *Música y Músicos Bolivianos.* La Paz, Bolivia: Los Amigos del Libro, 1995.
Rojas Rojas, Orlando. *Creadores de la Música Boliviana.* La Paz, Bolivia: Producones CIMA, 1995.

Brazil

Enciclopédia da Música Brasileira: Popular, Erudita e Folclórica. 3rd. ed. São Paulo: Art Editora, 2003.

Canada

Kallmann, Helmut, Gilles Potvin, and Kenneth Winters, eds. *Encyclopedia of Music in Canada.* 2nd ed. Toronto: University of Toronto Press, 1992.

Czechoslovakia

Gardavský, Čeněk, ed. *Contemporary Czechoslovak Composers.* Prague: Panton, 1965.
    Titles of works are in English only; thus this book can be used to determine what a composer has written, but not necessarily the form of the uniform title.
Ceskoslovenský Hudební Slovník Osob a Institucí. 1. vyd. Praha: Státní Hudební Vydavatelství, 1963-1965.

Cuba

Orovio, Helio. *Cuban music from A to Z*. 1st English-language ed. Durham, N.C.:
    Duke University Press, 2004.
    A translation of the *Diccionario de la Música Cubana*.
————. *Diccionario de la Música Cubana: Biográfico y Técnico*. Ciudad de la
    Habana, Cuba: Editorial Letras Cubanas, 1981.

Denmark

*Danske Komponister af i Dag: En Værkfortegnelse = Danish Composers of
    Today: A Catalog of Works*. Købenavn: Dansk Komponistforening, 1980-

Ecuador

Guerrero Gutiérrez, Pablo. *Enciclopedia de la Música Ecuatoriana: EMEc*. Quito:
    Corporación Musicológica Ecuatoriana Conmusica: Archivo Sonoro de la
    Música Ecuatoriana, 2001-2002.

England/Great Britain

Poulton, Alan J. *A Dictionary-Catalog of Modern British Composers*. Westport,
    Conn.: Greenwood Press, 2000.

Estonia

Eesti Muusika Biograafiline Leksikon. Tallinn: Valgus, 1990.
Eesti Tänase Muusika Loojaid. Tallinn: Eesti Muusikafond, 1992.
    Twentieth-century emphasis.

Finland

Hillila, Ruth-Esther, and Barbara Blanchard Hong. *Historical Dictionary of the
    Music and Musicians of Finland*. Westport, Conn.: Greenwood Press, 1997.
Suomalaisia Säveltäjiä. Helsingissä: Otava, 1994.
    Includes lengthy biographies of better-known Finnish composers; brief
    biographies for other Finnish composers are arranged alphabetically at the
    end of the volume.

France

Dictionnaire de la Musique. Les Hommes et Leurs Œuvres. Paris: Bordas, 2003.
Encyclopédie de la Musique. Paris: Fasquelle, 1958-1961.

Germany

Lexikon zur Deutschen Musik-Kultur: Böhmen, Mähren, Sudetenschlesien. München: Langen Müller, 2000.
Müller, Erich H., ed. *Deutsches Musiker-Lexikon.* Dresden: Wilhelm Limpert-Verlag, 1929.
    Includes biographies of many obscure German composers, with work lists for most.

Holland

Algemene Muziek Encyclopedie. Haarlem: De Haan, 1979-1984.

Hungary

Contemporary Hungarian Composers. 4th rev., enl. ed. Budapest: Editio Musica, 1979.
Ki Kicsoda a Magyar Zeneéletben? 2., bőv. kiad. Budapest: Zenemükiadó, 1988.
Zenei Lexikon. Budapest: Zenemükiadó, 1965.

Iceland

Podhajski, Marek. *Dictionary of Icelandic Composers.* Warsaw: Akademia Muzyczna im. Fryderyka Chopina, 1997.

India

Sambamoorthy, P. *A Dictionary of South Indian Music and Musicians.* 1st ed. Madras: Indian Pub. House, 1952-

Ireland

Klein, Axel. *Irish Classical Recordings: A Discography of Irish Art Music.* Westport, Conn.: Greenwood Press, 2001.

Israel

Tischler, Alice. *A Descriptive Bibliography of Art Music by Israeli Composers.* Warren, Mich.: Harmonie Park Press, 1988.
    This source does not use LC transliteration of the original Hebrew titles.

Italy

Dizionario Enciclopedico Universale Della Musica e Dei Musicisti. Le Biografie.
Torino: UTET, 1985-1990.
Enciclopedia Della Music. Milano: Rizzoli Editore, 1972.

Japan

Matsushita, Hitoshi. *A Checklist of Published Instrumental Music by Japanese Composers.* Tokyo: Academia Music, 1989.
In parallel Japanese and English.

Latin America

*Compositores de América: Datos Biográficos y Catalogos de Sus Obras =
Composers of the Americas: Biographical Data and Catalogs of Their Works.*
Washington, D.C.: Unión Panamericana, 1955-
    19 volumes with an index. The index serves as a locator for the entire set, which is not arranged alphabetically. A composer's country of residence must be determined before consulting the index, which is arranged by country. This set is particularly good for Latin American composers, but is out of date.
Diccionario de la Música Española e Hispanoamericana. Spain: Sociedad General de Autores y Editores, 1999-
Ficher, Miguel, Martha Furman Schleifer, and John Furman, eds. *Latin American Classical Composers: A Biographical Dictionary.* 2nd ed. Lanham, Md.: Scarecrow Press, 2002.
Lorenz, Ricardo. *Scores and Recordings at the Indiana University Latin American Music Center.* Bloomington: Indiana University Press, 1995.
Mayer-Serra, Otto. *Música y Músicos de Latinoamérica.* México: Editorial Atlante, 1947.

Mexico

Soto Millán, Eduardo. *Diccionario de Compositores Mexicanos de Música de Concierto, Siglo XX.* México, D.F.: Sociedad de Autores y Compositores de Música: Fondo de Cultura Económica, 1996-1998.

New Zealand

Norman, Philip. *Bibliography of New Zealand Compositions.* 2nd ed. Christchurch: Nota Bene Music, 1982-

Thomson, John Mansfield. *Biographical Dictionary of New Zealand Composers.* Wellington: Victoria University Press, 1990.

North and South America

Compositores de América: Datos Biográficos y Catalogos de Sus Obras = Composers of the Americas: Biographical Data and Catalogs of Their Works. Washington, D.C.: Unión Panamericana, 1955-
    19 volumes with an index. The index serves as a locator for the entire set, which is not arranged alphabetically. A composer's country of residence must be determined before consulting the index, which is arranged by country. Other sources are more current for American and Canadian composers.

Norway

Cappelens Musikkleksikon. Oslo: Cappelens Forlag, 1978-1980.

Paraguay

Szarán, Luis. *Diccionario de la Música en el Paraguay.* [Asunción, Paraguay: s.n., 1997.]

Poland

Encyklopedia Muzyczna PWM. Kraków: Polskie Wydawn. Muzyczne, 1979-
    Issued serially.

Romania

Cosma, Viorel. *Muzicieni Români: Compozitori şi Muzicologi: Lexicon.* Bucureşti: Editura Muzicală Uniunii Compozitorilor, 1970.
Popescu, Mihai. *Repertoriul General al Creaţiei Muzicale Româneşti.* Bucureşti: Editura Muzicală, 1979-

Russia/Soviet Union

Biographical Dictionary of Russian/Soviet Composers. New York: Greenwood Press, 1989.
    The transliteration of the names of composers and titles of work is not according to the LC style of transliteration.

Muzykal'naia Ėntsiklopediia. Moskva: Izd-vo. Sovetskiia Ėntsiklopediia, 1973-
   1982.
   In Russian (Cyrillic). This source should be used with care with
   composers from the former Soviet Union, as the titles are in Russian and
   not the original Ukrainian, etc.

Scotland

Baptie, David. *Musical Scotland, Past and Present.* Hildesheim: G. Olms, 1972.
   Reprint of an edition of 1894.

Silesia

Schlesisches Musiklexikon. Augsburg: Wissner, 2001.

South Africa

Malan, Jacques P., ed. *South African Music Encyclopedia.* Cape Town: Oxford
   University Press, 1979-1986.

Spain

Diccionario de la Música Española e Hispanoamericana. Spain: Sociedad
   General de Autores y Editores, 1999-
Musicos Españoles de Todos los Tiempos: Diccionario Biográfico. Madrid: Tres,
   1984.
68 Compositors Catalans. Barcelona: Generalitat de Catalunya, Departament de
   Cultura, 1989.

Sweden

Sohlmans Musiklexikon. Stockholm: Sohlmans Førlag, 1975-1979.

Switzerland

Schweizer Musiker-Lexikon. Zurich: Atlantis, 1964.

Ukraine

Sonevyts'kyi, Ihor, and Nataliia Palidvor-Sonevyts'ka. *Dictionary of Ukrainian
   Composers.* L'viv: Union of Ukrainian Composers, 1997.

United States

American Society of Composers, Authors and Publishers. *The ASCAP Biographical Dictionary of Composers, Authors and Publishers.* 4th ed. New York: Bowker, 1980.
> Brief biographical information; includes ASCAP members only.

Anderson, E. Ruth. *Contemporary American Composers: A Biographical Dictionary.* 2nd ed. Boston: G. K. Hall, 1982.
> On occasion, a person in the first edition is not found in the second edition.

Butterworth, N. *Dictionary of American Classical Composers.* 2nd ed. New York: Routledge, 2005.

Cattell, Jacques, ed. *Who's Who in American Music, Classical.* 2nd ed. New York: R.R. Bowker, 1983.

Hitchcock, H. Wiley, and Stanley Sadie, eds. *The New Grove Dictionary of American Music.* New York: Grove's Dictionaries of Music, 1986.
> The most well-established American composers are included. Entries for those of foreign birth include works composed after coming to the U.S.

Venezuela

Compositores Venezolanos. Caracas, Venezuela: Fundación Vicente Emilio Sojo, 199-.

Enciclopedia de la Música en Venezuela. Caracas, Venezuela: Fundación Bigott, 1998.

Yugoslavia

Leksikon Jugoslavenske Muzike. Zagreb: Jugoslavenske Leksikografski Zavod Miroslav Krleža, 1984.

Muzička Enciklopedija. Zagreb: Jugoslavenski Lekskografski Zavod, 1971.

Library Catalogs

Bayerische Staatsbibliothek. *Katalog der Musikdrucke: (BSB-Musik).* München: K.G. Saur, 1988-1990.

British Library. Dept. of Printed Books. *The Catalogue of Printed Music in the British Library to 1980.* London: K. G. Saur, 1981-1987.
> Known as CPM to 1980. Even though the cut-off date is 1980, this source is valuable for finding first edition titles and ascertaining how many of a given form a composer has written. It is good for titles of works by Russian composers, as they are given in Cyrillic.

Library of Congress. *Music and Phonorecords*. Washington, D.C.: Library of
   Congress, 1953-1972; and *Music, Books on Music and Sound Recordings*.
   Washington, D.C.: Library of Congress, 1973-1989.
   Known as MBMSR, this is a printed catalog of *cataloged* music in the
   Library of Congress and selected North American music libraries. Each
   entry is presented in card catalog format, according to pre-AACR2
   cataloging rules for the volumes from 1953 to 1981. Therefore, those
   uniform titles in MBMSR cannot be used as they appear, but may be
   useful in establishing current uniform titles.

Resources by Form, Genre, or
Medium of Performance

Stage Works

Diccionario de la Zarzuela: España e Hispanoamérica. Madrid: Instituto
   Complutense de Ciencias Musicales, c2002.
Gänzl, Kurt. *The Encyclopedia of the Musical Theatre*. American ed. New York:
   Schirmer Books, 1994.
Hamilton, David, ed. *Metropolitan Opera Encyclopedia: A Comprehensive Guide
   to the World of Opera*. New York: Simon and Schuster, 1987.
Parson, Charles H. *Opera Composers and Their Works*. Lewiston, N.Y.: Edwin
   Mellon Press, 1986.
Sadie, Stanley, ed. *The New Grove Dictionary of Opera*. New York: Grove's
   Dictionaries of Music, 1992 (2002 printing).
Steiger, Franz. *Opernlexikon = Opera Catalogue = Lexique des Opéras =
   Dizionario Operistico*. Tutzing: H. Schneider, 1977.
   Arranged in three sections, by title, composer, and librettist.

Vocal Music

Barlow, Harold and Sam Morgenstern. *A Dictionary of Vocal Themes*. New York:
   Crown Publishers, 1950.
   Particularly good for finding titles of opera arias in original languages.
Carman, Judith E., William K. Gaeddert, and Rita M. Resch. *Art Song in the
   United States, 1759-1999: An Annotated Bibliography*. 3rd ed. Lanham, Md.:
   Scarecrow Press, 2001.
Lincoln, Harry B. *The Italian Madrigal and Related Repertories: Indexes to
   Printed Collections, 1500-1600*. New Haven: Yale University Press, 1988.
   Organized by composer, with musical incipits, an index by first line, a list
   of the sources arranged chronologically, and a thematic locator.

Tiemstra, Suzanne Spicer. *The Choral Music of Latin America: A Guide to Compositions and Research.* New York: Greenwood Press, 1992.

Vogel, Emil, Alfred Einstein, François Lesure, and Claudio Sartori. *Bibliografia Della Musica Italiana Vocale Profana Pubblicata Dal 1500 al 1700.* Nuova ed. Staderini: Minkoff, 1977.

Wachsmuth, Karen. *A Bibliography of Twentieth-Century Hungarian Choral Music.* Lawton, Okla.: American Choral Directors Association, 2002.

Instrumental Music

Sartori, Claudio. *Bibliografia Della Musica Strumentale Italiana Stampata in Italia Fino al 1700.* Firenze: L. S. Olschki, 1952-1968.
    Arranged by date; includes works by individual composers and collections of works of multiple composers; includes content lists for some entries.

Band/Wind Ensemble

Gillaspie, Jon A., Marshall Stoneham, and David Lindsey Clark. *The Wind Ensemble Catalog.* Westport, Conn.: Greenwood Press, 1998.

Rehrig, William H. *Heritage Encyclopedia of Band Music: Composers and Their Music.* Westerville, Oh.: Integrity Press, 1991.

Suppan, Wolfgang. *Neue Lexikon des Blasmusikwesens.* Freiburg-Tiengen: Blasmusikverlag Schulz, 1988.

Chamber Music

Bunge, Sas. *60 Years of Dutch Chamber Music = 60 Années de Musique de Chambre Néerlandaise – 60 Jahre Niederländische Kammermusik: 1913-1973.* Amsterdam: Stichting Cultuurfonds BUMA: Stichting Nederlandse Muziekbelangen, 1974.

Cohn, Arthur. *The Literature of Chamber Music.* Chapel Hill, N.C.: Hinshaw Music, 1997.

Everett, William A. *British Piano Trios, Quartets, and Quintets, 1850-1950: A Checklist.* Warren, Mich.: Harmonie Park Press, 2000.

Secrist-Schmedes, Barbera. *Wind Chamber Music: Winds with Piano and Woodwind Quintets: An Annotated Guide.* Lanham, Md.: Scarecrow Press, 1996.

———. *Wind Chamber Music: For Two to Sixteen Winds: An Annotated Guide.* Lanham, Md.: Scarecrow Press, 2002.

Individual Instruments

Bassoon

Bulling, Burchard. *Fagott Bibliographie.* Wilhelmshaven: F. Noetzel, 1989.
Koenigsbeck, Bodo. *Bassoon Bibliography = Bibliographie du Basson = Fagott Bibliographie.* Monteux, France: Musica Rara, 1994.

Clarinet

Brixel, Eugen. *Klarinetten-Bibliographie.* Wilhelmshaven: Heinrichshofen, 1977-

Double Bass

Planyavsky, Alfred. *Geschichte des Kontrabasses.* 2. Aufl. Tutzing: H. Schneider, 1984.

English Horn

McMullen, William Wallace. *Soloistic English Horn Literature From 1736-1984.* Stuyvesant, N.Y.: Pendragon Press, 1994.

Guitar

Moser, Wolf. *Gitarre-Musik: Ein Internationaler Katalog.* Neuausg. Hamburg: J. Trekel, 1985.

Harp

Palkovic, Mark. *Harp Music Bibliography: Chamber Music and Concertos.* Lanham, Md.: Scarecrow Press, 2002.
———. *Harp Music Bibliography: Compositions for Solo Harp and Harp Ensemble.* Bloomington: Indiana University Press, 1995.

Horn

Brüchle, Bernhard. *Horn Bibliographie.* Wilhelmshaven: Heinrichshofen, 1970-1983.
Hornisten-Lexikon = Dictionary for Hornists. München: Hans Pizka, 1986.

Keyboard

Brookes, Virginia. *British Keyboard Music to c.1600: Sources and Thematic Index*. Oxford: Clarendon Press, 1996.
Includes extensive sections listing the manuscript sources and the printed sources, with contents and composers. The thematic index is arranged by composer. This is not a source listing *all* of a composer's keyboard music, but it is useful in identifying works.

Oboe

Hošek, Miroslav. *Oboen-Bibliographie*. Wilhelmshaven: Heinrichshofen, 1975-1994.

Organ

Arnold, Corliss Richard. *Organ Literature: A Comprehensive Survey*. 3rd ed. Metuchen, N.J.: Scarecrow Press, 1995.
Beckmann, Klaus. *Repertorium Orgelmusik: Komponisten, Werke, Editionen, 1150-2000, 57 Länder = Bio-Bibliographical Index of Organ Music: Composers, Works, Editions, 1150-2000, 57 Countries: A Selection*. 3. Aufl. Mainz: Schott, 2001.
Very good resource; organized by country and then chronologically by date of birth; with work lists and index.
Edson, Jean Slater. *Organ-Preludes: An Index to Compositions on Hymn Tunes, Chorales, Plainsong Melodies, Gregorian Tunes and Carols*. Metuchen, N.J.: Scarecrow Press, 1970.
Includes composers, with birth and death dates.
Henderson, John. *A Directory of Composers for Organ*. Wiltshire, England, 1996.
Includes composers' last names and initials, birth and death dates, and country; lists of works.
Hettinger, Sharon L. *American Organ Music of the Twentieth Century: An Annotated Bibliography of Composers*. Warren, Mich.: Harmonie Park Press, 1997.
Vessia, Gian Nicola, and Marco Rossi. *Le Firme Dell'Organo: Compositori e Repertorio Organistico Del '900 Italiano*. Bergamo: Carrara, 2003.

Percussion

Siwe, Thomas, ed. *Percussion Ensemble & Solo Literature*. Champaign, Ill.: Media Press, 1993.
———. *Percussion Ensemble Literature*. Champaign, Ill.: Media Press, 1998.
———. *Percussion Solo Literature*. Champaign, Ill.: Media Press, 1995.

Saxophone

Londeix, Jean-Marie. *150 Years of Music for Saxophone: Bibliographical Index of Music and Educational Literature for the Saxophone, 1844-1994.* Cherry Hill, N.J.: Roncorp, 1994.

Trumpet

Lowrey, Alvin. *Lowrey's International Trumpet Discography.* 1st ed. Columbia, S.C.: Camden House, 1990.
Intended as a discography, it is useful for authority work.

Viola da Gamba

Dodd, Gordon. *Thematic Index of Music for Viols.* London: Viola da Gamba Society of Great Britain, 1980-

Violin

Creighton, James. *Discopaedia of the Violin.* 2nd ed. Burlington, Ontario: Records Past, 1994.
Arranged by performer with a composer index.

Violoncello

Homuth, Donald. *Cello Music Since 1960: A Bibliography of Solo, Chamber & Orchestral Works for Solo Cellist.* Berkeley, Calif.: Fallen Leaf Press, 1994.

Bibliography

Anglo-American Cataloguing Rules. 2nd ed., 2002 rev. with 2004 update. Ottawa: Canadian Library Association; Chicago: American Library Association, 2004.

Fenske, David E., Michael Fling, Brenda Nelson-Strauss, and Shirlene Ward. *Using Uniform Titles.* 1998. http://library.music.indiana.edu/collections/uniform/uniform.html (accessed January 22, 2008)

Fling, R. Michael. "Computer-Assisted Instruction for Music Uniform Titles." *Public-Access Computer Systems Review,* no. 1 (1990): p. 23-33.

Lasocki, David. "When Is a Flute not a Flute?" (unpublished data, 1997)

Library of Congress. Cataloging Policy and Support Office. *Subject Cataloging Manual: Subject Headings.* Washington, D.C.: Cataloging Distribution Service, Library of Congress, 1996.

———. Office for Descriptive Cataloging Policy. *Library of Congress Rule Interpretations.* 2nd ed. Washington, D.C.: Cataloging Distribution Service, Library of Congress, 1989-

———. Program for Cooperative Cataloging. NACO. *FAQ on Uniform Titles.* 2002. http://www.loc.gov/catdir/pcc/naco/utfaq.html (accessed January 22, 2008)

Maxwell, Robert L. *Maxwell's Guide to Authority Work.* Chicago: American Library Association, 2002.

Music Library Association. *Music Cataloging Bulletin.* Middleton, Wis: MLA, 1970- http://www.areditions.com/mcb/MCB_List.html (accessed January 22, 2008)

Music Library Association. Working Group on Types of Compositions. *Types of Compositions for Use in Music Uniform Titles: A Manual for Use with AACR2 Chapter 25.* 2nd, updated ed. [S.l.: s.n.], 1997. http://www.library.yale.edu/cataloging/music/types.htm (accessed January 22, 2008)

Smiraglia, Richard P. *Describing Music Materials: A Manual for Descriptive Cataloging of Printed and Recorded Music, Music Videos, and Archival Music Collections: For Use with AACR2 and APPM.* 3rd ed. Lake Crystal, Minn.: Soldier Creek Press, 1997. Soldier Creek Music Series, no. 5.

———. *Music Cataloging: The Bibliographic Control of Printed and Recorded Music in Libraries.* Englewood, Colo.: Libraries Unlimited, 1989.

———. "Musical Works and Information Retrieval." *Notes* 58 (2002): 747-64.

Weitz, Jay. *Cataloger's Judgment: Music Cataloging Questions and Answers from the Music OCLC Users Group Newsletter.* Westport, Conn.: Libraries Unlimited, 2004.

————. *Music Coding and Tagging: MARC 21 Content Designation for Scores and Sound Recordings.* 2nd ed. Belle Plaine, Minn.: Soldier Creek Press, 2001. Soldier Creek Music Series, no. 6.

Wise, Matthew W. *Principles of Music Uniform Titles: A Brief Introduction.* 1995. http://www.music.indiana.edu/tech_s/mla/ut.gui (accessed January 22, 2008)

Index

271